just out of reach
the 1980s new york yankees

just out of reach
the 1980s new york yankees

by greg prato

Printed and distributed by Greg Prato
Published by Greg Prato
Front cover photo by Jim Accordino
Front cover design by Greg Prato
Copyright © 2014, Greg Prato. All Rights Reserved.
First Edition, March 2014

All rights reserved. No part of this book may be reproduced in any form or by any electronic or mechanical means, including information storage or retrieval systems, without permission in writing from the publisher.

ISBN 978-1494931230

introduction

It was during 1981 that I began following professional sports. And the first baseball team I rooted for was the New York Yankees. One of the main reasons was probably due to the scrumptiousness of the "Reggie Bar" that I would often purchase down at the corner delicatessen. And my selection appeared to be a wise one right off the bat - the Yanks zipped right through the playoffs (one of my earliest memories of watching a Yankees broadcast was the early innings of game three of the ALCS, a game which resulted in a Yankees victory over the A's, and a trip to their 33rd World Series appearance overall). I also recall feeling quite confident when they jumped out to an early lead in the ensuing World Series...before experiencing my first disappointment as a sports spectator.

    The following year, I found myself rooting for both New York baseball teams, and also taking in my first-ever game at Yankee Stadium (as a belated birthday present) - a twilight double header against the Chicago White Sox on August 3rd. Due to snarling traffic, my father (who was wearing a "Willie Randolph photo pin" that I had recently given him as a gift), grandfather, cousin, and I arrived late - so late in fact, that we showed up just as the first game was winding down (I recall having pretty sweet box seats not far from the field, between home plate and first). Bobby Murcer was called in as a pinch hitter in the bottom of the ninth of a 1-0 game, and with the scoreboard flashing "BOBBY!", the crowd grew rather excited. Unfortunately, Murcer committed the final out. First game over.

    Looking to kill some time, my small group went walking around famed Yankee Stadium (during this short journey, I was treated to a Yankee yearbook, while my father was lucky to spot a folded up 20 on the ground, that a vendor had undoubtedly dropped). Ultimately, we decided to try and grab a bite to eat at the Diamond Club. As soon as we entered this fine establishment, we were told by a rather gruff gentleman that we were not allowed to be admitted, as my just-turned-thirteen-year-old cousin was not wearing "proper attire" (which really made *a lot* of sense - how many kids do you see at a sporting event wearing a blazer, buttoned shirt, dress pants, and shiny shoes…especially on a hot summer night?).

Slightly disappointed, we made our way back to our seats for the second game. From a baseball playing perspective, the game couldn't have gone worse for the Yankees, with a final score of White Sox 14, Yankees 2. But there was plenty of "entertainment" provided by the crowd, including a woman partially disrobing at one point, Ken Griffey committing an error in the outfield and the crowd offering up chants of "REGGIE! REGGIE!" (since Jackson was the player that Griffey replaced that year in right field). At another point, when it was clear that the blowout was on (the White Sox scored five runs a piece in the fifth and sixth innings), a friendly vendor attempted to try to get a "Let's go Mets!" chant going. I even offered up several hollers of "Bring in the Goose!" (still somewhat new to the game of baseball, I had yet to realize that most professional clubs don't bring in their star reliever when the team is down twelve runs). With the crowd growing more and more displeased, an announcement was made over the PA system, that fans could exchange their tickets for another Yankee game (throughout the years, I have never heard of this happening again at any other pro sporting event). The crowd cheered, but soon after, we began our trip back to the suburbs of Long Island. And in case you were wondering, we chose not to accept the ticket trade-in offer.

I have to admit that over the next year or so, I wound up jumping ship to the Mets (who were in the process of putting together a world championship-winning team), although I did continue to follow the Yankees throughout the decade, and was intrigued about the prospect of a Mets/Yankees Subway Series during this era, which seemed reasonably realistic after the Mets acquired Gary Carter and the Yankees acquired Rickey Henderson in time for the 1985 season. Unfortunately, fans had to wait another 15 years for a Subway Series (which wound up not exactly living up to all the hype).

However, as the years went on, I found myself increasingly intrigued by the 1980s Yankees teams, and why/how they did not manage to put it all together and win a World Series (the only decade since the 1910s that did not include at least one Yankee World Series victory). Dave Winfield, Rickey Henderson, Don Mattingly, Willie Randolph, Graig Nettles, Goose Gossage, Tommy John, Ron Guidry, Dave Righetti, Phil Niekro…it was certainly not due to lack of talent (I've often felt that the then-non-option of a "wild card playoff team" robbed the Yanks of possibly multiple postseason and World Series visits during the '80s).

While flipping through Yankees history books, I notice that many tend to not pay much attention to the '80s, and focus more on the other decades. So I set out to put together a book I always wanted to read, that traced the ups and downs of the 1980s Yankees. After tracking down and speaking to many players that helped make those Yankees teams so memorable, there is now a book that solely chronicles this oft-overlooked era of the Bronx Bombers.

Enjoy!
Greg Prato

p.s. Questions? Comments? Feel free to email me at gregprato@yahoo.com.

p.p.s. I would like to thank the following people for their help with setting up interviews for this book - Rachel Levitsky at MLBAA, Brian Fisher at MSG Networks, Andrew M. Levy at Wish You Were Here Productions, Natalie Niekro at the Joe Niekro Foundation, Nancy Niekro, Scott Stimell, Louis John Rossi, and David Benjamin Kay.

cast of characters

Steve Balboni - Yankees first baseman/designated hitter from 1981-1983 and 1989-1990
Dale Berra - Yankees shortstop/third baseman from 1985-1986, son of Yankees manager Yogi Berra
Ron Davis - Yankees pitcher from 1978-1982
Mike Easler - Yankees designated hitter from 1986-1987
Brian Fisher - Yankees pitcher from 1985-1986
Barry Foote - Yankees catcher from 1981-1982
George Frazier - Yankees pitcher from 1981-1983
Goose Gossage - Yankees pitcher from 1978-1983 and 1989, inducted into the Baseball Hall of Fame in 2008
Toby Harrah - Yankees third baseman/shortstop in 1984
Fran Healy - Yankees catcher from 1976-1978, Yankees sportscaster from 1978-1983
Marc "The Hersch" Herschmann - Yankees fan, stand-up comedian
Rex Hudler - Yankees second baseman from 1984-1985
Steve Jacobson - Newsday sportswriter from 1960-2003, book author
Tommy John - Yankees pitcher from 1979-1982 and 1986-1989
Steve Kemp - Yankees left fielder from 1983-1984
Ron Kittle - Yankees left fielder/designated hitter from 1986-1987
Dave LaRoche - Yankees pitcher from 1981-1983
Billy Martin Jr. - Son of Yankees manager, Billy Martin
Rudy May - Yankees pitcher from 1974-1976 and 1980-1983
Bobby Meacham - Yankees shortstop from 1983-1988
Phil Niekro - Yankees pitcher from 1984-1985, inducted into the Baseball Hall of Fame in 1997
Mike Pagliarulo - Yankees third baseman from 1984-1989
Dave Righetti - Yankees pitcher from 1979-1990
Andre Robertson - Yankees shortstop from 1981-1985

Gary Roenicke - Yankees left fielder/right fielder in 1986
Scott Stimell - Sports memorabilia dealer/owner of Cardboard Memories store
Bob Watson - Yankees first baseman/left fielder from 1980-1982, Yankees general manager from 1995-1998

contents

Chapter 1: Late '70s..1
Chapter 2: The Boss' First Bonus Baby and a Pitcher Named Rags..6
Chapter 3: 1980...12
Chapter 4: 1981...19
Chapter 5: 1981 Playoffs...30
Chapter 6: 1981 World Series..37
Chapter 7: Farewell, Mr. October..50
Chapter 8: 1982...57
Chapter 9: 1983...65
Chapter 10: No-No...79
Chapter 11: 1984...84
Chapter 12: 1985...97
Chapter 13: #300...114
Chapter 14: Late '80s..118
Chapter 15: Back on Track..130
Chapter 16: The Boss..134
Chapter 17: Billy..153
Chapter 18: Winny...175
Chapter 19: Donnie Baseball..182
Chapter 20: Rickey..191
Chapter 21: Goose...198
Chapter 22: Other '80s Yankee Greats................................207
Chapter 23: The Ballad of George and Billy......................217
Chapter 24: The Ballad of George and Winny...................220
Chapter 25: The Ballad of Billy and Eddie........................227
Chapter 26: Some Struggle..232
Chapter 27: Managers..243
Chapter 28: Yankee Stadium...252
Chapter 29: Inside the Broadcast Booth and the Press Box...263
Chapter 30: A Fan's Perspective...269

Chapter 31: Booming Baseball Card Biz……………………278
Chapter 32: Old Timers' Day………………………………287
Chapter 33: Substances……………………………………..292
Chapter 34: Rivals…………………………………………..299
Chapter 35: Crosstown Nemesis…………………………...304
Chapter 36: Why Not?..310
Chapter 37: Today…………………………………………..328

1 Just Out of Reach: The 1980s New York Yankees

chapter 1:
late '70s

During the late 1970s, it all came together for the Yankees. After a dry spell of no World Series appearances between 1965-1975, a colorful cast of characters - owner George Steinbrenner, manager Billy Martin, catcher Thurman Munson, and pitcher Catfish Hunter - help return the Yanks to the forefront of New York baseball with an American League Pennant in 1976. A year later, the addition of slugger/outfielder Reggie Jackson proves to be the final piece to the puzzle - resulting in back-to-back World Series victories in 1977 and 1978...before tragedy strikes in 1979.

FRAN HEALY [Yankees catcher from 1976-1978, Yankees sportscaster from 1978-1983]: It was a chaotic time, an entertaining time, and a winning time. So you put those three things together, and you've got a very interesting team, and fans were more than interested. The players were even more than interested going to the ballpark, because so many things would happen...and could have happened the night before, after the game, in the morning. It was almost like the players unexpectedly would be caught, and didn't know that. But it was a fascinating time. It made for interesting baseball on *and* off the field - which is unusual.

STEVE JACOBSON [Newsday sportswriter from 1960-2003, book author]: In the late '70s, that's the "winning years." That was looking over your shoulder all the time, because you were interviewing somebody, and unknown to you, the story may be somewhere else in the clubhouse. Having [George] Steinbrenner and the free agency era cooking there, there was no off-season. You never could tell when the Yankees could be the story of the day.

TOMMY JOHN [Yankees pitcher from 1979-1982 and 1986-1989]: Well, the expectations rode with the Boss [Steinbrenner]. The Boss expected us to win. I mean, none of this, "Well, we played good. We fought hard and we finished second." No, there was none of that. You either won or it was a bad season. '79 was a horrible season because of Thurman's death [on August 2nd, in a plane crash], and then that coupled with Goose Gossage got into a fight with Cliff Johnson, and Goose broke his thumb [it was actually a torn ligament] hitting Cliff upside the head. So Goose was gone. And then to shore up the bullpen, we took [Ron] Guidry out of the starting rotation, and they pitched Ronnie out of the bullpen. If you go back and look at statistics of that, Guidry would pitch two innings about every other game - if there was a save going - and you couldn't score off Ronnie in two innings. You couldn't score off of him, because he was that devastating with his fastball and slider.

STEVE JACOBSON: Gossage got into a fight in the clubhouse with Cliff Johnson - there was a fight in the bathroom, which wound up pulling the toilet stall around Chris Chambliss' head, which made a funny scene...but it tore up Gossage's hand. The Yankees might have won another division championship going into the '80s if not for that.

GOOSE GOSSAGE [Yankees pitcher from 1978-1983 and 1989, inducted into the Baseball Hall of Fame in 2008]: Playing for George, first off, I always said, "If you were not going to be as demanding of yourself as he was going to be, it wasn't going to work out." Those Yankees of that era, those were great, great teams. The '77/'78...'79 was a disaster - losing Thurman. So the expectations were tremendous.

RON DAVIS [Yankees pitcher from 1978-1982]: We lost Thurman Munson, and then Catfish [Hunter] retired after the '79 season. So there was a lot of changes being made, that's for sure.

3 Just Out of Reach: The 1980s New York Yankees

TOMMY JOHN: When Thurman died, it took everything…we just played the season out.

TOBY HARRAH [Yankees third baseman/shortstop in 1984]: Having played against Thurman Munson [Harrah played for the Washington Senators, Texas Rangers, and Cleveland Indians before joining the Yankees] - who I thought was one of the best catchers of all-time - that was a big thrill. I always think of Mickey Rivers when I think of the Yankees when they were really at their best. He was such a catalyst for the teams back then.

RON DAVIS: I only had Thurman for a couple of years, in '78 and '79. He was an old veteran, so back in the day, the old veterans didn't hang out with the young guys that much, so I didn't really get to know him as good as I wish I could have. But he was definitely the leader and the captain of the team. He was just an outstanding guy in the locker room - as far as what I got to see of him. I was down there by Reggie, so he was at the other end of the clubhouse. I got to chat with Reggie a lot, but not Thurman.

FRAN HEALY: You could probably say it depended on the day [in response to being asked "Is it true that the clubhouse was divided between Jackson and the rest of the Yankees?"]. And I can't be specific, because it just depended on the day - on Tuesday it could have been divided, and Wednesday it could have been together. Winning cures all problems. The greatest example I can give is Reggie gets three home runs and Billy Martin and Reggie were hugging, as Reggie approached the dugout [in Game 6 of the 1977 World Series].

RON DAVIS: Reggie was in the locker next to me, because no one else wanted to be near him, because no one really cared about Reggie that much. The way it sounded, nobody liked him, but as a rookie, I didn't have any choice - I had to be in the locker next to him. So of course, he and I always had conversations together. He and I never really had any problems. I kind of enjoyed his talks. He was definitely full of himself, but it was fun listening to him and hearing the BS and his stories. But during that part of the time, with all the characters that we did have on that team - Sparky Lyle, Graig Nettles - he was just one of the characters. He was maybe a character people didn't like, but he was definitely a character that made our ball team 100% better. He would come up big in big situations. He would come up clutch.

What he did on and off the field, or his disagreements with George and Billy, well, that was a lot of stuff that took pressure off of me, because when I would screw up a game, they would read "Billy this" or "Reggie this." That would be the headlines instead of "Davis screwed up again." It definitely made the clubhouse a lot more enjoyable - to hear them always ragging each other and arguments. And yeah, there were a couple of close fights, but I think the pressure of New York City and the pressure of winning, it kind of got your mind off baseball a little bit. To me, that played a pretty big part, because you weren't always thinking about baseball, you were thinking about, "Hey, are these guys going to fight? What's going to be in the paper next? What is George going to say about Reggie or Billy…or what is Billy going to say about them?"

STEVE JACOBSON: I essentially wrote the framework for their baseball stuff [for the 2007 mini-series, 'The Bronx is Burning,' which focuses on the 1977 Yankees]. I thought it was pretty accurate, except the portrayal of Reggie [played by Daniel Sunjata], which I thought was a cheap shot and not at all accurate. The guy who played Martin [John Turturro] was terrific. Steinbrenner [played by Oliver Platt] is very hard to capture. It was OK. The series - in essence - was pretty good.

FRAN HEALY: Some of it was [in response to being asked "Was 'The Bronx is Burning' an accurate representation?"]. They said I was a consultant - I really wasn't, because I didn't see the script. Some day, I'm going to write a book. There's a lot of stuff

5 Just Out of Reach: The 1980s New York Yankees

in 'The Bronx is Burning' that wasn't accurate, but it was entertaining. But a lot of it wasn't accurate. I can give you one example, they had me saying to Reggie something about, "And if that happens, we'll just go hunting and fishing." Well, number one, I've never fished in my life, and number two, I'm not shooting any animal. So that wasn't even close. Although I did find it extremely entertaining. I did go over to the set - the set was not far from my house in Connecticut - so I went over there twice. Other than that, I didn't see a script, and they didn't ask me any questions about it. We did talk about certain things with the writer the first time I went over there. I think they did a good job and it was a very entertaining movie. But like any other movie, you've got to make stuff up.

chapter 2:
the boss' first bonus baby and a pitcher named rags

The stories behind two of the most highly touted prospects of the '80s Yankees.

REX HUDLER [Yankees second baseman from 1984-1985]: I was George Steinbrenner's first "bonus baby." Oh man, it was an exciting time. I had a full ride to Notre Dame to catch passes from Joe Montana as a football player. All the scouts kept calling for the draft, wanting to know if I was draft eligible, and my mom said, "You'll waste your pick if you draft my son. He's going to Notre Dame - he's going to get a college degree." So we never heard from the Yankees - we heard from a lot of other teams. And I was going to be one of the top picks in the country. I think some of the teams were scared off with my full ride. I came home from the draft from school, and I walked in after school was out - about 3:00 - and said, "Mom, did we get a call today?" She goes, "Yeah. *The damn Yankees drafted ya.*" I grew up in Fresno, California, so that was kind of a long ways away. I said, "Mom, what did you tell them?" She goes, "I told them they wasted their pick!" So a week or so went by, and I said, "Hey mom, I haven't heard from the Yankees at all. Did you scare them off?" And she said, "Son, don't worry. They'll call." They called, and said, "Hey, we're coming to town." There was no warning.

The next thing I know, I open the door, and Al Rosen - who was George Steinbrenner's vice president - came to the front door, along with Jack Butterfield, who was an executive of George's, who really was George's right-hand man. Unfortunately, a year later in '79, he got killed tragically in a car

7 Just Out of Reach: The 1980s New York Yankees

wreck. But it was something I'll never forget. My mom didn't want me to be a part of the conversation, because she was afraid I would jump at the first offer. So she sent me out to the local pizza place, and said, "Come back in 30 or 40 minutes." I came back, and my front door was locked. I knocked on my own front door and my mom answered the door, and said, "Son, congratulations. *You're a Yankee.*" My mother negotiated my first major contract ever, because I couldn't have an agent because I didn't want to lose my eligibility for college. I said, "Mom, what did you do?" She goes, "I got you a $125,000 signing bonus. I got them to pay for your education. Gosh, you're going to graduate next week, and then they're going to fly you out to Oneonta, New York."

I got on an airplane and they wanted me to go to New York City, to meet the Boss. Anyway, I got ripped off my first taxi ride in New York City. We pull up to Yankee Stadium, it was a $15 cab ride, and the guy goes, "That will be 30 bucks." I didn't know any better, I'm 17 years old, my first taxi ride I'd ever been in, and the first time I'd ever been in the Big Apple. I'd only been on an airplane one other time before that. So it was all new. I give the receipt to Mr. Steinbrenner's secretary, and she knew I got ripped off. She said, "Well, welcome to New York." Then George Steinbrenner opens up the door and comes out of his office, and says, "Rex, how you doing? George Steinbrenner." I stuck out my hand, looked him in the eye, and said, "Mr. Steinbrenner, thanks so much for giving me the greatest opportunity I will ever get in my life. I hope I can help you win a World Series some day." He showed me his pinstripe carpeting, his baseball gloves, his furniture. And then he opened up the drapes to his window, and there was Yankee Stadium.

The team was on the road - it was in June. I was beside myself. If that was some kind of a recruiting deal, it was the best one I'd ever been on. Because I took my five visitations to colleges for football - I was an All-American and had a nice future in football. And Notre Dame and Michigan State, y'know, Kirk Gibson, some of those guys showed me around their campuses. And those campuses were beautiful. But man, *nothing*

The Boss' First Bonus Baby and a Pitcher Named Rags

compared to George Steinbrenner and the New York Yankees. I basically said "Yes sir," "No sir," "Yes sir," "No sir," because I was raised with manners - my parents are from the south. I didn't realize it, but years later, they told me that George liked me because the first time we met, I had discipline and manners. And it turned out that all of George's kids went to military school. And he liked football players. So there was the reason that they drafted me. I was a shortstop. So the media took pictures around Bucky Dent's locker. I'll never forget it - they took me in and said, "We want you to pose right here." There I was, right in front of Bucky Dent's locker. "The Next Yankee Shortstop" - all that stuff. Left, and went off and really had my eyes opened wide about professional baseball and being a Yankee and the commitment to winning.

The first class buses, the uniforms were hand-me-downs from the big league Yankees - that had Bobby Murcer's name inside the waistband, Roy White. This was very classy. You had to show blue in your socks. There was obviously a chain of command. And the Yankees, they took pride. And I didn't know it, because this was my first organization - I was fortunate to play 21 years through six organizations. So I got to see the other organizations, and how lesser they were - as far as their commitment to winning and championship products, by the fact that George spoiled me for seven years.

Anyway, every spring, Mr. Steinbrenner would come to the minor league complex, and the organization and coaches and managers in the minors, were always aware that he was coming a week in advance. And they were scared to death of their jobs. They were worried - "Oh, he's coming. Make sure all the helmets are polished, make sure everyone's wearing blue." Because of the way he ran his ship. He ran a tight ship and he demanded excellence. Once every spring, he would come and watch the games, and he would pull me aside - he would pull up his lawn chair down the third base line, and he would say, "Rex, come here! How are we treating you? I just want to make sure that everything's OK." I loved it. Now, there were probably 500 guys in their minor league camp, 400, I'm not sure how many there

9 Just Out of Reach: The 1980s New York Yankees

were - but it was a lot. Every spring when that happened, he would always pull me aside. All the teammates would go, "Hey, *your daddy's* coming. [Makes kissing noises] Go kiss up to him!" In fact, they were giving me a hard time, because he liked me and I was his #1 pick.

It was really fun. I got to go to big league camp. My first year they took me there and introduced me to Thurman Munson - it was right before he passed in the plane wreck. Reggie Jackson. The CBS cameras were behind me, because of my #1 pick status, they made a little special about it. It was an honor for me to get my first sunscreen poured into my hand by Whitey Ford. Mr. Steinbrenner had all of his Yankee greats that came to camp in Fort Lauderdale. That's back when they trained in Lauderdale. Because Whitey Ford had light skin and I was a redhead too, he goes, "Hey kid, come here - let me show you something. Open up your hand." He poured some of this stuff out of a bottle into my hand, and goes, "Rub it all over your skin. It'll keep you from getting sun-burned." It was like when they first came out with sunscreen. I'll never forget that. But they all treated me like I was part of their family.

And I truly believed that they expected me to be like a Derek Jeter. But it just wasn't meant to be, because physically and mentally, I wasn't prepared. I was not ready for that. It took me a long time. Eventually, I did get my ten years - but not with the Yankees. But anyway, the cream did rise to the top eventually for me. I remember getting called up - my first "cup of coffee." Going to spring training, Yogi Berra was the manager. This was 1984. I had been up for the strike they had [in 1981]. They would call up some of the minor leaguers to play in these games, to get the big leaguers ready to go - when the strike was over. So, they started giving me a little taste of it. But I'll never forget that first trip to Yankee Stadium, that was really cool. And getting all fired up to play with them.

DAVE RIGHETTI [Yankees pitcher from 1979-1990]: I was in Double A, in Tulsa, Oklahoma [as a member of the Tulsa Drillers]. Ada, Oklahoma is just outside of Tulsa - Ada is the

The Boss' First Bonus Baby and a Pitcher Named Rags 10

home of Jerry Walker, who was then a scout, and he was scouting for the Yankees. I only found this out later - in fact, Jerry wound up being one of my coaches. But I was pitching a Double A game in Tulsa for the Rangers - I was a Texas Ranger - and had one of those days. I had a 21-strikeout game [on July 16, 1978, against the Midland Cubs]. I think I had one more start after that and I got called up to do an exhibition game for the big league team, against the Triple A All-Stars, in Columbus, Ohio. And pitched in that game and during the game before, it was in Amarillo, I had hurt my arm...I'm just going through this because it ends up tying in. I had hurt my arm and I had tendinitis - I had never had that before, I was only 19 years old. So all I knew was that it hurt, and I couldn't throw the ball and hardly get loose.

It was funny - I got home that winter and I'm watching the Yankees play the Red Sox, of course, the big one-game playoff. And then the Yankees went on to beat the Dodgers in the World Series. And I think a couple of weeks later; I'm traded to the Yankees! I couldn't figure out why - there were ten of us in the deal. It was the Sparky Lyle deal, and that was the purge of...every free agent in the world went to Texas for the next four or five years. They tried to get everybody. And they pretty much got rid of their farm system the next two or three years - the Rangers. There were about ten of us that all pitched in the big leagues. There were all Ranger pitchers in the minor leagues then, including Ron Darling, Walt Terrell, Danny Darwin, Lenny Barker, David Clyde, and myself. There was just a ton of us. For whatever reason...I'm sure it was money-related.

So anyway, I ended up with the Yankees. The next thing you know, I'm in the locker room of the two-time World Series champs, and I'm 20 years old. I was a baby. That was 1979, but of course, didn't make that team. I went to Double A for half, and then pitched the second half in Columbus, and we won the championship there. I got called up late [to the Yankees], and that was obviously a tough year for everyone - it started with Goose breaking his thumb [it was actually a torn ligament] in a fight with Cliff Johnson and then the next one was Thurman's

11 Just Out of Reach: The 1980s New York Yankees

passing. Which was ironic, because I was in Richmond, and they flew me into New York that day - they were going to check my arm and see how things were going. I don't know if I was going up or not, but got to the ballpark, and of course, everybody was very upset. I think I ended up seeing the doctor, but they sent me back. They of course needed a catcher the next day - I think Brad Gulden came up. Jerry Narron and him were the catchers [after Munson's death]. So that's how I joined the team. And then Billy Martin took over, late in the year. When I got there, he gave me the ball, and he wanted me to go ahead and start the last three games, and I did that. That was my introduction to the big leagues with the Yankees.

Billy called Ron Guidry and myself into his office at the end of the '79 season. He knew Gator [Guidry's nickname] was kind of a mentor to me. At that point, he asked Guidry, "What do you do in the off-season to stay in shape and ready to go?" And Gator goes, "Well, I just hunt." Of course, I didn't do any hunting in California - I was going to play some golf and work out or whatever. But Billy goes, "Well, do whatever *he's* doing, because I'd like you to be one of my starters next year." So I went home thinking that I had a chance to make the team. And…I think that was the marshmallow salesman he punched or whatever that winter [at the Chez Colette Bar, in Bloomington, Minneapolis], and Dick Howser was the new manager. Which, I figured the same thing stood - they feel pretty good about me, and if I pitch and have a good spring…I was one of the first cuts. I think they just wanted more of a veteran [roster]. They brought in Jim Kaat, Luis Tiant, Rudy May - they went for it. And having a rough season in '79, they had plenty of time for a guy like me to go get his seasoning. Most of that season, I didn't pitch well at all. It was actually really bad. So I went to instructional league and had a good instructional league. I think I was trying to live up to the "hype," so to speak, and trying to throw too hard and all those other things - instead of just pitching. So I got back into my groove in the instructional league.

chapter 3:
1980

The '80s start off promisingly, with new manager Dick Howser guiding the team to a 103-59 record, and a first place finish in the American League East.

FRAN HEALY: I'm sure that the expectations - plus the demands - were high. And justifiably so, because one thing that George Steinbrenner did is he wanted to win, and he would do *anything* to win. He treated his players extremely well. Not that that translated into wins, but he didn't cut back anything - he took care of the players. He was a sideshow unto himself - off the field. He wanted to win, and he wanted big stars. And he did both.

BOB WATSON [Yankees first baseman/left fielder from 1980-1982, Yankees general manager from 1995-1998]: The only reason I went to the Yankees is because in '79, I was traded from Houston to Boston, but there was a trade to the Yankees that I declined. I had very, very low thoughts and respect for the Yankees because of their manager, and that was Billy Martin. The only reason I went there in '80 was a real good friend of mine, Elston Howard, came to me and said that Martin was gone, and they were definitely headed in another direction. And that he was going to be part of the baseball operations, and he would really want me to come to the Yankees. So that's how I ended up with the Yankees. The 1980 team was probably the best team I played on in my 19-year career. And one of the best managers, and that was Dick Howser.

RUDY MAY [Yankees pitcher from 1974-1976 and 1980-1983]: I didn't break camp with the ball club - I stayed behind in spring training. As far as I was concerned, when I did get to the

13 Just Out of Reach: The 1980s New York Yankees

ball club - and I was able to get into it physically and mentally speaking - I realized and understood that we had some players on our team that were stars. But that the entire club - for the most part - was extremely unselfish, and willing to do whatever it took to win. So that was the attitude that I got right when I got out of spring training. And when I did, I started in the bullpen. We had a bunch of players on the ball club that were not superstars - Ruppert Jones, Bobby Brown, Bob Watson. We just had a lot of everyday players and guys that went out there and did the job. They platooned and they just went out there and did the job. It was an unselfish feeling about that, and I think that all started from Dick Howser. That's what contributed to me having the successful season [May led the American League that year in several pitching categories, including lowest ERA, with 2.46]. When it was over, when everything was all said and done, I had no idea that I had that good a year - until you look at it, and go, *"Whoa!"* The only thing that I didn't do that I normally did was pitch a lot of innings, because I was getting a little later in my career.

RON DAVIS: The 1980 season was great for me. I had another pretty good year. We won 103 games that year. We had Dick Howser at the helm. Everything - to me - was going great. I know that I had pitched a lot that year. It might have been one of my most [pitched] years - I think I had 130-odd innings that year as a reliever, so I know I was used a lot. He was throwing me in there, so I didn't mind it. Mr. Howser had such a great team that no matter what he did - whoever he put in there to pitch or the line-up he made - it took care of itself. And I think that was the reason he got fired - not because we didn't beat Kansas City. I think George saw, "Hey, with this kind of line-up, I know I won 103..." but I think George wanted *113*.

TOMMY JOHN: Dick and I played together in 1963/1964, with the Indians. So I'd known Dick for 17 years from that time. He was a good baseball man. In fact, when Billy managed, Dick did all of the spring training stuff - Dick had all the workouts, all the plays, all this, all that [Howser was the Yankees' third base coach from 1969-1978]. He'd bring it in, show it to Billy, Billy said, "Yeah, that's good." Essentially, it was Dick Howser running the Yankees under Billy's auspices. And we had an awesome team in '80.

BOB WATSON: We had a team that everybody knew their job playing-wise, and we had quite a core of talent. Veteran talent. We had pitching - both starting and relief. We had a platoon system going in the outfield - especially left field - between Lou Piniella, Bobby Murcer, [and] myself. And like I said, I thought Dick Howser did one heck of a job. He was able to handle George Steinbrenner - who as everybody knows, was a guy that was "hands-on." He was micro-managing everything. He had him under control, for the most part. He communicated well with the veteran ballplayers, and he had one or two rules - do your job and show up on time.

RUDY MAY: Dick just kind of instilled that kind of responsibility on us as players. And we held one another accountable during a ballgame, like, "You guys are going to do *this,* you guys are going to do *that."* And it wasn't a coaching staff thing - it was just us players. I think that was the thing that attributed to us playing so well that year.

TOMMY JOHN: Nobody talks about the 103 wins, all they talk about is the three loses we had to Kansas City [in the American League Championship Series]. And Guidry pitched well out at Kansas City [in game one]. They didn't want to pitch me. Now, this is the thinking then, and I don't know if this came from...well, I don't think it came from Howser, but it came from the general manager, the owner, the scouts and all that. "You can't pitch Tommy John on AstroTurf. Sinker ballers on AstroTurf...no, no, no." When I'm good, I pitch *better* on AstroTurf than I pitch on grass, because the hops are truer.

So anyway, be that as it may, Guidry in game one got beat [7-2], Rudy May pitched game two and got beat [3-2], and

15 Just Out of Reach: The 1980s New York Yankees

then I come back and pitch a pretty good game in game three at the stadium, and Willie Wilson leads off the seventh or eighth inning with a double down the right field line. They take me out, they bring in Goose, and then UL Washington gets a base hit up the middle, that they knock down to keep in the infield. Now there are runners on first and third and Brett's at the plate. And Goose threw him a fastball and Brett it in the upper deck [which led to the Royals winning, 4-2, and sweeping the Yankees in the ALCS, 3-0].

I heard through friends of mine that George - the Boss - was questioning Howser's strategy at taking me out, because I pitched very well against George Brett. But the thing was, if they left me in and George Brett hit the home run off me, then he's got the second guesses - "I've got the best closer in baseball, and you've got a tired left-hander on the mound. Why is he out there?" So this way, it was fastball against fastball hitter, and this time, fastball hitter won. We ended up losing, and we went home. But we had a very, very, very good team.

GOOSE GOSSAGE: First of all, you're talking about a Royals team that was always a great team. And we were the ones that kept them out of the postseason most of those years [the Yankees beat the Royals in the 1976, 1977, and 1978 ALCS's]. '80 was a year that I ended up giving up the home run to Brett into the upper deck. Anything can happen in a five game series. The best of five, whoever gets the best pitching and timely hitting is going to win it. Not necessarily does the best team always win. I'm not taking anything away from the Royals, because those were great teams and they deserved to be there. Brett was the "Yankee killer." He was a one-man wrecking crew, and it was no different in the '80 playoffs.

RON DAVIS: And then, getting beat by Kansas City…but Kansas City had a great team and great pitching staff. We were primary left-handed oriented, number one. I remember Larry Gura and Paul Splittorff - two pretty good left-handers for Kansas City. And when they come into a short series - a five-game series - anybody can beat you. I went later on in my career to Minnesota, and I was one of the older guys over there. And I told them, "There is not a team that you played this year that hasn't lost three games." Or, for arguments sake, like the Minnesota Twins, I said, "Look, we swept Milwaukee four straight games. They made it to the playoffs and the World Series [in 1982]. That means they're not that much better than us - they're just more consistent than we are." When you're talking about a five game series, anybody can win it. Baseball is the only sport that defense has the ball.

RUDY MAY: We had good pitching, but we didn't hit. I think that's what lost the playoffs for us. I pitched really well I thought and didn't win, and we had many scoring opportunities, but we didn't capitalize on them. So we didn't hit, and that's why Howser got fired. I was a little bitter about that, because I wasn't ready to go home. I wasn't ready to finish.

BOB WATSON: Actually, I'm the guy that caused the whole uproar with Steinbrenner, Dick Howser, and Mike Ferraro [in game two]. Mike was the third base coach, and in Kansas City, I hit a ball off the wall in left field. If I hit that ball a hundred times, I probably would have hit it out of the ballpark 99 times. But this time, I hit it with topspin, and it didn't leave the ballpark. It hit the wall and bounced to Willie Wilson, who threw it over the cut-off man, UL Washington, and right to George Brett, who threw out Willie Randolph, who was on first base, and two out.

I think that whole play caused a chain of events to happen. We lose the game, we go in and George is in the clubhouse yelling at Mike Ferraro, telling him that he was fired, and Dick Howser grabbing George by the lapels and yanking him into the manager's office, slamming the door, and then they yelled and screamed. It just went downhill. Yes, we were down two games to none, but we got back to New York, and we didn't play well that night. George Brett hit a home run off of Goose that might be *still* going into the upper deck. We lose, and he fires Howser - or Howser resigns. That's when the real

17 Just Out of Reach: The 1980s New York Yankees

"manager-merry-go-round" started.

Oh yeah, without a doubt [in response to being asked "Would the Yankees have continued to thrive had Howser stayed on as manager?"]. He played with the Yankees [from 1967-1968, as a shortstop], he was a coach there, he knew the lay of the land, he knew his players, his players respected him, and I really think Dick Howser...he left the Yankees and went to Kansas City, and did well before he passed away [Howser won the 1985 World Series as manager of the Royals, before passing away in 1987 from cancer].

STEVE JACOBSON: As the crowd was leaving the ballpark [after game two], Steinbrenner got up and ranted to Ferraro's wife - *"Your husband cost us that game!"* One of the things that people didn't...why they couldn't go to play for the Yankees, it was they were subject to that abuse.

FRAN HEALY: As far as a short series, anything can happen. You can go cold for one week and be out of a playoff, or you can go cold for one week and have a bad World Series. I know that people say that for in order to establish a reputation and head for the Hall of Fame, you have to win. But I don't buy it. To get to the playoffs, to get to the World Series is the toughest thing, and then you've got to remain hot.

STEVE JACOBSON: Howser had a pretty good season and there was a press conference. There were ongoing negotiations. I remember speaking to Steinbrenner just about every day about how things were going, and what the give and take was. And Steinbrenner was always cagey about what was going to happen. So eventually, a couple of weeks after the season, the Yankees had a press conference that a lot of us assumed was rewarding Howser for winning all those games, and giving him an extended contract. Instead, Steinbrenner proposed that Howser - who was a Florida college player and a college coach in that interim - had been presented with a "fabulous real estate offer," that he couldn't turn down. Well, in effect, Steinbrenner had fired him, and wanted to make it look pretty. And throughout the day there, there were questions and answers that Howser wouldn't give a direct answer to [both Howser and Steinbrenner were present at the press conference], but let us all know that it wasn't his decision to go. And Steinbrenner kept urging us to eat some of the sandwiches...

chapter 4:
1981

Many figure the arrival of one of the most talented players (and sought-after free agents) in all of baseball, Dave Winfield, will put the Yankees back over-the-top. But a strike in the middle of the season and the hiring of two different managers (Gene Michael and Bob Lemon) gets things a bit out of whack.

BARRY FOOTE [Yankees catcher from 1981-1982]: It was interesting, because their big star signing that year was Dave Winfield, and I played against Winfield for eight years in the National League, so I knew Winny.

RON DAVIS: I liked Dave a lot. He brought a great outfielder in right field, so that kind of took Reggie out of right field and made Reggie just a DH. And Winfield being a lot younger at that time [Winfield was 29 years old and Jackson was 34 years old], just a tremendous defensive player and a great arm out in right. Well, he's a Hall of Famer, so that explains how good he was. But again, chemistry. Nothing wrong with Dave - Hall of Famer - but teamwork and chemistry is what wins a lot of ballgames. If you look back at the Minnesota Twins I played with, those guys position to position weren't the best ballplayers, but they were definitely the best team-oriented chemistry-type guys.

FRAN HEALY: Probably the best athlete ever to play baseball. Although Ralph Kiner disagrees with me - he says it's Jackie Robinson. But the reason I give is because Dave is about 6'7", and I did a 'Halls of Fame' show on him, in college I was told he threw like JR Richard as a pitcher. He had a magnificent arm, he could run, he could hit, he could hit with power, he could catch. He was an underrated great athlete. And he brought that to the Yankee ball club.

BOB WATSON: The guy was probably the best player in the game at the time. He was going to solidify, plus, they gave him a ten-year deal [for $23 million]. I had never heard of a ten-year contract until then. He was going to anchor the middle of the line-up. He was the leader, a spokesperson. And I thought it was going to go well.

GEORGE FRAZIER [Yankees pitcher from 1981-1983]: [The vast difference in salaries between the star players and lesser players] never interfered with what we were trying to accomplish as players - which was win a world championship. I never felt Dave Winfield treated me any different than Reggie Jackson, Ron Guidry, or Goose Gossage, because I was making a hundred and they were making nine hundred or a million. I got treated the same by those guys, because we all had one goal - to win a World Series. I've never begrudged a guy for the money they make. I never begrudged a guy now making the money they make, and having the same role I had as a pitcher. God bless 'em, glad they're making it.

ANDRE ROBERTSON [Yankees shortstop from 1981-1985]: There was a big division. I think when I first went up, the minimum salary was $33,500. So when Winfield had the contract for $2.5 million a year, that was kind of the difference back then. But if you performed, you were treated just as equally by the players as anyone else. They wanted to win. That is one thing, the Yankee tradition - teams want to win. Everybody wants to see you lose, so you pull it together to get those wins in.

DAVE RIGHETTI: In '81, they brought in a bunch of young pitchers, and said two of us were going to make the team. But they wanted to see how we all responded. Well, I ended up pitching well, and Gene Nelson pitched really well, and Gene made the team and I didn't - they had a situation in the bullpen with Doug Bird and Billy Castro, and trying to move one of those guys, and they couldn't do it. So I ended up going back to Triple A. But instead of being disappointed, I kind of put my

21 Just Out of Reach: The 1980s New York Yankees

nose to the grindstone and had a great start there, and they finally made room for me. And I came up in '81.

STEVE BALBONI [Yankees first baseman/designated hitter from 1981-1983 and 1989-1990]: When I was in college, there was an article written, and when I got to Nashville, Nashville got a hold of the article and started calling me ["Bye Bye Balboni"]...because the headline of the article was something "Bye Bye Balboni" or "Balboni Says Bye Bye." I don't know. But it was an article they did on me, and Nashville got a hold of it, and they started saying it, and it caught on with the Yankees and other people. I signed with them in '78, so I was in their minor league system. I came up through their system, and '81 was my first invitation to spring training, so I went with them to spring training. It was great. They had an All-Star team on the field.

I spent a lot of time with Gossage - we just happened to hit it off a little bit. He kind of took care of me coming up. He was the kind of guy who would go out and have a few beers. But they were all great. Lou Piniella, all those guys. It was just a great experience to listen to them. They loved to talk about hitting. It was a lot of information on how to play the game. Spring training was funny, because it's nothing like it is now. Guys came and they would get in shape, so it worked out well for me, because I got to play a lot. Bob Watson and Jim Spencer were platooning at first base that year. So one of them would go in and play a couple of innings, get an at bat, and then I'd finish the game. And then they took me to New Orleans with them at the end - they played a series in New Orleans before the season started, a little exhibition thing [from March 27-29, the Yankees played three different teams - the Pittsburgh Pirates, New York Mets, and Philadelphia Phillies].

TOMMY JOHN: And then in 1981, we didn't have as good [a team as the 1980 club], but the cards fell our way with the split season [due to a strike which lasted from June 12 through July 31, with play resuming with the All-Star Game on August 9]. In

'81, opening day was postponed for a week almost. I think we were supposed to open on a Tuesday, and it we ended up opening at Yankee Stadium on a Sunday, because we had 15-16 inches of snow in April.

STEVE BALBONI: Well, '81 they called me up - my first game I hit a triple my first at bat, and I walked in the winning run. And the next game, I hit a go-ahead double and we ended up winning in Detroit. So I was 2-4. And they sent me down after the game, because they made a trade - they traded some minor league guys for Barry Foote, because we needed another catcher [starting catcher Rick Cerone had broken his right thumb]. They sent me down because they needed the roster spot. That was the reason. They were apologetic. I was just the low man on the list.

BARRY FOOTE: My first game was on the road, and my first at bat as a Yankee, I hit a home run [April 28, vs. the Detroit Tigers]. I was going from the Cubs, who were dismantling the ball club because that was the time frame that Wrigley was selling the team to the Tribune company. They were getting rid of all their players, so I was going from a team that was headed to last place to a team that was fighting for the pennant right out of the gate. The thing that was most surprising to me was I was an eight-year Major League veteran when I went to the Yankees, but my first game when we finally got back to Yankee Stadium from the road trip, I was very nervous playing in Yankee Stadium for the first time. I think it was because of all the great players who had been down those hallowed halls. So it was a lot different experience than I had imagined playing the first game in Yankee Stadium.

DAVE LaROCHE [Yankees pitcher from 1981-1983]: I was just messing around in the bullpen [which led to LaRoche developing his "Eephus pitch"]. Actually, I got loose real quick. With three or four pitches, I was ready to go - most of the time. Especially with the Angels [for whom LaRoche played from 1970-1971 and 1977-1980], because most of the time we played

23 Just Out of Reach: The 1980s New York Yankees

it was warm - especially at home. I'd get loose quick and I was always working with my curveball. So I would just lob it in there because you were supposed to stand on the mound and keep throwing a little bit - throw pitch for pitch with the starter. Because back then, not very often did you start an inning. You usually came in when the starter got in trouble, because they would go nine - there weren't "pitch counts" or anything. You just went along with the pitcher - whoever was in there at the time. So I was always working on my curve, and so as not to wear my arm out, I started lobbing it in there, working on the rotation. And then the other relievers - because I was probably throwing it eight or ten feet, trying to get it to home plate - they said, "Well, how high can you throw it?" Then it was like, "Well, what's a strike? If it bounces on home plate, is that a strike…or comes down through the strike zone?"

Anyway, probably for parts of a couple of years - '79 and '80 - worked on throwing it higher and higher, and trying to throw strikes. And I got pretty good. Then the guys dared me to do it in a game. The last game I pitched with the Angels, I came in - in like the first or second inning, the starter got in deep trouble - and I went about six innings in relief or something. So I threw eight or ten of them on the dare. I probably got four or five outs with it, and gave up one hit. And no one said a word - the writers didn't say a word, except the guys in the pen. I don't know what they thought, so I didn't think much of it.

And then the next spring training, I got released by the Angels, and ended up signing with the Yankees. Somehow, I said, "I've got this pitch that works pretty good," and showed it to [Yankees pitching coach] Jeff Torborg down in the bullpen, who I had been with a lot off-and-on in Cleveland and with the Angels, and now back with the Yankees. Barry Foote was one of the catchers, and all of a sudden, they said, *"Use this"* - especially if I happened to come in, in middle relief. So I started using it in New York. It was fun and the fans liked it, the guys on the team. Several times, we were behind early, and I'd come in and kind of get the fans going, and get the guys laughing and relaxing, and we came back a bunch of times, to get back in the ballgame. Now, we didn't win them all or anything, but it loosened everybody up and kept the fans in the game at home. So it was fun. And it worked. That was the biggest thing - it worked. I had a lot of success with it. And the New York writers had to have a name for it. I'm kind of shy talking about myself usually and didn't say much. Barry Foote or somebody was next to me, and I said, "It's just my lob," and one of them said, "La Lob." It stuck [as a nickname for LaRoche].

RUDY MAY: We knew there was going to be a lockout or a strike. I remember going to the ballpark in Chicago that morning, and I remember getting there really early, and Stick [nickname for then-Yankees manager/general manager, Gene Michael] was there. I said, "Stick, what you doing here, man? You never get here this early." He goes, "You don't either!" And I said, "Well, I had nothing to do and we have a day game." He said, "Well, I don't think we're going to play today. Because there's going to be a strike. That's why I'm here early, because I'm going to announce it." At that point, when we found out there was a strike, I stayed at the New Jersey house for about a week or so. And then I came back home to Thousand Oaks [in California].

BOB WATSON: It's a baseball season, and the reason there were halves was because there was a strike or lockout, or let's put it this way - a "work stoppage." I didn't play the first half of the season. I got hurt opening day - I tore an adductor muscle, that didn't heal. I didn't start playing until, gee whiz, I want to say in late August. I was just getting my legs under me when the playoffs started, and I had a good playoff run.

What do you think [the strike] was about? It was about money - the owners and the players! [Laughs] I don't know all the details; I wasn't the player rep then [the strike was due to a disagreement over free agent compensation]. I had come from Houston where I was a player rep for seven of those work stoppages or strikes or whatever. All I know is we didn't play. It wasn't pretty, but at that time, I didn't think it would go long, because I didn't think they were going to stop a playoff or a

25 Just Out of Reach: The 1980s New York Yankees

World Series. Well, in '94, they did all of that, so I was wrong. It was about money. The divvying up of the pie. The owners, until I want to say '97 or '98, didn't realize how powerful the players union [the Major League Baseball Players Association] was.

RON DAVIS: The 1981 season was going well for us. It was definitely going well for me [in a game against the California Angels on May 4th, Davis set a Yankees record for most consecutive strikeouts in a single game, with eight]. At the time of the All-Star break...and I didn't even know this, but my best man in my wedding, [pitcher] Jerry Narron, we were in Seattle, and he goes, "Do you know you're leading the league in strikeouts?" So I'm probably the only reliever in baseball history that led baseball in strikeouts until the middle of August. Because of the strike, remember, we had the All-Star game on August 9th, and I was still leading the league in strikeouts at that time as a reliever. I don't know what happened to me that year - I was striking out more people than I was accustomed to, for sure, and had a blast doing it.

I think [the strike] hurt the Yankees. We were on a roll and pretty hot, and I think it lasted closer to 50 days. After about 30 days, I know I shut down. It's like, "This thing is going to go on all year. *We're done."* So I stopped running and throwing. When we came back, I know I never regained the same stuff I had going into the strike. I was feeling good when I left, but when we started up again, I just didn't have the same stuff as when I left. It's not that I quit, just, "OK, the season's over." I just had my first son, so I started taking him everywhere and doing things with him, and stopped playing baseball.

BARRY FOOTE: The star players were getting older - it probably affected us a little bit more than some teams, having the strike. It knocked everything out of balance. It was just one of those things that was kind of strange - they never had a strike that long in the middle of the season before.

RON DAVIS: I got a job - I was a waiter in Downtown Manhattan. It was a place called Oren and Aretsky, and shoot, I made more money there than I did in baseball! You've got to remember, when I broke into the big leagues, it was around $17,000. My son's rookie [year], it was almost $500,000 [one of Davis' sons, Ike, began playing Major League Baseball with the New York Mets in 2010]. A little bit of different change going in there. It got publicized that I was working there, and I would have people coming in and leave a hundred dollar tip and just order water and sit there and talk to me. Don't get me wrong, I had some people that would come in and order dinner, but the majority of the people came in to say, "I just want to have Ron Davis wait on me," so to speak. *A Yankee.* It wasn't so much "Ron Davis," more the Yankees.

GEORGE FRAZIER: I got traded [from the St. Louis Cardinals] the day the strike hit. And I actually was pitching in Columbus. So I didn't miss a paycheck, but I felt like that probably benefited me more, because I was in better shape than anybody else when they brought me up. And all of a sudden, I was on the ball club in August or whenever we kicked back in to start playing again. I was ahead of everybody else, because I was already in shape and ready to go.

It affected everybody. And it affected - more than anything - the timing, the desire maybe, a little bit. It was just weird. A lot of great teams didn't get in. I think it affected more than anything you get two months off in the middle of the season, and all of a sudden, "Hey, we've got to go play baseball again." It was like spring training basically, because the Yankees, we were already into the playoffs with Milwaukee. It was kind of weird - it was like spring training for the first two weeks when you came back. Guys were still trying to get in shape. I mean, you could go throw. In the early beginnings, people thought, "This is going to last a week. This is going to last ten days - we'll be right back to work." Then when it lasts two months, obviously, there are guys like, "OK. I'm going to go

27 Just Out of Reach: The 1980s New York Yankees

on vacation." At that time, some guys had to go get a job to keep their houses, keep their cars.

DAVE RIGHETTI: The whole year, everything went well - starting with that instructional league. And then I think I was 5-0 in Triple A when I got called up, and won my first three games, and was pitching very well...and then the strike hit. I thought they were going to send me back. At that time, there wasn't a whole lot of savvy about the strike and how things would work. But they certainly didn't want their young pitchers stuck on a strike, instead of being in Triple A or whatever, and continuing to pitch. But that was the first major one - in-season, anyway. And that thing lasted, gosh; I don't know how many starts I missed. Maybe eight or ten. So I just tried to stay ready. I figured I knew darn well from past history, if I came back and I didn't look good at all, they were going to pull the switch on me quick. So I really busted my rear end the whole time, trying to stay ready to go. I was throwing a lot and wanted to make sure I had my arm strength.

RUDY MAY: The way I stayed in shape was that there is now a scout for the St. Louis Cardinals, Chuck Fick, and he was a catcher at Pepperdine University, near Thousand Oaks. When I bought the Thousand Oaks house, I built a mound in the backyard - it was funny, I got that clay from Dodger Stadium...OK? [Laughs] I had that mound there, and Chuck used to catch me and I would throw. I would get my running in, up and down the hills there of Thousand Oaks, and Chuck used to catch me every other day or two days. I'd get in a good workout. I did that for about a few days before the strike ended. I know Dave Winfield called me, and said, "Hey Rudy, the strike is going to end soon. You'd better get your butt back to New Jersey." So I was there in a couple of days, and the strike ended.

DAVE LaROCHE: I don't think it affected us any different than anyone else. For the first time in our careers, we got a break during summer. I think everybody took advantage of that and stayed in shape, because we knew it could end at any time. And we were on a roll when it happened. After we started back up again, we knew we were in the playoffs. Of course, I'm not involved with management, but I'm sure that some things were done to ready ourselves for the playoffs - not necessarily to win every single game - just got get ourselves healthy and ready for the playoffs.

TOMMY JOHN: We played just well enough the first half to win, and then the second half, we played terrible [the Yankees finished the first half in first place at 34-22, and the second half in sixth place at 25-26]. We just played terrible baseball.

GEORGE FRAZIER: When I first got there, I was in awe of everything, to be honest with you. To walk in that locker room with Yogi Berra in there and Mickey Mantle was around at the time, and Goose Gossage, Bucky Dent, Tommy John - the list is long. Graig Nettles. One thing I noticed right off of the bat is it was all about winning. Regardless of what your friendship was off the field, if you weren't friends or were friends, when you crossed the lines, there were 25 guys trying to kick the other team's butt. That was the biggest thing that really jumped out at me more than anything else. And the leadership that Goose brought, that Guidry brought, that Nettles brought into those ball clubs.

DAVE RIGHETTI: Fortunately, when I came back, I pitched well right away - but I think I lost 1-0 my first game. So I was fortunate to stay there, which was my whole goal. And because of the strike situation, they named us the first half champions, so we knew we were in. The goal there was to make it through the season and stay sharp. There were two or three games in a row where I had shutouts in the seventh and eighth inning, and I remember Reggie diving for a ball in Minnesota. It was like 8-0. I'm like, *"What are you doing?"* He goes, "Hey, you're going for your first complete game shutout!" I appreciated that a lot - he didn't have to do that. And the first one's a big one, just to get it out of the way, so you don't have to think about it.

We were trying to get ready for the playoffs, and Goose hadn't pitched in a few days, so he wanted to get Goose an inning, so they took me out. They did that three games in a row - including the last one in Baltimore, where I had a shutout going, too. And I was way ahead in the ERA race, and ended up not qualifying by an inning. So I missed out on that. In fact, it got down to the point where we clinched and we were getting ready, and it was the last day of the season in Baltimore, and they were talking about giving me an inning, just so I could do it, and I said, "That's crazy with the playoffs coming up. It's a little late now - I could have stayed in those games." So that was the only disappointment.

[Third base coach] Joe Altobelli and Bob Lemon called me in the office in Baltimore, and Lem was the greatest - he had that way about him, and he was a Hall of Fame pitcher. He goes, "Hey, nobody cares about the ERA." So I said, "Geez...*I kind of do.*" It would have been four years in a row a Yankee would have won it - I think Guidry won it in '78, Tommy John in '79 [it was actually Guidry again, with John in second place], Rudy May in '80, and I would have been '81. So that would have been four Yankees and four different guys, and all left-handed. I thought that was a nice thing to be able to have. Of course, I didn't say any of that, I just kind of accepted it. I said, "You're the boss. We have bigger fish to fry here." But it was funny, he said, "Oh, you'll get another chance at that." Little did I know that I was going to be a reliever in a couple of years, so I never got that chance.

BARRY FOOTE: We won what you could call "the first half" [of the season], and then they had a second half winner, which was the Milwaukee Brewers. We had to play the Brewers for the Eastern Division, which was a tough series.

chapter 5:
1981 playoffs

The Yankees square off against two teams in the playoffs - the slugging Milwaukee Brewers and the speedy Oakland A's.

GOOSE GOSSAGE: Man, that Milwaukee ball club...the whole Eastern Division was off the charts tough-wise. The Brewers, that was an exciting series with them. We pulled it out, but man, beating the Milwaukee Brewers was no easy task. That was a tremendous ball club up there. They had great pitching and they had tremendous hitting - a tremendous offensive ball club.

DAVE RIGHETTI: We were in Milwaukee, and it was a day game [game two]. Back then, there were a lot more of them. And there were maybe 25,000 people in the stands. I bet it was half empty. That was kind of weird. It was probably a weekday, I guess, and here it is a day game. So that's what does happen, I guess - fans can't always go to a game. But you're figuring a big, crazy, full house. We had won the first game [5-3], and I knew what the script was, because Clyde King was the pitching coach and he walked up to me and said, "If we win the first game, you'll pitch game two. If we don't, Tommy John will pitch game two." So we ended up winning game one, and game two, I pitched six innings and Ron Davis and then Goose finished it - we won 3-0. Coming home, we just need to win a game. We had a couple of crazy games - we didn't run the bases well.

RON DAVIS: We won the first two; they won the next two [5-3 and 2-1]. Then we won the last one, but it was nip and tuck again. With the Paul Molitors and the Robin Younts and their left-handed pitching staff, it was a great battle for us. It was definitely a hard-nosed fought battle, and we got lucky...not *lucky,* but in these five game series, anybody can win.

31 Just Out of Reach: The 1980s New York Yankees

DAVE LaROCHE: They probably had the best team. They had outstanding talent, and one of the toughest line-ups I've ever faced. I would rank that year with facing Cincinnati in the '70s or Pittsburgh in the '70s - they had a really, really tough line-up. And they probably should have beaten us.

GEORGE FRAZIER: The thing that sticks out for me is they were tied with us [2-2], and I remember Steinbrenner coming into the locker room and saying, "I want nothing but baseball. You focus on baseball. If I catch any of you at a Broadway play, at a theater, you sitting at a restaurant, anywhere else - I'll fine you $10,000." He was so dead-set on winning this series. We won it, but it was funny how he said it. I'll never forget it. I hadn't been in New York very long, and I'd gotten my wife tickets to 'Cats,' and I go, "We ain't going to the theater. We'll just have to cash them in." I was making $33,000 - tickets to 'Cats' was a lot of money. But she always wanted to go, so I got her tickets. It was pretty funny. I didn't go to 'Cats' - I went home, ate bologna, and went to bed.

BARRY FOOTE: Steinbrenner was in the clubhouse, waiting for us when we came in [after Milwaukee had evened the series]. And in that clubhouse, he started jumping on the ball club, and he and Rick Cerone got in a verbal yelling match. It was good, because all the players felt what Cerone was saying. Y'know, "What the hell do you know George? You're not out here trying to play!" But one of the funniest quotes I've ever heard - especially if you think of it in the context of the future that happened - Bud Selig was the owner of the Milwaukee Brewers, and Steinbrenner's comment was, "I can't believe you guys are going to let *a used car dealer* beat us like this!" [Laughs] And he's gone on to become one of the most successful commissioners in baseball. I think he and George actually became good friends. I just thought it was a real funny comment, especially in light of what happened in the future.

DAVE RIGHETTI: Milwaukee was a great team. We found out over the years that we were playing against World Series caliber teams in our division, constantly. We just got beat a couple of games - that was when Mr. Steinbrenner went nuts. And I was in the clubhouse when it happened. He came in and he was pissed off that we lost. I'd never seen him in there before. Ever. I just sat at my locker, and wondered what was going on. He was just concerned about how we were running the bases and how we played. It didn't matter - Cerone told him [allegedly, Cerone verbally "flipped the bird" to Steinbrenner], and Bobby Murcer calmed him down. The next day, George apologized or whatever.

Another funny thing happens, here I am a rookie, and again, Clyde King comes up to me for game five and he says, "Guidry's going four, you're going two or three, and Goose is going the last two." I said, *"What?* Has anyone told Guidry that he's only going four?" He said, "No, this is how we want to run it. And that's exactly what they did - they took Gator out after four. I think Reggie and Gamble went back-to-back, and I pitched the fifth, sixth, and seventh coming out of the bullpen, which I'd never done before. Goose finished it up and we won. It was a great game - and Cerone ends up hitting a home run, which made it even more fun. And it made a great story of course - George "motivated him." It was great stuff and I was lucky to be a part of it. I was excited about where we were at.

RON DAVIS: And then we went out to Oakland, and we swept Oakland.

ANDRE ROBERTSON: That was kind of unexpected. The thing was, we had a lot of veteran players - Graig Nettles, Goose Gossage, Ron Davis. Those type players. They had a lot of younger guys, and I think that's what got us through that - the older guys knew how to play, weren't doing the "running-and-gunning" like Oakland did, and got the job done.

33 Just Out of Reach: The 1980s New York Yankees

TOMMY JOHN: I remember I opened up the Championship Series against the Oakland A's, and Billy was managing Oakland then. I remember him saying, "We've got Mike Norris going against Tommy John," and something about "It's a long season and he's older, and I've got the best pitcher in baseball in Mike Norris, blah blah blah." And I don't remember the score, but I think they got one run off me [the final score of game one was 3-1, Yankees over the A's] in the game I pitched.

GEORGE FRAZIER: I warmed up in the Milwaukee series, and then when I came in against Oakland [in game two], Rudy May had gotten tattooed, we were getting beat. I came in with the bases loaded. Rickey Henderson was hitting, and I got a double play back to me. I threw it to the plate, and over to first. I can't remember who was umpiring at first base [Jerry Neudecker], but I thought Rickey was safe by about a foot-and-a-half, and they called him out. An argument ensued, and we came in and scored seven runs, and I ended up going five-and-two-thirds innings of relief that day and getting the win.

And what really kind of touched me more than anything was that in the ninth, I remember stepping off the back of the rubber, and I think Dwayne Murphy was the hitter if I'm not mistaken - the center fielder for Oakland. I found my mom and dad in the stands and it was kind of like, all the bus rides, all the little league baseball games, all the American Legion games - it kind of came to a head right there. At the time, I just had a record for strikeouts for a single appearance by a relief pitcher in an American League playoff. So all those things kind of came to a head. I got the last out, and the game ended. Everybody was pretty excited. I took my dad into the interview room and of course, in New York, there's like ten thousand reporters. It was just a really cool experience. And then to win it in Oakland, and to know you're going to a World Series. It all happens so fast when you're in a World Series, that you don't really realize it until it's over and you're sitting at home.

DAVE RIGHETTI: I live in the Bay Area, so it was a big deal for me, too. All these years, I was watching the A's play World Series and playoffs, and watching Catfish and Reggie. Now, here I am, I'm in it. Right in the middle of it. I was fortunate enough to pitch the clincher in that, too. That was strange, because it was the ALCS, and it was still only three out of five games. So we were fortunate enough to get ahead of those guys and beat them. You win a pennant and go to the World Series, and it's in your hometown…there were friends of mine jumping on the field. Even in Oakland, after we clinched it, the people jumped all over the place and were all over the field. That was as good as it gets. And that was the first game my parents had seen me pitch.

RON DAVIS: I know for sure that we were a lot better team going into it - they were a bunch of young players, and we had a lot more veterans on our team. I think we were definitely a heavily favored team - even though Billy doing "Billyball" [a style popularized by Martin, in which he would have his players run the base paths aggressively] and all that kind of stuff that year, and they set a record for winning eleven games in a row opening a season. Those guys had a bunch of great pitchers on that team, but I think with our veteran leadership, it ended up being a 3-0 sweep. But just going back and playing Billy and those guys, that was more the excitement than actually the game itself.

BARRY FOOTE: It was good, because we wanted to beat them, and he *really* wanted to beat the Yankees, obviously. And being able to sweep them was pretty sweet for us. It was good, because of Billy being who Billy was, he had a real strategy of his team, of how he was trying to mess up Ron Davis, who was our guy who set up for Goose Gossage. He had all his guys stepping out of the box and really messing up Davis' timing. And it worked to a certain degree. Billy was a smart strategist - anything it took to win, he would try. It was always real sweet for us as a ball club to beat him, three games to none.

35 Just Out of Reach: The 1980s New York Yankees

BOB WATSON: I had a good series, Graig Nettles had a good series [Nettles would be awarded MVP of the ALCS]. We hit. We really took it to the Oakland club. If I remember correctly, they were playing what they call "Billyball." Well, we took that right away. *We were the Yankees.*

BILLY MARTIN JR [Son of Yankees manager, Billy Martin]: My father always wanted to win. [Umpire] Durwood Merrill told me a funny story about him one time, how he was a different guy between the lines than he was after the game. And several umpires told me similar type stories. Ken Kaiser was actually the first guy, and I don't know if you remember Kenny, but Kenny was a wrestler in the off-season. He would do the WWF-type wrestling stuff. He was a really big guy. And he'd tell me these stories about my father - "Billy, your dad would be screaming in my face. I'd want to *kill him* after the game. But two hours later, I'd see him at the hotel bar. He'd sit down, buy me a beer, ask how my family was doing - and never say a word. It took me a while to realize that that was who your father was. He left the game at the field. Between the lines, there's no telling what he would do to win. But as soon as the game was over, all was forgotten, all was forgiven. There are managers out there that still give me a hard time about calls I blew 20 years ago. But your father wouldn't even bring it up the same night. But between the lines, there were no friends. It was all about winning." And that's something that a lot of guys I don't think understand very well. They have a hard time differentiating what's right and what's wrong, and how between the lines, those things were real easy for dad. It was about winning.

RON DAVIS: Probably my biggest thing remembering that playoff series is instead of "THE YANKEES WIN, GO TO WORLD SERIES," it was "NETTLES AND JACKSON FIGHT AT VICTORY PARTY." I just think headlines, again [was the cause of the ruckus]. The Yankees - between George, Reggie, Billy, and a lot of guys - they loved the headlines. Nettles was MVP of that [ALCS] playoff that year, and in my opinion,

Reggie didn't do anything, so, "Hey, if I get in this scuffle with the MVP, the headlines are going to be, 'JACKSON AND NETTLES SCUFFLE AT VICTORY PARTY' instead of 'NETTLES GETS MVP'." All it did was take a headline away from somebody. And I think a lot of the guys on our team were definitely "headline-oriented."

DAVE LaROCHE: That was blown out of proportion. They had a couple of beers and then getting on each other, but it wasn't any big deal. Nothing that lingered on to the next day or anything. And everybody knows Reggie could be high-strung. Great player obviously and a great guy, and he was great for the team, because whether he played or not, he took the pressure off everyone else. He loved to be in the limelight and loved to answer questions. Guys like Nettles and Gossage could skate by real easy - as far as pressure from the media. Reggie was always available and loved doing the interviews. Everybody liked that - it was easy on them.

FRAN HEALY: I was with Harmon Killebrew, having something to eat after the game, when the engineer from the radio told me. There was a party - it was a celebration. And there was a skirmish at the celebration. It might have been over-emphasized. Believe me, there are *a lot* of skirmishes that nobody hears about. You go to some of the small towns that have teams, there are skirmishes and nobody hears about them. That's what makes New York special.

DAVE LaROCHE: We did sweep Oakland and we were on a roll…until we got out to LA.

37 Just Out of Reach: The 1980s New York Yankees

chapter 6:
1981 world series

Things are looking promising for the Yankees, as they do battle with a familiar foe, the Los Angeles Dodgers, and take a two games to none lead early in the Series. But then...well, read on to find out.

TOMMY JOHN: What's it like with me pitching against the Dodgers in the '81 World Series? [John played for the Dodgers from 1972-1978, before coming to the Yankees] Truthfully, it was like an inter-squad game at Vero Beach, because I used to pitch against those guys in inter-squad games all the time when I was with the Dodgers, and now I'm with the Yankees. I know Guidry pitched game one [a 5-3 Yankees victory] and I pitched game two - I shut them out [a 3-0 Yankees victory]. I think Goose got a two inning save - I pitched seven shutout innings.

DAVE RIGHETTI: Things are flashing before your eyes [as a rookie pitching in the World Series]. But we won the first two games. We pitched really well - Guidry and John. And played great defense. But in game two, Nettles broke his thumb. You're around things during a season, but being a rookie, I don't know all the little things - the guys talking in the showers and this and that. I know he hurt his thumb diving on a ball, but he also got in a fight with Reggie two days before that. So I don't know if he had hurt it then and then aggravated it again diving - only Puff [Nettles' nickname] would know. I just remember him being out. He was such a "mental block" for the Dodgers - this I know for sure. The Dodgers didn't like playing in Yankee Stadium, they couldn't believe every ball they hit near him he would catch...and he's still doing it - he did it in those first two games. They figured, *"Here we go again."*

BARRY FOOTE: We won the first two games of the World Series at home against the Dodgers, and we were up 4-3 in the fifth inning against the Dodgers and Fernando Valenzuela [in game three]. It really felt like there was a good chance we were going to sweep. And then suddenly, we lose that game late, and we lose the next game late, and we lose the next game late, and we're down 3-2 going into Yankee Stadium...and we lost the next game in New York.

RON DAVIS: We started off and we won the first two. It was pretty easy - it was almost like a cakewalk. And then we went out to their place for three games, and I forget who we had ready for them, but Gator was pitching and he got beat 2-1 [in game five]. And Reggie makes an error in right that costs us a couple of runs [in game four]. Every game, we were kind of in it, and they got on a roll, and then went to our place and just beat the hell out of us one game [9-2]. But they got hot at the right time, and our bats shut down a little bit in those first three games. I think Gator pitched an outstanding game - he pitched the first and fifth game. Every game was a pretty tight knit game - it wasn't like they were crushing us. It's just that we didn't have a lot of breaks go our way right then, and then all of a sudden, we find ourselves, "OK, they won the first one [game three]. No big deal, it's 2-1. Then it's 2-2, then Gator pitches an outstanding game, and I think that's the game that Goose comes in and hits Cey in the middle of the head [game five], and then they end up scoring some runs there. And then coming back into New York, they had the momentum, and they crushed us.

DAVE RIGHETTI: That game three, when I pitched against Fernando out there in LA, that was a critical game. Of course, he hung in there and pitched the whole way - I don't know how many he walked. But he pitched all nine innings. I got caught in the first inning with one bad pitch [Ron Cey hit a three-run homer], and didn't really get my feet on the ground, and we ended up losing that game 5-4, with again, a couple of bad base running things. Either way, the series kind of turned.

39 Just Out of Reach: The 1980s New York Yankees

They got some momentum and they beat us three games all by one run. The Guidry game [game five] was tough too - it was 2-1. And George breaks his hand and gets in a fight in the elevator [Steinbrenner claimed he got in a brouhaha with some Dodgers fans]. It was funny, on the way to the World Series - this is back then now, it's done all the time now - we always used to get our bags no matter what. You did it on your own. You went to the World Series, and somebody is taking your bags to your room in the hotel. You couldn't believe it, it was a big deal - especially to me. Well, when we lost those three, we were out there picking our own stuff off that conveyor belt in the middle of the night back in New York!

Our rear ends were against the wall. We got caught early, we got behind. Tommy came out of the game for a pinch hitter in a close game. We had bases loaded and a chance to break it open, but it didn't happen. The Dodgers beat us. That wasn't a whole lot of fun. From one of the greatest years and have one bad game, and you just don't even want to think about it anymore. That's the sad part of sports, but that's the way it goes.

BOB WATSON: We really swung the bats well. That continued into game three of the World Series, where I hit a home run my first at-bat in '81 against the Dodgers [in game one, off Jerry Reuss], and a home run in Dodger Stadium off of Fernando [game three]. I think we were doing well in that, until they asked Bobby Murcer to bunt, and he popped up a bunt. The wheels came off, and then we never regained any momentum at all.

BARRY FOOTE: I was on deck to pinch hit for the pitcher [in the eighth inning of game three, with the Yankees down a run, and with runners on first and second]. And they called Bobby Murcer in to pinch bunt - I never got in the game - to bunt the runners over, with no outs. Murcer bunts the ball down the third base line, close to the foul line, and it ends up being foul. Ron

Cey makes a diving catch, gets up, and doubles the guy off first. So we had a great rally killed there, and we went on to lose that game [5-4]. And I love Bobby Murcer - one of my favorite guys that I played with, with the Cubs and the Yankees - but if anybody was being fair about that whole Series, I don't think it was Bob Lemon's greatest moments as a manager, as far as the way he strategically managed. And it's nothing bad about Bob - I love Bob Lemon. But I don't think he had a great managerial series.

TOMMY JOHN: We go out to LA, and there were two Italians on the mound that day - Mike Scioscia and Tommy Lasorda - and Lasorda was going to take Fernando Valenzuela out of the game. He had runners on first and second. And Scioscia talked him out of it. Son of a gun - if Mike would have kept his mouth shut, we might have won that game! But Scioscia talked him out of it, and Murcer popped up into a bunt foul - Cey caught it and caught the guy off first base, which is bad base running. And then they hit a groundball to third base, and Willie Randolph ran into the out at third base. And Valenzuela, as he did back then, shut the door on us. And then the next day, I ended up pitching 2 2/3's innings out of the bullpen at Dodger Stadium, and then I got food poisoning that night - we went out to eat at this very nice Italian restaurant, and I got food poisoning. Monday I went to the doctor to see what was wrong, Tuesday we were rained out, and I pitched Wednesday.

RUDY MAY: Every time I go to the Angels' games and see Mike Scioscia, he always reminds me...I think he was the hitter that was up when I came in [in game three], but I had the bases loaded and no one out, and the game tied at 4-4. And Scioscia hit a ground ball to Willie Randolph. We turned a double play. And of course, the run scored. Scioscia didn't get an RBI - the way he looks at it, I got him out. I was out there to strike him out, or maybe get a double play on the next hitter. But he always reminds me of that. [Laughs] And I also remember Pedro Guerrero hitting a home run off of me in game six of the World

41 Just Out of Reach: The 1980s New York Yankees

Series in Yankee Stadium. I won't forget that. There wasn't much of the series to remember - *we lost it.*

ANDRE ROBERTSON: I got in a couple of the games - I think Bucky Dent had gotten hurt, and I was kind of an insurance policy. Larry Milbourne actually did most of the playing. I actually stayed with Bob Watson. He had a home run in that first game, and everything looked good. What I can best remember is we went out to LA, that infield was hard, we didn't get the bounces. They were three very close games they had - they got the lucky bounces. I think Dave Winfield did struggle, but it was because Reggie was hurt. So they were kind of pitching around - it was [Winfield's] first Series and he was pressing. They just ended up getting the best of us. But when they came back to New York, they really put it on us.

  I think it was just putting a lot of pressure [as to why Winfield struggled in the World Series, going 1-22]. It was his first Series. He'd just signed that big contract which by today's standards wasn't that big, but back then, it was $25 million for ten years [the figure was actually closer to $23 million]. And I think that's what he did - put the pressure on himself. I don't know of anyone that played harder than him. He ran, he dove for balls, he jumped on fences. I mean, you couldn't ask any more from the man. He just had a struggle. And I can remember when he finally got his hit, I think out in LA, it was a little bloop over first. He wanted the ball, and everybody made a big deal about that. But hey, you may never get back there again. He played as hard as he could. When they're pitching around you and I think he was trying to make things happen, he got out of his game a little bit.

DAVE LaROCHE: All three [games in LA] could have gone either way. I think Reggie lost a ball in the sun in right - that was instrumental. It's not like he did anything wrong, it's just that was a key play in one of the games. And George Frazier just had terrible luck - he was pitching good, but had some bad bounces and high choppers. He was a sinker baller, and got a lot of ground balls, but they went in the holes and different things. They were all tough. It felt like we were still in it coming home, but we got blown out that last game.

BOB WATSON: I think George Frazier - who had a heck of a season - lost all four games in the World Series [three games]. And things just didn't go our way - balls fell in and balls took bad hops. We lost Nettles - he broke a hand or something. Things just didn't go well for us in that World Series.

GEORGE FRAZIER: Well, obviously, I lost three games. One thing that kind of stuck in my craw a little bit for a long time, I remember in Dodger Stadium, there's a left-hander coming up, and they brought Tommy John in to relieve and he didn't want to relieve. He didn't want to be in the game. I remember telling Bob, "Hey, if he doesn't want to be in here, leave me in here." It was kind of one of those deals, because Tommy wanted to start all the time, and they brought him into that situation just to get an out. And I think they ended up getting two base hits and a run scored. So I think when you start to look back at that, do I feel like…me and Lefty Williams are the only two guys to ever lose three games in a World Series. Well also, he bet on it, I didn't [Williams was involved in the infamous "Black Sox Scandal," in which several Chicago White Sox players - including Williams - were accused, but later acquitted, of intentionally losing games in the 1919 World Series]. I look back at it and I must have been doing something right - Bob put me in those situations every time. I can't even remember that much - I think I gave up ten hits, and four or five of them didn't even leave the infield. It wasn't like I gave up *25 home runs.* It just snake bit me on that side of it. But a lot of people forget the playoff against Oakland and winning that ballgame. They only remember the three World Series games.

DAVE LaROCHE: But the biggest thing was pinch hitting for Tommy John [in game six during the fourth inning, when the score was 1-1] when it was still a close game and it was early in

43 Just Out of Reach: The 1980s New York Yankees

the game. And Tommy was one of our top starters, and they pinch hit early. Everyone was like, *"What is going on?"* Still, we had to go out and play and we still had good pitchers, so it wasn't anything other than, "What's he doing this for?"

TOMMY JOHN: When Lemon told me he was talking me out, I said, *"What?!"* He said, "Yeah, I'm taking you out. I'm going to pinch hit for you." And I said, "Lem, you wouldn't do this during the season." He said, "This is more important than the season." And I said, "But you're taking your best pitcher out of the game - because the starter is your best pitcher that night, if not, he shouldn't be starting - and who are you bringing in?" And he said, "I'm bringing in Frazier." I said, "Frazier hasn't pitched well all series." And then Lem got mad at me.

Lasorda walked Larry Milbourne to put runners on first and second, and then they pinch hit Murcer. He flew out, and we ended up losing 9-2. Managerially, it might have been the worst managerial move in the history of the World Series. It made no sense. Now, this is my logic - "If what you're saying is you need a run in the bottom of the fourth…so what you're saying is it's not the bottom of the fourth, but it's the bottom of the seventh or the eighth. Because you need a run to get up. OK, who would you bring in? Would you bring in Frazier or would you bring in Gossage?" And they said, "Yeah, but it wasn't a save situation." And I said, "Yeah, but you're managing as if it is." So if you're going to take your starter out that early, then you've got to go with your closer, and he pitches two innings, three innings." And they said, "But who do you bring in?" I said, "You bring in your next best pitcher." Your next best pitcher was Righetti, he was going to start the next night. Well, Righetti's next start was in the spring - because there was no "next night."

I said, "Because he managed himself into a box, you've got to manage *out* of the box. That was the only thing that made sense - if he told me, 'Tommy, I'm pinch hitting for you. I want to get a lead, I'm bringing Gossage in." OK, I have no problem with that. But what you're saying, at that point in time, is "George Frazier is the better pitcher than Tommy John." And if that's the case, then George Frazier should have been pitching at the start of the game. Later on, I found out from Doug Melvin, who was our "eye in the sky spy" or whatever his duties were - he was the batting practice pitcher for us then - that George had meetings with his staff, and they went over a game plan. To George's credit, he is a football man. And you have a game plan - "OK, we're going to pound the ball to the left side of their line. Their left side of the line is weak. We're going to continually pound it."

Well, in baseball, there is no game plan. Your game plan is you start the best pitcher, and then the game takes the game plan. If you're up five, six, or even runs, the game plan is easy - you try not to give up runs, you try not to give up bases, and you get outs. If you're down runs, you try not to run into outs, you try not to do anything to give up outs, because you want to try to get all your outs. The game plan changes as the game goes along. "Well, I don't need my closer. I don't need to bring Mariano [Rivera] in - we're up seven runs." Now, the other team scores five, and now you've got to bring Mariano in a game, or you've got to bring Gossage in a game. That's the game plan - it changes as the game changes. But George wanted, "Get a lead early and go to the bullpen and win the game out of the bullpen." OK, so Lemon - being a good soldier - did what he was told to do. But it was the worst managerial move in the history of the World Series.

I had a golf tournament out in LA [after the '81 season]. When I went back out to look at all the celebs, I didn't see Bob Lemon saying that he was going to come and play. So I called him up, and I said, "Lem, Tommy John." And he said, "You're still speaking to me?" [Laughs] I said, "Yeah! Lem, that was then, this is now. Are you going to play in my golf tournament?" He said, "Are you going to poison me?" I said, "No, but I've got a bottle of VO that will be in your cart for you." He said, *"I'll be there then."* [Laughs] So Lem came out and people made a big thing, but that was in October and this was in November, and one's baseball and one's golf.

45 Just Out of Reach: The 1980s New York Yankees

GEORGE FRAZIER: Fernando was Fernando. The greatest pitcher at that time. You look back at it, what he accomplished, what he did for LA and selling out the ballpark and the whole deal. He was just a phenomenal pitcher. A great story for him, obviously. And as much as you hate losing, I admire guys who can do what he was able to do for the number of years he did it [Valenzuela pitched for the Dodgers from 1980-1990, eventually retiring from baseball after the 1997 season].

ANDRE ROBERTSON: The man could pitch. You look at him, you don't think he's that kind of player - he was kind of chubby, I guess is a good way to put it. But he had that screwball working, he could swing the bat, he could do it all. When he was on the mound, I think it was one of those things, he had everybody playing above par. And so, that's the kind of things you have to have when you're in a Series, going for wins. Everybody was having career years - that's what they had that year.

DAVE LaROCHE: Obviously, that was the first time we had seen him in person. He looked hittable, but from the bullpen and from the dugout. Except his ball was moving and he had a screwball, which very few people had seen - not many pitchers...I don't think anybody has it now. He had that, he was effective, the fans were into it, and got them going. He did a great job for them. I think he and Righetti matched up - two kids. It was a good match up. Fernando was impressive.

BOB WATSON: You knew Dave Righetti was going to be a good pitcher - he was left-handed and had good stuff. For a youngster, he pitched beyond his years. I think all of that caught up with him in the World Series [Righetti did not complete three innings in his lone World Series start]. But during the season, he had one heck of a season. One thing I was surprised about, they took him from a starter and made him a reliever [after 1983], and the next thing I know, he had forty-something saves. Again, that was George and his brainchilds or whatever. But Dave Righetti, you knew he was going to be a heck of a pitcher [Righetti won the American League "Rookie of the Year" Award in 1981].

RON DAVIS: We all know what [Fernando] ended up being - a great pitcher. But the bottom line is any time anybody threw a left-hander against us, they had a chance to beat us back in the day. Back when I played, they had trouble beating a left-hander. So him being a left-hander, and of course, there weren't a lot of videos on him back in the day, or we didn't have pictures of him or games of him, to see what he did. He definitely had an advantage on us and he was dominating.

DAVE LaROCHE: Well, I wish there would have been! [LaRoche's response to claims that Valenzuela would have started game seven, against Righetti]

RON DAVIS: [Game six] was at home, and seeing somebody celebrate on your home field, that's hard. It's heartbreaking. It's devastating. You never want to see anybody beat you on your own field. And of course, they did. And they whipped our butts on it. It was like, "Dang, *here they are.*" But you know what? I look at it like, "OK, '77 we did it to them. '78 we did it to them. They owed us one." You never like it and you hate it, but you've got to roll with the punches. You can't win them all.

GOOSE GOSSAGE: George was probably at his peak of being crazed. That's why in the '81 World Series, I said, "When my contract is up, I'm going to leave." Because I wasn't having any fun...*we* weren't having any fun. I believe at that time that George just stepped over the line. As crazy as he always had been, it just seemed like he was getting crazier. And taking all of the fun...we went to the '81 World Series, it still sticks in my craw that we lost that Series, and I think it was a lot of distractions. And a lot of focus was lost - I believe - with kind of the way George acted. He came in the clubhouse and told Righetti, "This is the biggest game of your life. *Don't fuck it up."* Here's a kid that's scared to death anyway. He's in his first World

Just Out of Reach: The 1980s New York Yankees

Series, he's scared to death. I really wanted to throw him out of the clubhouse, because it happened right by my locker. It was just unfortunate that that was the way it was. And then after the '83 season, my contract was up, and I ended up leaving for San Diego.

DAVE RIGHETTI: He definitely said it [in response to being asked if he recalls Steinbrenner's advice/warning of "Don't fuck it up"]. He was kind of building up. He didn't just say it out of the blue - he was talking about Valenzuela getting all this press, and "We've got a guy who is just as good. This is a big game. *Don't fuck it up."* That's kind of how George talked at times. That was my first experience of it...first or second - he had at other times done some things similar. Some of the guys heard it, which I remembered. It didn't bother me pitching - I could give a shit. In fact, it was the opposite.

The biggest problem I had before the game was, Graig Nettles might remember this - his cousin, Tom, was a sportscaster in the Bay Area on Channel 7. I had about 20-something tickets, and I left them for my parents, family members, and people that were going to go down to the game. Everybody got in...but my dad. Well, I don't know this [at the time], but my dad told everybody to go in, he would find his way in - which he did. In fact, he called the Dodgers and he knew Monty Basgall [a then-coach for the Dodgers] - my dad had played with him in the minor leagues. And he knew Lasorda. He got a message somehow to Monty Basgall, and anyway, my dad got a ticket and he got into the game. But again, I don't know any of this. The only thing I know is I'm walking out to the pen, and Nettles has got this cast on his hand or wrap, he's running out as I'm walking to the bullpen, going, *"Rags! Rags! You've got to get your tickets in!"* I go, "I left my tickets." He goes, "My cousin told me the problem." And I said, "Well, I can't do shit - I'm walking out to the bullpen right here." That was about my only distraction. I don't know if that distracted me much. It might have helped me relax.

I just made one bad pitch. I had almost gotten out of the jam - I struck out Steve Garvey and popped up Dusty Baker, with an open base. Cerone had come out to talk to me, and we talked about basically pitching around [Cey] - we had Rick Monday on deck - and what to use. It was the first inning, and I didn't throw a whole lot of change-ups and things like that, and I figured the best thing to do was locate a fastball in a tough spot, and that was the easiest thing to locate. Throw it down and away. I made a bad pitch - the damn thing cut and he knocked it out. They weren't real happy about that. [Laughs] Before, here I was the guy coming out of the bullpen, I was "the guy," and I was going to be the big sparkplug. And I didn't pitch well - they didn't even use me out of the pen the next three or four days, either. And then they were contemplating saving me for game seven. That we'll never know.

But yeah, Goose probably did hear it. I don't know if you remember the old stadium and the old locker room, but in the middle of the clubhouse, when you went toward the bathroom, there was an opening and there were no doors or anything. He caught me in that opening between going to the bathroom area and in the locker room. Almost anybody could hear it, I guess. But that was a workout day, and I guess Goose did hear it.

I was, of course, happy [about winning the 1981 AL Rookie of the Year]. But really disappointed. The World Series thing was tough. We got there and lost. A lot of teams, it would be a great achievement. But in New York, supposedly, you can't lose. You get there and lose, and it's thought of as, "You're a loser," in a sense. So instead of thinking you're great, you're a winner, and you just came up short, it's the opposite. So now, the hammer comes down even harder. It made '82 kind of a rough year.

RON DAVIS: After losing it in '76, winning it in '77, winning it in '78, getting beat in the playoffs by Kansas City in '80, and then losing the World Series in '81 - it was only one year there out of six years that we weren't in the playoffs. You don't realize it at the moment, you just think it's going to continue. But as we all

49 Just Out of Reach: The 1980s New York Yankees

know, things change. Other teams get better, and we might have got a little older.

chapter 7:
farewell, mr. october

One of the greatest players in baseball history decides to bolt from the team that gave him his famous nickname.

BOB WATSON: I knew with Winfield being there, Reg was going to probably have to be a full-time DH. He wasn't going to probably play outfield with Winfield being the right fielder. And Winfield just signed a ten-year deal for however many millions.

STEVE JACOBSON: Let's see, I was at the Super Bowl in Detroit [Super Bowl XVI, at the Pontiac Silverdome on January 24, 1982], and he was gone. There had been rumblings about that, but I didn't - and a lot of people didn't - think it was actually going to happen. Reggie only played five years here, and he said, "I didn't come to New York to be a star. *I brought my star with me.*" And that's the way he went about that period of time. George was very big on the theater concept of having a "star." You put your star on your marquee, and you sold tickets and put fannies in the seats. And Reggie did that for him. Winfield didn't quite do that.

GEORGE FRAZIER: Obviously, there was so much media around it. So much pressure on it. At that time, we'd signed Dave Winfield for $20 million for ten years [$23 million], Reggie was making $600,000 [Jackson's exact 1981 salary was $588,000] - a lot of jealousy, envious. Reggie hurt his calf in the playoffs. At that time, I think him and George weren't getting along very well. "If you want to leave, *leave.* Go out on the free agent market." Obviously, Reggie is a Hall of Fame player. You take somebody like that out of your line-up, it makes a big difference.

51 Just Out of Reach: The 1980s New York Yankees

FRAN HEALY: I've never heard him say, "I want to renegotiate." He's probably one of the few players that said he signed a contract, that's a contract.

RUDY MAY: I saw it coming, because we lost the World Series, number one. And I don't remember exactly how it happened, but I do remember Reggie was pretty elated about it, because he was getting back here to California. But he loved the Yankee mystique behind "#44" and "Reggie Jackson."

TOMMY JOHN: Whatever you say about Reggie, there's pros and cons about him. As a pitcher, you did *not* want to see Reggie come up in a game that was on the line, because you may get him out, you may strike him out, and he may hit the ball. But he brought fear into the pitchers. Reggie got into a fight with Graig Nettles at the '81 playoff party in Oakland, and George then said, "That's it. I've had enough of Reggie." Just taking that bat out of the line-up…guys were still going to hit, but Reggie in the line-up made hitters around him better, because of the respect and the fear factor that he put into the opposing pitchers.

BARRY FOOTE: [Reggie and George] had whatever the relationship was that we may or may not know what was real and what was in the press. But all I can say is that Reggie has been around the Yankees ever since he signed. If George didn't have a great deal of respect for him and like him, he wouldn't have been there. Listen to what a man says, then watch what he does. And the fact that he's allowed Reggie to be a part of the Yankees for 30 years or however long it's been - maybe longer than that now - I think that pretty much says it all right there, about their real relationship.

FRAN HEALY: He wanted to leave, and he wanted to go to the Angels. He was frustrated. In New York - not only for Reggie, but everybody - there is a lot of pressure there. And I always felt that he was frustrated. Before Cable TV really took off, I used to kid him when I was with the Yankees and was broadcasting - I said, "If you leave and go to California, when you hit a home run on Tuesday night, nobody's going to care in New York, because it's going to be the Wednesday afternoon edition when they see it, and they're on to the next game." He led the league in home runs the next year [Reggie tied Gorman Thomas for the most AL home runs in 1982, with 39]. And he told me that the reason George gave up on him was Charley Lau said he wouldn't hit anymore - Charley Lau was the hitting instructor. He was a little bit off with that, I think. And it's funny, because you knew that Reggie was going to have a big year, when he came into New York, and I believe the first guy he faced was Guidry [on April 27th], who had great stuff. And he hit a home run off him. I'm sure George wasn't happy that night either. George loved Reggie. He didn't go along all the time with his baseball people, but he has to listen to them. Gene Michael was his best baseball guy. I think George would get hot and cold on his baseball people.

ANDRE ROBERTSON: In that Series, he didn't play. He was hurt. They had Winfield and they had some younger guys coming up. I think he thought it was time for him to go. And judging from what I can remember, he had a contract about so much money over what their highest attendance was, and I think he dealt with his contract. Reggie was a good businessman. I think he was trying to use what he had done - "Mr. October" and all that stuff - to get him some financial security. It played out well for him.

RON DAVIS: I don't know if it was a surprise. I think Reggie was at the end of his career. When he went to Anaheim, I can't remember how many years he played there - probably two or three years [five years, from 1982-1986]. But you could see the numbers weren't very good afterwards...*as good,* I should say. I think George said, "Hey, I'm not going to pay him that kind of money - which he's probably demanding - at the end of his career." And so I think that was part of, "OK, that's part of a baseball type deal there" - just the business aspect of it.

53 Just Out of Reach: The 1980s New York Yankees

As far as hurting our team, again, as far as his hits and his at-bats or his bad defense didn't hurt us...Ken Griffey Sr. [who joined the Yankees in 1982] was out there in right, and numbers-wise, probably had a better year than Reggie. I'm just guessing at that, because I was traded, too. But I'm assuming he probably had better numbers [Griffey Sr. hit .277 for the Yankees that season, while Jackson hit .275 for the Angels]. But the chemistry of Reggie being there, and the Catfish Hunters and the Thurman Munsons and the Lou Piniellas and the Bobby Murcers, when you have this "family tie" - even though there is some good, bad, and ugly in there - when some of the good, bad, and ugly disappears, it can hurt the family.

BARRY FOOTE: I think it negatively impacted the team. I wasn't a long-term member of the ball club, so I didn't see the good, the bad, the ugly, and some of the other things that went on with Reggie there. I just know that in '77 and '78, they won the World Series with him. In '81, he got hurt, and that hurt us - it kept us from probably having a good chance to win that World Series. How it affected the ball club is that New York City is a very tough place to play, because the press is always on different players. But because Reggie was on the ball club, he had absorbed a lot of that - he was a guy they always went to, and he liked that whole thing. I think that really was as important as anything. Having him not on the ball club allowed other guys to absorb the criticism that usually went to Reggie, and he handled it real well.

DAVE LaROCHE: Sometimes it can be the presence - just the presence. Sometimes you can cut back your playing time, and maybe the total numbers aren't the same per games played, but still be productive. Like Frank Robinson in Cleveland - just his presence and when he was in the line-up, he had that chemistry that could make a team be better than they were.

FRAN HEALY: Well, [Steinbrenner] signed him. He wanted pizzazz, and he got pizzazz. George had his own pizzazz. George is underrated with pizzazz. Reggie had it and George had it. In fact, they may have had more pizzazz than Martin. Martin was a good foil for George, and because of George and Reggie, Martin got sympathy. And Martin was a very popular manager - feisty, he wasn't going to take anything…but he did. He took stuff, believe me. As far as Reggie and George, I thought the relationship was very good. To this day, Reggie speaks fondly of George. Even when they were having their ups and downs, he spoke fondly of George. George came to Reggie's defense. George had a lot of guts. George - as an owner - had a lot of guts and defended Reggie. Everybody has a lot on their plate when they own a team, but George stood there with Reggie. There were certain times when it didn't look like that, but he stood there with Reggie. And Reggie - to this day - is very fond of him and the Steinbrenner family.

DAVE LaROCHE: Probably a little bit like Billy's [is how LaRoche describes George's and Reggie's relationship]. I think Reggie loved playing in New York, and I think George loved having him, but I think George expected Reggie to hit a home run every time he got up for something. [Laughs] Or they were going to win every single year, and if they didn't win, he probably blamed Reggie…or the manager…or both.

BILLY MARTIN JR: I would describe [Billy's father's relationship with Reggie] as my father respected his ability to play big in big games. And that's about it.

GOOSE GOSSAGE: Oh, I don't think it affected us. Reggie was gone and I don't think there was any love lost or any real feelings towards Reggie from anybody that he left. Like, "Oh well, he's gone. Neither here nor there."

BARRY FOOTE: I think you always knew that you were going to have a shot at winning, because George was the kind of guy that was going to try and get the right players in there. But I think there was something not having Reggie for the first time

55   Just Out of Reach: The 1980s New York Yankees

around, because he was a big-time player. "Mr. October." There were probably some veteran guys that knew Reggie a long time that were maybe glad that he wasn't on the ball club. But myself, I had played with the Phillies part of my career, and in my time in the major leagues - spanning a ten-year period of time - I felt Mike Schmidt was the best player in the National League and I felt Reggie was the most dynamic player in the American League. He may not have been the *best* player, but he was a guy who could do some things that may help you win, and he absorbed a lot of criticism that a lot of guys that might not have been able to take the kind of criticism, allowed them to play better. Not having him, I think that was a big deal. I think it was a bigger deal than anybody would have thought it was going to be. Not so much because of his performance, but the other things that he brought to the ball club. As an outsider…or even guys on the ball club might have thought were negatives, I think were really positives.

ANDRE ROBERTSON: My first experience [with Jackson], I went up to spring training in '81. They introduced me. I said, "Hi, I'm Andre Robertson." He shook my hand and looked me from my head down to my feet and back up. And I'm like, "Well shucks, what is he doing?" He didn't say a whole bunch. But that was in spring training, that was my first experience. I played in spring training, I think I was the best rookie in camp that year. I forget the name of that award - the James P. Dawson Award [it was actually in 1982 that Robertson won the award].

The thing that did occur when they called me up, I joined the team in Minnesota in September, well, I didn't play that first night, but the next night, we traveled to Kansas City. My first game they put me in, he actually came up and said, "Come run with me." I said, "OK." Well, we went out running, and he knew it was my first game. He told me, "I know this is your first game. What you do is just go out and relax and play like you've been playing all year. You should be fine." I think I went 2-3 that game - got a hit my first two times up. The only one I didn't get, Willie Wilson robbed me in deep left center. But those words, when they're coming from the superstars like that, he did take me kind of under his wing for that first game. And that eased the tension of playing the first game, and I went up there and had a good game.

STEVE JACOBSON: Reggie was gone, and Steinbrenner conceded that that was the biggest mistake he made as owner of the team. It may not have been - I thought his handling of Dave Winfield may have been the worst mistake that he made.

chapter 8:
1982

Several new players are welcomed aboard, to hopefully replace their departed star and get the Yankees back to the World Series.

DAVE LaROCHE: It seems like we lost a few pieces of the puzzle, because we had some new guys. The chemistry is big, I think. You can look at the Giants now - for two years they've won the World Series [2010 and 2012]. They had a very good pitching staff, but they didn't have the best team. But, they play good enough to win their division, they play good enough each playoff series. They have really, really good chemistry. And the Yankees - for a lot of years - had the highest payroll and some of the best players in the game. But it takes that one person or something that kind of brings them all together, or somehow, you get that chemistry going, where no one's thinking about any one guy - good or bad. They're not thinking, "Oh man, I hope Reggie doesn't get hurt or we're really screwed." It's, "OK, we're playing - all's going well, as far as on the field." It's like the Dodgers now, last year, they have all the talent - great talent. And it looks like [Hyun-jin] Ryu might be that little sparkplug that brings the whole thing together.

GEORGE FRAZIER: Oh, you're going back to the World Series [was Frazier's mindset going into '82]. I think as a player, every time, that's what you think you're going to do. You automatically think, "We're going back." And then everything fell apart. Everything just got destroyed. People were hurt. I remember we traded for John Mayberry - he was at the end of his career, and played first base. We were making trades for guys and doing everything we could to win. We just couldn't win. We just weren't a very good baseball team. I can remember George telling me personally, "Hey, we're going to fix this. And you're going to be a part of it." I was like, "Great!" Because everything I ever did in my life as a player, I won at. Two state championships in high school, four college World Series, winter ball championships, summer ball championships. I didn't like to lose. And he was the same way, obviously. And he was going to fix that ball club…but that ball club was not a very good baseball team.

TOMMY JOHN: Then we started making some trades that were absolutely horrible trades. *Horrible trades.* We traded and got Roy Smalley, traded Bucky Dent to Texas. Somebody had told George that Smalley being a switch hitter would hit really well in Yankee Stadium. Roy was a good offensive player, but he was not a good defensive player. His range was not real good. They made that trade, and then they kept making trades to try and make up for *that* trade. Then they traded Ron Davis, and he was an integral part of our bullpen. Being that guy that could pitch the sixth, seventh, and eighth innings, and turn the game over to the closer. Back in those days, the closers didn't go three outs - they may go six outs, they may go seven outs, they may go five outs. Whatever needed. But Davis was an integral part of our bullpen. And then we got Lee Mazzilli - they started making a series of trades. Then they traded me to the Angels for Dennis Rasmussen, and then it was like, "We've got to rebuild the pitching staff." From that point on, they just kept making trade after trade after trade.

DAVE LaROCHE: You never know what's going to happen. Of course, we thought we had a good team and we were hoping we could stay pretty much intact. It was kind of disappointing. But that's baseball - we learned quick, you deal with the cards you've got. You can't say, "Goshdarnit. It would have been nice if we had him." But then it's over - you go out and play. Once the season starts, you don't look back and say, "If we only had *him.*" You play. You work with what you've got and deal with what you've got and play the game.

Just Out of Reach: The 1980s New York Yankees

BOB WATSON: I had gotten in trouble with Steinbrenner, because he wanted everybody to show up on February 4th or something like that for spring training, to have two or three weeks of "bunting practice," before regular spring training started. And I told him I wasn't coming. It got him in trouble with the Players Association, so he told me he was going to trade me. And I was like, "OK, fine." But he said, "Before I trade you, you've got to teach Dave Collins how to play first base." That experiment didn't work very well, because they ended up trading for a number of other first basemen during the course of that '82 season. But he did what I asked him to do - trade me to a good team. He traded me to Atlanta. I ended up being a player/coach for Atlanta for three years with Joe Torre. We won the Western Division [in 1982] and we finished second the next two years. I was grateful. But did I keep up with the Yankees? No. Did I keep up with Reggie in Anaheim? No. I really had other priorities. Joe, when I came over, asked me to take over the hitting duties. He was the hitting coach, but he said he didn't have time - being manager. So I said I'd be glad to learn that as a player/coach. And that's what I did.

TOMMY JOHN: George [and Tommy] had a fight in '82. We had a "lover's spat." [Laughs] I was trying to get him to uphold a clause in my contract that we negotiated in that he agreed to, and he said, "No. I'm not paying it." It was a loan for a house - to buy a house. And I said, "But it's in the contract." "Yeah, we know. But the boss won't OK the check. Here's the check, the check's written, but he won't OK it and we can't give it to you - unless he OK's it." So the only way I was going to get my contract enforced was I had to ask for a trade. So I asked for a trade, they traded me to the Angels, we got into the playoffs that year, and got beat by the Brewers. But we had a good team. Had the 1982 Angels had Rich Gossage or Dave Righetti as our closer, we may have won 130 ballgames. Because I think if you go back and look at the statistics, the '82 Angels, our save leader had seven. *Seven.* Which means one, they weren't closing games. Secondly, starters were left in the games to win or lose them.

STEVE BALBONI: Spring training was weird for me. '81, I played all the time. '82, I never stepped on the field in spring training. I played in two B games, and then they sent me down. I never stepped on the field. It was strange. And I think it was because he brought in Davey Collins to play first base. I don't think he ever played first base. I know it had something to do with more speed…I don't know exactly what it was. He came in to play first base, and when the season started, I don't even know if he ever did. It was a weird season - I did get called up off and on throughout the season. I was platooning, so if we went on a road trip, I just played against the lefties. I couldn't tell you how many games it totaled out to [33 games]. But I think probably close to half the season I was out, because I only played about half a season in Triple A.

'82 and '83 I was up and down a lot. '82, there is a pitcher, Dave LaRoche…it was funny because we were both in Columbus and with the Yankees, and we hardly ever played together. It was pretty much we were switching. I was called up mostly on the road - which was fun for me, because I was going to be in a hotel anyway. It was better to be on the road where everyone else was in a hotel, too. But yeah, it was like every time we went on a trip, we were going to face left-handers. Because mainly, I was just platooning against left-handers. So '82 and '83, that's pretty much what it was. It was very frustrating. But there's nothing you can do about it. I had to resign myself to the fact that this was the way it was - I just had to make the best of it, wherever I was. It was more about every time I got sent down, it was like, "You can't make them right. You've got to try and prove them wrong." Just the way I was - I was competitive and wherever I was playing, I wanted to compete and win.

DAVE RIGHETTI: It started in spring. *I knew George was after me.* The coaches had arguments and meetings - and I know this to be true - over me. George didn't even want me on the team in spring training. Typical of how he used to run things. He threatened the coaches - "If he doesn't do well, it's your ass" kind

Just Out of Reach: The 1980s New York Yankees

of thing. I knew that, and I knew Yogi and Bob Lemon and those kind of guys were sticking up for me. He was mad at me for not pitching a good game [in the World Series]. I felt it all spring. I could tell by the tone of the writers' questions. Certain guys - not the real classy guys - he used some guys I won't mention, to come up to me...you could tell it was almost like a set-up deal. They were always edgy. I said, "Christ, he really wants my ass." So anyway, I pitched good coming out of spring, and I started the season off well. Somehow, someway, they decided to...we were a bad team that year, and I think I was .500 at the time, I was 5-5. It basically came down to my wildness. Trying too hard, not using my other pitches a lot. Getting a lot of deep counts. He decided to send me down.

That was a big deal. It was big because the team got involved in a sense - players were pissed, and "Why are you doing this?" At the time, I think I was third in the league in strikeouts and I think .500 on a team that was under .500. I'm a young guy...am I going to develop? I'm not going to develop at Columbus. But he didn't care. He sent me out for exactly 19 days, and back then, you could do that, because the 20th day, you would use up one of your moves, going down to the minor leagues. And not only that, it kept me away from arbitration in those days. I didn't care about all that. At that point, they just sent me down. I pitched well when I went down and came back - I finished out the season pretty strong.

Yeah, '82 was ugly. We had three managers [Bob Lemon, Gene Michael, and Clyde King] and five pitching coaches [Jeff Torborg, Jerry Walker, Stan Williams, Clyde King, and Sammy Ellis]. Players were coming and going. The sad part was our minor leagues were so good - I mean *really* good - and every player down there was a winner. We won at every level, every team won. They were cocky, strong, hard-willed guys. Not a lot of flash, but all good players. And they're all over the big leagues coaching and managing now. Guys that all played in the big leagues. And we never used them. Just constantly didn't have any patience. We were lucky to get the Donnies [Don Mattingly] of the world later on. And he had to be great just to stay there.

Everybody else got traded away, until they finally had to do something about it, and some of the older guys couldn't do it anymore. And quite frankly, guys stopped coming to us, too. We had to use the system a little bit more. So that was too bad, because we had some great players.

GOOSE GOSSAGE: I think a lot of it had to do with the Eastern Division. Oh my god - that Eastern Division hasn't been as good since. It was known as the "beast of the east." There was not a weak link in the whole division. There might have been a lack of a little pitching here and there, but that was it. All were great offensive teams - Cleveland even had a great offensive ball club. They may have lacked a couple of pitchers that kept them out of the playoffs, but it was just such a tough time to win, because the division was just so, so tough.

GEORGE FRAZIER: It's kind of funny, because Bill Bergesch was the GM at the time, and I loved eating at Carmine's downtown - over in the Theater District. I loved their Italian food. And I remember I was sitting there, and here comes John Elway [who was going through turmoil finding a suitable NFL team to quarterback, and instead, played on the Yankees' Single A team in '82, after being drafted in the second round of the 1981 MLB Draft]. He went to the bathroom and I went to the bathroom and I introduced myself. We're standing there talking, and he's a junior or senior at Stanford. But he says, "Oh hell, I'll take the money and I'll buy me a Porsche, and I'll go on down the road and play somewhere. It's just added pressure on the football side of things." And it was kind of funny - it was kind of like, *"Do you really even want to go play?"* I think he just wanted the $125,000 that Steinbrenner was giving him, to come out and play.

And I've seen John here out in Denver where I work now, and we kind of giggled and laughed about it a couple of times. Football was I think his love, baseball was a hobby. He never really brought up too much the baseball side of things, other than he didn't like his slider. Fastballs were fun, sliders

Just Out of Reach: The 1980s New York Yankees

were no fun. You're talking about a college guy that was playing in a high school league, too [Elway had a .318 batting average, with four home runs, thirteen stolen bases, and a team-high 25 RBI for the Oneonta Yankees in 1982, having played the outfield for 42 games]. Most of the players in that league were high school guys. He was in the New York-Penn League. When I first signed I went there, and I only stayed seven days. But that league is made up of a lot of young Latin players and a lot of high school players.

Once again, you start to look at some of the drafts and things that didn't happen and where they were, and I think at that time, Bo [Jackson, who was drafted by the Yanks in the second round of the 1982 Major League Baseball Draft, but didn't sign] probably didn't realize how good he was going to be in both sports. People don't realize how good this guy was at baseball. They really don't. Because he was playing two sports at the time in the big leagues when he got there, and people don't realize how good Bo was at baseball. I mean, how far he could hit a baseball, how good of an arm he had, and speed in the outfield. They had no clue how good this guy was. He was *really* good.

DAVE LaROCHE: That was the year I went up and down, so I was with Don [Mattingly, who made his Yankee debut in '82] in Triple A, too. I was going up and down, trying to help the team. So I saw a lot of him in Triple A. He had very little power, but he was *an RBI machine.* He hit more doubles, and he was kind of like Rod Carew - he really had that topspin through the infield, and he hit a lot of line drives. He was a line drive/groundball [hitter]. He was really a tough out with runners in scoring position. It seemed like every year in the minors, he drove in a ton of runs - and he continued to do that. Always a good clutch hitter and an RBI man. I was surprised and pleased when Piniella worked with him - and of course, his talent was there - and he learned to pull the ball in Yankee Stadium, and he started to hit a lot of home runs. It just made him the great player that he was.

GEORGE FRAZIER: Bobby Murcer was from Oklahoma and

a really good friend of mine. I remember when Donnie got called up for good, George told him, "I'm going to put you up in the TV booth." He goes, "I had never done that. Why are you going to do that?" He goes, "Well, there's a pretty good player coming up from Triple A. *So you need to go to the TV booth.*" And that's how Bobby's TV career was launched. But Donnie was a great player. When Donnie first came up, he and his wife stayed with me, and the friendship remains today, as a manager of the Dodgers. But you just watched Donnie play, people always ask me trying to compare him to other players, and it's hard for me to compare. He was as good a first baseman as you'd want defensively. As I watch the game today, Todd Helton is Don Mattingly. But Donnie, you could tell was going to be a great, great player. And that was the cool part about it for me - Donnie stood out to me as a guy that worked countless hours to make sure everything was right. Because we'd had Bob Watson when I was there, and like I said, we had Mayberry there - we played different guys over there. But when Donnie came in, it just kind of put a calm at first base.

RUDY MAY: I don't know if you can relate the 1982 Yankees as a "rebuilding season." But if I remember correctly, there weren't very many players on that ball club that had good years. I just know we didn't have a good team, we didn't win, and it wasn't very much fun playing on the ball club that year. And I was hurt. A bad taste - you don't remember things because you don't *want* to remember.

chapter 9:
1983

One of the more interesting/unpredictable seasons the Yankees have ever endured, where seemingly, there was never a dull moment.

GEORGE FRAZIER: I was excited, because Billy was coming back. I'd always heard all the stories about Billy - all the negative side of things. But I also knew that he was a pretty good manager. And he seemed to get an awful lot out of his players, and he managed the game great. I always had the ultimate respect for Billy. A funny story - we were in Anaheim, and Bob Boone was the leadoff hitter. It was 5-1 or 5-2, and he got a bloop hit off me in the ninth, and he didn't want to pitch Goose that day. Then, the next guy I think got a base hit, then I got a double play. Then a guy was on third. He got mad at me because I didn't throw a certain pitch, and he came out to the mound, and we got into a big argument on the mound. He took me out of the game and the argument continued in the dugout. And then after the game ended, I didn't pitch for like, thirteen days.

I think we were playing again against Anaheim, Reggie was in, and I remember Righetti started the game. Again, it was one of those situations where he brings me into the ballgame, hands me the ball, and then walks off the mound. I think I struck out Reggie, and I got two more outs, and then pitched the ninth. We came back and won the game. And then all of a sudden, I get called into Billy's office. He looks at me, and says, "Why haven't I pitched you in two weeks?" I said, "Hell, I don't know. You're the manager." He goes, "Alright. Well, I'll pitch you to wear you out." And he did. I mean, I pitched *a lot* the rest of the year and kind of became a favorite of Billy's. I think that group of guys we had there was a very good baseball team, but we came up short - Baltimore that year won the World Series. I remember going into Baltimore, I think we were three back in September, and they beat us and we didn't win it. But we had a very good baseball team that year - a really good team.

STEVE KEMP [Yankees left fielder from 1983-1984]: I knew guys that were on the existing team, just from playing against them. I had a ton of respect for all of the guys on the Yankees in previous years. Going there was what I expected - they were professional guys who loved to have fun and play. I think the players were happy and accepted me, and liked the style of play that I brought to the Yankees. As a rookie in my first year playing [1977] - I will never forget this - this is when the season was halfway in, we were playing the Yankees and I stepped up to home plate, and Thurman Munson said, "Hey, kid. I really like the way you play the game. You're going to go a long way." To me, coming from Thurman Munson - who was an icon at that particular time - was pretty moving to me. So I was happy to be a part of the Yankees. The guys I played with over there were the best. If I had to say it, looking back, it would have been great to play with one team for your whole career. It doesn't happen very much. I loved Detroit, but looking back, going around after the White Sox and the Yankees and a couple of other teams, it gave me the opportunity to meet some quality people, great people, and people that I may have played against and respected as an opposing player. But then having the opportunity to play with them on the same team and be teammates with them was worth it, also.

BOBBY MEACHAM [Yankees shortstop from 1983-1988]: For me, it was brand new - it was my first time up. I was in A Ball in 1982 with the Cardinals, so I was traded over and had a great spring. It was a new experience to be around big leaguers and big league camp. I saw a lot of the older, veteran players that we had - guys I remember watching on TV. It was one of those things where now I'm playing next to or seeing guys like Randolph, Winfield, Guidry - people like that. It was eye opening. I thought we had a real good team just based on what I

Just Out of Reach: The 1980s New York Yankees

saw in spring training. I got called up in June of '83, because Randolph got hurt, I believe. One of the other infielders was on the DL too, and was coming back in a couple of weeks. I was just a sort of stopgap for two weeks, and then I came back up for September.

I was on the team for Righetti's no-hitter [on July 4th, against the Boston Red Sox at Yankee Stadium - the first Yankee no-hitter since Don Larsen's perfect game in the 1956 World Series]. That was exciting for me. I didn't play in it - I was sitting on the bench, wondering if I was going to happen to get in. It was one nerve-racking game. I remember being real nervous in the last inning. I remember we had one out, and it was a ground ball. Andre Robertson was playing second - it was pretty far to his left, so he ended up getting it and throwing to first. I was like, "Oh man, maybe that would have been two outs on a double play if it was a little bit closer to second base." And then I remember the last hitter being Wade Boggs, and kind of going, "It figures - a good young hitter coming up to the plate here. Hopefully Rags has enough to get him out." It was great to see him get him out. I remember Rags just being mobbed by all of us. Actually, I think it's my best memory as a Yankee - watching him throw a no-hitter. Great guy, great game - in front of a full house at Yankee Stadium [interesting factoid - former US President Richard Nixon was in attendance that day].

STEVE KEMP: I was playing in that game, and the opposing pitcher was John Tudor, who was one of the top left-handers in the American League at that particular time. I remember having a big hit in that game, that drove in a run or two late in the game. But then I also made a catch, which was a foul ball - it was in the stands, and I leapt up into the stands on the right field line. It didn't matter if I caught it or not because it was a foul ball, but the person that was batting was Wade Boggs, who in those years, Wade could get a hit off of anybody. So who's to say what would have happened?

Dave was an awesome teammate. He was just great to play for - the same thing with Guidry. Those guys were gamers.

If you made a mistake, they didn't sit out there and glare at you. They just went from there and tried to bail you out if you made an error. That's the great thing about me going to New York - I just met some awesome people, and played with some great players. I think Dave was always tough to beat if you were an opposing hitter. But he was "on," and to throw a no-hitter, I'm trying to think if I've ever been part of another no-hitter, and I don't think I was. He deserved it, and had a very good career. He was a great teammate. It was an exciting Yankee memory for me, just to be able to participate and be a part of that. He's the one that did all the work - we just happened to be a part of it.

GEORGE FRAZIER: What I remember the most about it was just the total dominance of a great baseball team in the Boston Red Sox. You're talking about Carl Yastrzemski, Jim Rice, Dwight Evans - you can go on and on with their ball club, about how good they were. And he just took it to them.

RUDY MAY: I remember Righetti's no-hitter, and I remember it from my hospital bed on the 4th of July in New York [May had injured his back]. I forget which hospital it was - maybe it was New York University Hospital. And I was also there with Lou Piniella...and Gerry Cooney, the heavyweight. After I had hurt my back, I knew that my '83 season was over, and there was a possibility that my career was over, as well.

STEVE KEMP: I was in right field [on July 24, 1983, for the infamous "Pine Tar Game," vs. the Kansas City Royals at Yankee Stadium]. All's I remember is that George Brett hit the ball [a two-run home run off Gossage, to give the Royals a 5-4 lead in the top of the ninth inning] to right field. It was in I think the third deck. And then the next thing I knew, there was all kinds of commotion going on. I think Nettles is the one that brought it to Billy's attention [the fact that pine tar exceeded the 18-inch limit on the handle of Brett's bat], and then Billy went up and talked to the umpire. That's kind of my read on it - I can't tell you if that's how it totally came down. It was entertainment - let's

Just Out of Reach: The 1980s New York Yankees

put it that way. George went off and wasn't too happy with the call the umpire made.

GOOSE GOSSAGE: It wasn't Billy Martin - it was Graig Nettles that spotted the bat, that brought our attention to it. In Kansas City [during an earlier game], I came in with the game on the line in the ninth inning - it was the bottom of the ninth. Brett was at the plate with the tying run at second base - he was the winning run at the plate. Graig Nettles came over to me and said, "Hey, if he gets a hit here, we're going to get his bat, because he's using an illegal bat." And that is the first I had heard of it. So he hits a ground ball I believe to second base for the final out. No harm no foul - we didn't say anything. Then they followed us into New York, and the same scenario comes up, where Brett is at the plate and Nettles is at the mound again, telling me, "Hey, remember - if he gets a hit here, we're going to get his bat." And then he hits the home run, and the rest is history. That's the maddest human being I've ever seen.

BILLY MARTIN JR: [Martin] and Graig talked about it a lot. They had a list of players. They had a player or two on several different clubs. And something else people don't realize about my father - my father would read the rulebook. He'd go through it and look for little nuances. Look for rules to take advantage of. But he had a list of guys, and he just wanted to wait for the most opportune moment to take advantage of that rule. He loved George Brett. As a guy off the field, they were pals. But like I said, he didn't have any problem trying to pull a home run away from the guy, that could help his team win.

ANDRE ROBERTSON: Tim McClelland was behind the plate and he made a decision - it was too high. I thought George Brett was going to run out and kill him! But Billy got a kick out of that. He says, *"That's one for us, boys."*

STEVE BALBONI: I started the game, then I came out of the game when it happened. I was on the bench for the Yankees when it happened. I ended up playing for Kansas City [from 1984-1988], and I became friends with George Brett. But I didn't know him back then. I thought he was going to hit the umpire when he came charging out. But the thing is, we were just in Kansas City, and everybody saw the bat. I heard them talking about the bat. We knew that if he did anything, we were going to check the bat. So it wasn't like, "Oh, he hit a home run, what can we do?" It was planned all along - if he got a game-winning base hit, that's when we'd do the bat. Why do it before, y'know? It was a plan right from the start, as soon as they saw the bat in Kansas City, it was like, "OK, as soon as he does anything, we'll check it."

STEVE KEMP: It was reversed and we finished the game at a later date [August 18th, with the Royals holding on for a 5-4 victory]. I just thought it was kind of funny. I think most of us were laughing when we were in the locker room, about the whole situation and how it came down.

GOOSE GOSSAGE: They reversed the call - Lee MacPhail did - and went against...well, I have a rulebook, and I never understood that move right there. Tim McClelland, the home umpire, did his job - called him out. It's in the rulebook - "If you have pine tar above the label or 18 inches above the handle..." I'm not sure exactly how it reads, but you couldn't have any substance on your bat, or you were called out. Nettles knew about the rule because Thurman Munson had been called out on a similar play. He got a big hit in a ballgame and he used a lot of pine tar. These guys were such good hitters, they didn't break a lot bats. That's when bats were *bats*. They were not making them out of that balsa wood like they are now, or whatever they're making it out of. They never broke bats, so all that pine tar would build up on their bats. So that was the deal there. But we had a lot of fun with it.

BILLY MARTIN JR: That's what bothered me so much about it - obviously, the rule was the rule. They should have upheld the rule, and then said, "You know what? This is a stupid rule" - because it is. I mean, come on, how is pine tar going to help anything? If anything, if that pine tar gets on the barrel, how is that going to help the ball?

FRAN HEALY: It doesn't make sense the rule, because the flight of the ball would be *hampered* by pine tar. It's just like they talk about the bat being loaded with cork doesn't make sense. They say it makes the bat lighter…then just go to a lighter bat. It's never been proven scientifically. Even if it was, I wouldn't believe the scientist.

BILLY MARTIN JR: That's such an antiquated rule. It's so old. I'm sure whoever wrote the rulebook thought, "Oh my gosh, that would put a funky substance on the ball, and make it harder to throw for the fielder." That's just my guess - I don't know that. But it's got to be, why else? It's a very silly rule, but the funny part to me is they did - in a weird way - the oldest street ball rule there is…they did a "do over." [Laughs] They didn't really even do the do over, they just did the rest of the game over. I don't know, that's goofy. I don't know if I've ever seen a player more angry than George Brett was at that particular moment.

GEORGE FRAZIER: I was just the guy that hadn't pitched in the game yet, so that's why they had me pitching later [on the 18th], when we came back from Baltimore on the off day to have us play the game. And George didn't even come to the ballpark - I remember Hal McRae popped off and said, "I didn't come all the way from Baltimore to strikeout. *I'm going to take Frazier deep."* And I ended up striking him out to end the inning. But it was funny because he had me throw to every base, because there was a different umpiring crew - they all had an affidavit signed, saying that they saw George touch all the bases. If I remember correctly, Mattingly was at second, Guidry was in center. We kind of made a little bit of a farce of the whole deal. We ended up losing the ballgame and going on forward, but that whole pine tar thing…it's funny, Brett says, "I'm remembered for hemorrhoids [Brett had hemorrhoid troubles during the 1980 World Series] and the Pine Tar Game, versus 3,000 hits." It's kind of one of those silly things that's part of baseball that happened, and every year, I get calls about the Pine Tar Game on the anniversary. Every year I do interviews about the Pine Tar Game. It's kind of weird that it's still going on, since 1983.

GOOSE GOSSAGE: I ended up getting the loss. We ended up losing the ballgame.

ANDRE ROBERTSON: They did come and play one inning and a third, and that was the morning that I had the car wreck [which occurred on the West Side Highway, and left Robertson with a broken neck, and his passenger, Shenikwa Dawn Nowlin, a paraplegic]. I missed that game and the rest of the season.

TOMMY JOHN: The one thing that I think hurt them in the early '80s - '83, '84 - Andre Robertson was the shortstop and Andre was in that horrible car wreck with his girlfriend on the West Side Highway. He was good - he was *really* good.

GEORGE FRAZIER: He was a great player. He was a very good player. Came out of Texas. One of those guys that's young in the face and young in the heart. Played the game right, played hard. I think being around all these other guys helped him become a great player. One other thing I remember is funny, we had a rain delay one night, and they ended up canceling the game. And Andre went out to his car in the parking lot. In the old stadium, they had these pull-down garage doors that players came in and out. And he forgot something and he came running back in, and when he did, the cops thought he was one of the street kids trying to get back into the stadium and they slammed the door down - hit him right across the forehead! He had to get fourteen stitches right across his head, because they didn't even think he was a Yankee - they thought he was just some kid trying to break into the stadium.

Just Out of Reach: The 1980s New York Yankees

ANDRE ROBERTSON: A few people did [come visit Robertson in the hospital], but the first three or four days, I was out of it. My parents were there, and they told me a few of the [players] came. I know Willie came up. I didn't remember a lot of other people, because like I said, I think they had me pretty much sedated to get through that. But I did hear when people would call the hospital, and it was kind of funny, because no one could find me - I think they had me under a name, "Joaquin Murphy," or something like that. So that did make it more difficult for people to find me when I was there. That was pretty good because I did get the rest in. I got out of there in probably about ten days. I didn't really get back until the next year. That was August, it was going into September. So when I got out of the hospital, I actually came home. I had to go back up there for a couple of visits, but I didn't get back until spring training. I had hurt my right shoulder - I was really struggling trying to throw, but I played in one of the pitcher's games. And I ended up hitting a home run down there in Fort Lauderdale, and that made big news - here I am with glasses on, sore shoulder, and hit a home run. I think everybody got a big kick out of that.

    I think it was right away [that Robertson realized that the accident had hampered his playing ability]. When I was playing shortstop, there was a guy down in Triple A named Roy Staiger. He had played with the Mets, and I had seen how he'd went about things, and I tried to do the same thing. When I was throwing the ball to first, there were no short hops - the ball was right there, people were out. And what I noticed [after the accident] was I was struggling to get the ball to first. And I think that hurt me more than anything else - it hurt my arm. When you're a shortstop going in the hole, doing all these other things, that was the hardest part for me to get back from - trying to get that throw back over to first.

BOBBY MEACHAM: I just remember all the hype - how everybody was pretty excited about him playing. Heck, maybe that's when I got called up, I don't even know - when he got in the car accident. But I remember the hype and the excitement over him, and hearing all the good stuff that he could do. We ended up being friends, and I remember when he got sent down - I want to say it was '84, he got sent down in June and I came up - basically, we switched apartments. It was one of those things, kind of like, he really helped me with the living situation in New York and helped me with whatever I needed when he came back up. We were both kind of in the same boat, of trying to get back to our strengths and get back to playing every day in the big leagues.

GEORGE FRAZIER: That was just disheartening. It was so sad that it happened. And then basically changed his whole career - of what could have been a great player. [Randolph] felt like they would become Alan Trammell and Lou Whitaker, y'know? They were playing about that same time - that they could become a "Trammell/Whitaker" for another five, six, seven years, because Andre had such quick hands and great range, and handled the ball around the bag so well, that Willie was looking forward to playing with him every day. Bucky Dent was a good shortstop - Bucky's remembered more for hitting the home run in Boston [in 1978] than he is for anything else. And Bucky was a very solid shortstop, that could make all the plays hit right at him. But Andre had tremendous range, arm, and the whole deal. He had the makings of being a superstar.

ANDRE ROBERTSON: I even came up with this little nickname for us, "Give the pitchers 'R and R' - Robertson and Randolph." They hit to the infield, double play, we're out of the inning. Willie, everybody knows he could play. He's proven it over a long period of time. And I was hoping to get there. It just didn't work out. I was planning on being there, and like these days, that injury I had, you can get back a lot quicker. But back then, I think a lot of it was it's a business, and I think Bobby Meacham was coming up then, so he was playing. I ended up playing third in '85 for half of the year. I thought I did a good job over there. I always could catch the ball and I could hit. I was

Just Out of Reach: The 1980s New York Yankees

doing things in my mind to help the team win. I consider myself a team player and that's what I was trying to do back then.

A lot of things I think back on now. I couldn't see well, and I played all of those years, they were telling me I had 20/20 vision, but I had a stigmatism - I got contacts I think in '85. I didn't play every day, but I hit .328. Also, in '81, I was put on the indefinite disabled list - I had a bad left knee, and I came to find out I had a partial tear of my ACL. So I played from '81 through '85 with that partial tear in there. There were a lot of things, looking back on it, I could have played a lot better than I did. But you don't know those things. The technology these days, they can see stuff a lot better than they could back then. But hey, I enjoyed my time. I met some great people and I have no qualms about what happened. I just know if I could have gotten those things done, I could have had a very long career.

STEVE KEMP: Actually, I was the one Winfield was playing catch with [on August 4, 1983, in Toronto]. I was in right field…which is weird, I don't know how much center field he played. I remember him being right there. I think he was in center field that game. So if he was in center field and I was in right field, we were playing catch in between innings, and the seagull…I remember the seagull was on the turf, and he was far away from the bird. He threw the ball, and I don't know, maybe the bird was sick or something - the bird had time to react, and it didn't even move. He didn't really even hit the bird - I mean like, "hit it" hit it. The ball just kept coming to me - it grazed the ground and the bird just fell over. I was kind of laughing to myself. The next thing you know, I heard a couple of people booing. I'm sure people said, "Oh my god! Winfield just threw the ball and hit that bird and killed the bird!" The next thing you know, it got louder and louder and louder. I don't think they did anything until after the game, when they came in and supposedly, if you want to call it, "arrested" him. Actually, I thought something that was a little bit more funny about the story was I think the next day in the New York papers, it just said "WINFIELD INDICTED ON MURDER CHARGES." I guess that will sell papers, won't it? Winfield had no intention of trying to hurt or kill the bird. The bird was on the ground - the ball didn't hit the bird, if it did, it grazed him. The ball didn't like, hit the bird, and then the ball ricocheted, and then went into the infield - the ball kept its same movement.

GOOSE GOSSAGE: A lot of mixed feelings [Gossage had when he left the Yankees after '83]. When I finally made the decision, I had to hold a press conference, because it was the first time that we knew about collusion. Nobody was knocking my door down to talk to me, because they knew George - they weren't going to get in a bidding war with George. So what happened was I called a press conference and said, "Under no circumstances, I didn't even *accept* an offer from Steinbrenner or the Yankees." I just made the decision that I was going to leave. And that's when the phone started ringing. I ended up signing with San Diego. But that night that I had that press conference, I actually cried, because I was leaving the Yankees, and I didn't want to leave. I loved the Yankees. I just felt that George was over-the-top with his antics and all the things that happened with the distractions at the World Series. And then he apologized for us to the fans - not to us, but to the fans *for us* - telling the fans that he was sorry that we didn't perform. And I just felt that it was unfair because of all the distractions that he caused during the World Series. There was a lot of just uneasiness. Just really the bottom line was George I felt was the worst that he had ever been since I had gone to the Yankees.

STEVE BALBONI: I kind of did [see Balboni's trade from the Yankees to the Royals coming, in December]. It was good and bad - I loved the Yankees, I loved being a part of that organization, I loved the players that I was up there with. It was kind of bittersweet, but I didn't feel like I was going to get a chance to play there, so going to Kansas City was my opportunity to play. It was good *and* bad. The Yankees were the best organization - it's the "class organization." It's hard to go anywhere else. But yeah, I had a feeling - I was out of options at

Just Out of Reach: The 1980s New York Yankees

that point. So they were either going to have to keep me the whole year or not. I had a feeling something might happen. After Dick Howser called me with the Royals, I was pretty happy where I was going. I'll tell you, it surprised me, what a class and competitive organization it was. I mean, it wasn't the Yankees, but it was the same idea - veteran players...really good veteran players. Guys that wanted to win, an organization that wanted to win. The fans were different - they were nice and friendly. [Laughs] But I grew up in the northeast, so the New York/Boston fans, that's normal to me. These fans were *not* normal to me, but they were just incredibly nice. It was different.

That was weird [a baseball superstition dubbed "The Curse of the Balboni"]. I hit 36 home runs in '85 and [the Royals] won the World Series. And I guess it wasn't until when Arizona beat the Yankees [in 2001], Luis Gonzalez had 57 home runs, and that was the first team that won the World Series since '85 that had somebody on the team that hit more than 36 home runs. The Yankees won like four times [in 1996, 1998, 1999, and 2000], and they hit home runs, but they didn't really have a "big home run guy" those years. They were just an excellent team. They did everything - they hit for average, they drove in runs. A great team to watch, but they didn't have the big home run hitter. It was through the steroid era, too. Steroids had been in, so 36 home runs wasn't even that much. That's the funny thing. I still can't believe it's still a record in Kansas City [for most home runs in a single season]. It was the way it worked out - the teams that won, really didn't have anybody that was doing it. That just goes to show you, it's more about pitching than it is about anything else.

No, that was the furthest thing from my mind [if Balboni felt he "showed" the Yankees by winning the 1985 World Series with the Royals]. Going to the Royals, actually, '84 was the surprise [when the team finished first in the Central Division, but lost in the playoffs to Detroit in the ALCS], because they had just gone through that drug issue, and they lost some players. It was really kind of a rebuilding year. But it turned out to be just a great, young pitching staff. And we won it in '85. It was a great experience and I have a lot of good friends who were on that team. It really worked out well for me. And it was a great organization to be part of. We had an owner [Ewing Kauffman] who was kind of the same as George, only not as extreme - but on the "nice" side. [Laughs] He wanted to win and he would go above and beyond, even though it wasn't financially the smartest thing to do as a businessperson. It was more about, "This is my baby. If we need more money, let's put it in there to get whoever we need." It was more about winning to him, too. And I'll tell ya, I like and respect both of them, and those kind of owners are good for baseball - that go in there, and it's not about a business, it's not about a company. It's about the team and winning, and looking at it that way.

chapter 10:
no-no

Dave Righetti helps put some extra sizzle in Independence Day 1983.

DAVE RIGHETTI: The whole year, I was confident. Billy had come in again - I had in a sense missed him - and [pitching coach] Art Fowler. They just handed me the ball, and said, "Go get 'em. We've got your back." It made you feel like you were ten-feet tall, because with Billy, it was either you were on one side or the other in a sense. And if he didn't like you, things weren't good probably for you. But when you got him backing you, you really felt like you were ten-feet tall. And at that time, I needed that. The whole season, I was pitching well up until that point. It was just before the All-Star Game, and I couldn't pitch in it, because it was the last day and they didn't want me pitching on Tuesday, if I threw a bunch of innings. And I just wanted to make the team and go - to be an All-Star. So I was upset about that, disappointed that that couldn't happen. It was my mother's birthday, so it would have been nice to do and be a part of. But the biggest thing that day was Boston was of course a rival, and they had knocked us around for a couple of days. I just wanted to get after them early in the game and show them that they weren't going to walk through us that day. The no-hit thing just kind of evolves. You have a few games like that, and you never expect it to carry out through the whole game. You just keep pitching and try to not let them get on - especially in a close game.

    Fortunately, a couple of balls went at some guys, and Steve Kemp made a great play down at the foul line. I didn't run out of gas - I had a lot of strikeouts early and was really over-throwing, probably. I was in great shape then. But probably wasn't going to be able to keep that pace up. Two years before that, I probably would have kept trying to strike everybody out.

But I backed off, got some easy outs on some change-ups and some breaking balls. The next thing you know, it started getting later in the game and I had a legitimate shot, but with the score so close, I really didn't care about it at that point, because number one, I didn't think it was going to happen. And number two, up to that point, I just wanted to finish that game and us winning it, because we needed a win against these guys. The big deal was getting the two extra runs in the eighth inning. I think Kemp hit a double with the bases loaded. And that made it 4-0. 4-0 back then was a pretty big lead, especially with Goose down there. I think the biggest play, again, I mentioned the Kemp play, when he went down there and caught that foul ball, it was the first pitch of the inning [in the eighth], and Dwight Evans, who was in the meat of the order, popped it up right away. That really helped, because I didn't have to grind through him, because here I think comes [Tony] Armas, Rice, and those guys. That was a huge out at that time. Getting a quick impact, the next two outs were quick - I think I got a quick grounder and a pop-up. So I had some gas left - I think I came close to throwing 140 pitches. But it was a hot day, and again, it was building.

It started in '82, when we had the five pitching coaches. It was pretty obvious they were getting fired because of me - I was the young guy, we weren't pitching well. Doyle Alexander I think broke his thumb [Alexander broke a knuckle on his little finger, allegedly after punching a dugout wall]. There were all kinds of young guys coming in and out. You kind of felt like it was your fault - you're the young guy, and Guidry doesn't need any help. You felt like you were the weak link. I didn't feel real good about some things about that, when these guys are getting fired. You get close to them, because they're working hard to help you. Anyway, I would leave the dugout for at least two outs, and the reason why I did is because I got tired of walking off the mound every inning and having the pitching coach coming up to me like it's an instruction league. So I got to the point where I said, *"The hell with it."* I'd go up in the clubhouse and sit up there for two outs, and I'd come back down. But on that day, it was even better, because it was hot, and I'd get up

Just Out of Reach: The 1980s New York Yankees

there, and that's when Nettles came up to me, because me and him were going to Atlantic City for the All-Star break. He couldn't travel home because he had pink eye, and in fact, he wasn't playing because of it. I said, "Can you drive?" I don't know if he can see or not! I'm trying to pitch a game and what he was trying to do was get me relaxed I think. I said, "Well, we'll worry about that after." And then I went in and I'd always get a piece of gum. There was no spreads or anything like that, or big club house stuff. I got some gum and I heard Fran Healy say something about the no-hitter, and "He hasn't given up any hits." I knew it then, but I had a 4-0 lead now, and I know I've got Goose. If I give up a hit, I'm out of the game, he's going to finish the ninth.

    You're feeling pretty frisky now. It was the first time in the game I kind of pitched all around the zone, and I shouldn't do that with the first hitter. And I did - I walked [Jeff] Newman in about nine pitches. Here I am, I'm gassing myself, and I threw him all fastballs. That wasn't real good. Because I know now, if I give up a hit, Goose is coming in with men on base. But I think I got a ground ball quick on [Glenn] Hoffman, I think on the first or second pitch. And then the first pitch to [Jerry] Remy, he hit it [but made the second out] - again, I'm fortunate because these guys put the ball in play really quick, so I had something left against Boggs-y…and I got him out [on a strikeout].

    For the most part [Righetti was thinking], "He's going to hit it somewhere." There were two things in the back of my mind - first of all, he didn't have a lot of power to left. You could do it in Fenway and hit that wall, but that's going to be an out against us in our park. So I'm thinking, "Left field." And the other thing in the back of my head was getting over to first base on a ball between me and Donnie, because I threw a hard breaking ball, and if it broke and he got out in front…it's almost like a swinging bunt. And that's a nightmare for a lefty like me - especially for a guy that falls off a little. And I really had that in the back of my head. In fact, when I got the second out, people say I was doing these knee bends and all that. It was not because I was nervous - I was doing that because I knew I was going to have to run to first base to cover, and I was *not* going to be late. That's the reason why I was doing those knee bends. I was as shocked as anybody [that Boggs struck out]. I had thrown him hard sliders early in the game and he hit them both to center. But I threw them too hard and they weren't breaking enough, and they stayed in the middle of the plate. That last one, fortunately, I don't know where it went. I thought I had him struck out on an outside fastball, but I got him out. It was nice.

Any of those guys - him [Butch Wynegar, who caught the no-hitter] or Cerone-y were great. Butch, he was a classy catcher. Great hands, really good hands. I trusted those guys tremendously. I threw a lot of sliders in the dirt and those guys sucked them up with no problem. Wynegar was special because he caught both the Niekro brothers, and I remember Phil talking about how good he was catching him. He was worried about his knuckleball that it wasn't moving enough - because Wynegar was handling it so well. That was just Butch. He was just really hands-y and a good athlete. And a switch-hitter, of course. I never had a problem with getting along with those guys in a game, and it was nice to have them back there. Nowadays, one way I can get in Cerone-y's craw a little is I say, "Hey, you missed a game, huh?" [Laughs] Because we were pretty close, me and Rick. But that was nice - Butch was a hell of a catcher.

Relief [is how Righetti describes feeling after the final out]. As soon as it went by him, I just kind of dropped my arms and wanted to collapse. I didn't have any energy to jump around. Plus, I don't know how to put it, but you've still got that loss of the World Series in your head - the only jumping around you do is when you win it all. And when you do something on your own, you kind of still don't feel like jumping around. Nobody does that in a sense. So that was my way to react in a sense. I hugged Butch and kind of collapsed in his arms - which guys have a lot of fun copying and making fun of me a lot. But I was just tired. The coolest part was walking off the field with your teammates. The saddest part was it was a get-away day - on get-away days, guys can't wait to take off. Either the last day of the year or the All-Star break, guys are gone. And I never saw my

Just Out of Reach: The 1980s New York Yankees

teammates. They wouldn't let me go in the clubhouse - Fran Healy stopped me and I think John Gordon stopped me to do the radio. So I never got a chance to go in. And when I did, most of them were gone. So I never got to really share it with them.

And anyway, I had to get ready for my next game. I just remember that whole thing, at that time, it turned into a little bit of a...I just wanted to pitch the next game and, "Let's go. We've got a big season here." And all these TV people wanted me [in the ensuing days], and I didn't do any of them. And again, that was a lot of the structure of the Yankees. Back then, George [said], "Players have got to play during the season. I pay them to play and you don't do any off-field stuff and this and that." So that's kind of in your head all the time. And so I told Nettles, "We're *still* going! If they want to follow us, they can gas up those news trucks, but we're going to Atlantic City." So we did. And it went away in a couple of days, because back then, there wasn't a whole lot of media stuff. There was maybe a little ESPN, but that was about it. There was local, but once you got out on the road, nobody cared that you threw a no-hitter.

The Yankees doing so well, and Jimmy Abbott, David Cone, Dwight Gooden, and David Wells doing what they did [subsequently, Abbott and Gooden would pitch no-hitters, and Cone and Wells would pitch perfect games], it kind of brought it back to light, and they show it more and more. The most special thing outside of winning these World Series, without a doubt, people feel real close to it because it was the Red Sox, it was July 4th. If I'm on the field [nowadays], every day, somewhere along the line, somebody mentions it. So that means it was pretty cool to a lot of people and a lot of people remember where they were. That's the way I've got to take it. I'm glad I was able to do something like that, that people remember. But at that time, I was in a mindset of, *"We've got to win the next game."*

chapter 11:
1984

A season best known for an intense batting championship battle - between two Yankee teammates - that comes down to the final game.

PHIL NIEKRO [Yankees pitcher from 1984-1985, inducted into the Baseball Hall of Fame in 1997]: The Braves called me and told me they were going to release me [Niekro had been a member of the Braves since 1964]. I think John Mullen was the general manager at the time, Ted Turner owned the ball club, Joe Torre was the manager, and Bob Gibson was the pitching coach. At the end of the season [1983], it was the end of my contract, and I thought for sure I was probably going to come back - I didn't have a great year, but I had a decent year to today's standards [Niekro went 11-10, with a 3.97 ERA]. Ted called me over to his office, I went in and John Mullen was sitting there, and says, "The organization has made a decision - we're going to release you." I remember John Mullen saying, "We know you can still pitch but we're just going to go with a younger guy." That was it and I left. I went down to the stadium and cleaned out my locker, which was one of the tougher days in my career in baseball - cleaning that locker out. And just kind of mystified as to why they let me go - they told me I could still pitch and I could still win. I remember they told me that. And then as the news hit, the papers and everybody was talking about it, I remember Ted telling me after that, "If you want to go to spring training, I'll take you to spring training with our ball club." I said, "You can't do that Ted. I'm not going down there, and you're going to baby-sit me or hold my hand?" Torre and the staff made a decision, and I was gone - that's all there is to it.

I remember Steinbrenner calling and said he was interested in signing me to a two-year contract. Which was good news, because I was hoping *someone* would pick me up. But here's the New York Yankees - one of the greatest franchises in the history of baseball - wanting me to come play for them. I did not know George - I had never met him. Just heard about him, and saw him on TV a lot, and knew some of the Yankee players. But never ever thought that the Yankees would call. I remember waiting for spring training, went to Fort Lauderdale. The first week that I got there, one day during practice, Ron Guidry says, "What are you doing after practice?" And I said, "Nothing," and he says, "Well, George wants you and I to go someplace." I said, "I'm really not dressed. I didn't wear a tie or anything to the ballpark." He said, "No, you're fine."

So as soon as that was over, we walked outside the clubhouse - there was a limo there for us. Ron and I got in the limo, went to the Fort Lauderdale Airport, which is five minutes from there. Got on a plane and flew to I think Tallahassee. When I got on the plane, George was there - that was the first time I met him. Talked a little bit, not a whole lot, because it was a short flight. We got to the airport in Tallahassee - in his private jet. A limo picked us up there, drove up to a hospital, we got out of the limo and the staff - a doctor and a couple of nurses - were waiting for us. We went in the elevator, went up to I think the second or third floor, walked down the hall and into a room, and there was a young boy - thirteen or fourteen years old - having yellow jaundice, and needing some kind of a transplant. I'm not sure what it was. And talk about yellow, he was as yellow as a lemon. And me and Ron sat there and talked to him, signed a baseball and a picture, and while we were doing that, George was talking to his mother, and I remember George reaching into his sport coat, taking out a checkbook, writing a number down, and handing it to the lady. I thought she won the world's biggest lottery. George handed it to her, and said, "Hope this will help. I'll be in touch. If you need help, I'll be glad to help."

And right there, I realized what kind of a man George was, because he does so many things that people don't write about, or seems like they always speak the bad parts about George. And that was never written, no one ever knew that -

except for me and Guidry and George. Those are the only three people that ever knew about that. It was never brought up again. I'm saying, "Boy, this has got to be some kind of a good guy to play for."

TOBY HARRAH: I was with the Indians, and Gabe Paul had come to me and mentioned the fact that they were going with a lot of young players, and that the Yankees were looking for someone that could play third and back-and-forth, and a right-handed bat. My name had come up, and Mr. Steinbrenner, being from Cleveland, he had always kept a big eye on the Cleveland Indians and the players. It just worked out that the deal was made that I ended up going to the Yankees for the '84 season.

MIKE PAGLIARULO [Yankees third baseman from 1984-1989]: I got drafted in 1981 [by the Yankees], went to Oneonta, New York, and played there for a half season, then went to Greensboro for a full season, Nashville the next season, and then Columbus, Ohio, for Triple A. I got called up around halfway through the year or so [July 1, 1984]. Yogi Berra was the manager and Lou Piniella was the hitting coach. For me, I was standing around these MVP's - Don Baylor, Ron Guidry, and all these stars. But they made me feel right at home. I had been to spring training earlier in the year, and that was quite an event. Actually, I was at spring training with Graig Nettles. Graig Nettles was the greatest and a super-classy guy. That was the first impression that I got, was how classy they were. Being brought up in Boston, you're thinking they're all these big, mean guys. And they were the classiest bunch of guys - the most professional bunch of people. I was a little surprised at that.

Graig Nettles, as a young third baseman coming up, he could have made it tough on anybody - but he was great. I mean a great help and support. Even when he was gone [Nettles would be traded to the San Diego Padres on March 30th] and I would play third base and I'd make an error..."BRING BACK NETTLES!" And he knows how difficult it was to play there at

87 Just Out of Reach: The 1980s New York Yankees

times. But he also knew that it didn't really bother me much at all. That was normal for me I guess, growing up in the northeast. It helped me understand how to play in New York. I learned a lot of that from guys like Don Baylor, Ron Guidry, and some of the veteran players - Dave Winfield and Willie Randolph. They really helped me and helped some of the younger guys. Because it could be tough - it could be tough on some free agent veterans, like Eddie Whitson [who joined the Yankees in 1985]. But it wasn't difficult for me - I felt like I was part of that culture and guys showed me the way. And I listened - I was coachable. I just did what they said. I didn't say a word for about a year and a half. So I enjoyed it very much, and they had some great people - teammates, front office men, coaches - around me all the time. You couldn't help but learn and get the most out of it. So I did. I felt like I got the most out of it.

REX HUDLER: So we go to spring training. Me and a guy named Matt Winters - who was another #1 pick - we're in spring training. We were at the hotel bar. I think I'd just turned 21. Maybe. And Yogi Berra was sitting with his wife. Of course, me and the other rook were sitting at the bar, looked over there and saw Yogi. The next thing you know, Yogi saw us, gets up, comes over to the bar, and he gets between me and Matt Winters and he goes, "Hey Rex, hey Matt. How ya doin'?" And I couldn't believe that he knew our names - let alone would come over and leave his wife to greet us. So obviously, Yogi knew something about managing players. I could tell that right away. I'm going, "I love this guy already. He knew my name!"

So then I got called up in '84. That ended up being Yogi's last year - they fired Yogi in '85. Ended up having fun there - a little cup of coffee in September with them. And then the next year, they called me up…actually, let me share this story with you that I forgot about Mr. Steinbrenner. Mr. Steinbrenner had more class than any owner - and now that I'm 53 and I've been through a lot of organizations, he was so classy by the way he treated me. After six years in A Ball, I was doing parts of six years in Fort Lauderdale - it was a struggle for me - I was hitting .300, it was maybe the middle-late in the season...I want to say in 1983 it was. I'm back in Fort Lauderdale again. Stump Merrill was my manager there, and I said, "Stump, this is unbelievable. I'm going to write Mr. Steinbrenner a letter and I'm going to ask him for a promotion. What do you think?" He goes, "Whoa. Better be a short letter - *he don't like long letters."* So I wrote, "Dear Mr. Steinbrenner, I'm currently in my sixth year in the Florida State League. I'm ready for a promotion. I'm hitting close to .300, I'm having a good season. Would you please consider moving me up somewhere? I appreciate the opportunities you've been giving me, but I'm ready to move. Thank you, Rex Hudler."

So I took it to the Bay Harbor Inn - that was George's hotel, and we would always stay there when we played St. Petersburg or Tampa. And so, I remember taking the letter to the front desk, and I told the lady, "Mam, could you give this letter to Mr. Steinbrenner when he comes to town?" And she goes, "I'll take it up to him. *He's here."* Oh, man - then my booty got tight, thinking, "Shoot, I wasn't expecting him to be in town." So, went to the ballpark in St. Petersburg at Al Lang Stadium - we were playing the Cardinals. They had an A Ball team there. I come out ready for batting practice, and in the stands, sat George Steinbrenner and Stump Merrill. The only people in the stands at that time - at an A Ball game. This is batting practice time. And man, I got nauseous. I got nervous. It took a lot of courage to write a letter to George Steinbrenner, and ask him for a promotion. I'd never done anything like that before. So I had a real stomach problem. Stump comes out of the stands, and I went over to him, and said, "Stump, did Mr. Steinbrenner mention anything about my letter?" He paused, he chewed his tobacco and he spit, and he goes, "Yeah, kid. *He loved the letter."*

So I went into the locker room and relieved myself, because I had diarrhea. I was nervous man, I was worked up. So we bus back to Fort Lauderdale after the game, and the next morning, at 8:00, I got a phone call, and it said, "Get on a plane. You're going to Columbus - you're going to Triple A." So, forget about Double A...you're going to Triple A. I get on the plane

Just Out of Reach: The 1980s New York Yankees

and I'm flying there, and I had a little conversation with myself. I'll never forget it - "Self, look, you pop off to the Man, you better be able to back it up. Don't go up there and lay an egg...or you're in trouble." Sure enough, I went there and I dealt - I hit .300, and the next year I hit .300. Now, all of a sudden, they're talking about possibly moving Willie Randolph for this young prospect. I had a couple of call-ups.

TOBY HARRAH: [Yogi Berra] was bigger than life. My first year in the big leagues, I was fortunate enough to play for Ted Williams, who to me was bigger than life. Well, Yogi Berra is the same. And him being the manager and me being a player, you just had to impress him and be the best player you could possibly be. But at the same time, realize he's the manager. I always went by two rules. Rule #1, your manager's always right. Rule #2, revert back to rule #1. And that gives you a good chance at staying out of trouble. But Yogi was fine, we had a very good ball club. He was easy to read and he made it easy for you to get ready to play in the ballgame at any time.

PHIL NIEKRO: The first spring training was with Yogi, and I didn't know him a whole lot. I certainly knew *of* him. I was just trying to have a good spring, keep my head above water, and make the ball club - even though I signed a two-year contract - and just hope that I could have a good spring training, have some good showings there and be a part of the ball club and pitch well for them. I really did feel bad in one area, because they took Dave Righetti out of the starting position, and made him a reliever. For a while, I had a hard time even being comfortable around him. But we talked about that and it was fine. Once I got into the feeling that I was welcomed - even if I was taking Righetti's spot in the rotation - nobody said anything about that. So I felt comfortable in a very short time.

DAVE RIGHETTI: Well, why? Because they asked me...they kind of *told* me [to transition from starting to relieving]. That was the mindset of all of us - Ron Guidry in 1978 had one of the greatest years of any pitcher in the history of baseball [going 25-3 with a 1.74 ERA, and winning the AL Cy Young Award], yet he volunteered and closed in '79 when Goose got hurt. So that's in your head. You should try to do whatever you can to help the team. And that winter, when Goose didn't sign back, there wasn't a whole lot of short guys available. They didn't just grow on trees back then. You didn't have a bunch of minor league kids throwing one inning and getting ready for closers jobs. There was no such thing as that. So, the odds were they were going to ask somebody - they asked Gator first, and at that point, I don't think he wanted to do it. And they came to me, and I was bummed. I was upset. I finally got my feet on the ground. I was a starter - I felt like that was my niche. And I was a young guy and I could help the team transition through Guidry. And we had young guys coming up - José Rijo, Jay Howell. I just felt pretty good about where things were.

But they asked me to close, and that's probably *the* most important job on the team - nowadays it is. Back then, you were used a hell of a lot different. But you just can't turn it down. Goose had done it, and to me, it was like an honor. But there was a lot made of it - there were a lot of people fighting over it and arguing about it. It made for a lot of press but a lot of tough questions for me. I just thought I was doing what I was getting paid to do. To be the closer, my responsibility went up quite a bit. So I did not take that lightly at all. I of course didn't know how to deal with some things, so everything was new to me. Yogi's the one that asked, and Sammy Ellis and Jeff Torborg. I just wanted those guys to feel good about their decision. I knew what it meant. I heard all kinds of rumors and stuff. Everybody was fighting over it in the front office. Anybody that weighed in on the situation had an opinion.

It wasn't the easiest thing to deal with, but at that time, privately, I felt like it weakened our starting staff, which is what we needed. I thought that the bridge to winning all those games was a great starting staff - and I still do. But hey, again, you just do what you've got to do. It was funny, it was ironic - they thought it was going to be saving my arm by putting me in the pen, and I think my first five years I averaged close to a hundred innings every year. We do that now, and we'd all be fired. You can't even pitch the closer 50 innings without somebody getting all upset. So yeah, I was pretty much done by the time I was 30, in terms of my arm. But that's why I did it, and I trusted them and Yogi. Of course, Yogi got fired soon after. But again, I'm glad I did it. I'm glad I had that responsibility and they trusted me for seven years of doing it. So that's the way I look at it.

RUDY MAY: I got out of the hospital, and I think I did play after I got out of the hospital. My back was really, really bad. So the [1983] season was over, I went home, and what happened was my left leg atrophied. And I lost about 75% use of my left leg. During the off-season, Gene Monahan, our trainer, we set up a training regimen. And he said, "You have to rehab and get this leg back strong again. So I worked my tail off the winter of '83. I just worked and worked and worked. And I got it back to about 90%. Which, is not good. So I struggled in spring training to get in shape. I never will forget, right at the end, I had pitched a game against Cincinnati, and really pitched well. By "well," I mean I pitched six or seven innings, I think, and had double-digit strikeouts. Had good stuff and pitched well, and I was very pleased. I remember Steinbrenner came into the clubhouse after the game, and said, "Damn it lefty, it's about time you showed up!" He was so elated, and I was too. So, I go home and go to bed that night.

The next morning I wake up, and I pull a hamstring getting out of bed. To the point where it was bleeding - there was blood down at the bottom of the back of my knee. Finally I get up and into the shower, and I get it all squared away, and I go to the ballpark, and as I'm getting out of my car going into the clubhouse, I slightly pull the calf muscle in my right leg. Now, if that happens to a guy just walking and getting out of bed, you can't count on him. So I get it all wrapped up and I go out to right field to shag [fly balls]. I'm standing out there, and I'm just distraught. Yogi comes out there, and says, "Hey left-hander, what's going on?" I said, "Man, I'm not going to do this anymore.

I quit." So I went in the clubhouse and it was either Yogi or Torborg said, "Hey, you better talk to that left-hander, blah blah blah." So George called me in there, and said, "What's going on?" I told him, and he said, "OK." I quit, that was it. I walked away from it right then. And it was proven correctly - I still have problems with my back.

PHIL NIEKRO: I think spring training, we didn't have a starting shortstop. I think every position was taken, and it was someone's job to take the shortstop position. And Meacham won it over Robertson, I believe. Then, I think it was our first road trip - it could have been our first game - in Texas. Bobby was playing shortstop, and we were winning 1-0, maybe 2-1, with two outs in the bottom of the ninth. We were up one run, and they had a man on second and third, if I remember correctly, and the ball went to the right of Bobby Meacham. He went and backhanded it, threw a short one-hop to Mattingly, and it got by Don - both runs scored and we got beat by one run.

    I remember sitting in the clubhouse, and somebody came out and told Bobby Meacham that Yogi wanted to see him, and he came out with his head down. Someone said, "What's up?" He said, "They're sending me to Triple A tomorrow." I'm thinking, "Uh-oh…if I make a bad pitch and give up a home run, they're going to send *me* to Triple A." But that was George - he expected his players to play well, and I guess right there, he just didn't like what he saw. He told Yogi I guess on the phone in the clubhouse, and Yogi had to tell him. And then Bobby was back not too long after that.

    You just don't hit, that's all - the designated hitter [Niekro's response to the question, "How does pitching in the American League compare to pitching in the National League?"]. The game's the same - you've got four umpires, fields are fields, you've got home plate and three bases, three strikes, four balls, the pitcher's mound is 60 feet and six inches, play nine innings. So the game doesn't change. I guess for a pitcher if you moved the pitching mound to one side or the other, or forward or backward, it would change the pitcher's view of the game. The game stays the same.

TOBY HARRAH: The things that stand out in my mind are Don Mattingly and Dave Winfield battling for the batting title, and then Mattingly winning it the last day of the season. Both of these guys - to me - are Hall of Fame players. It was just a privilege to be a part of that team and watch them - really at their best - play baseball that year with the Yankees.

STEVE KEMP: That was pretty cool. Winny was a perennial All-Star, and one of the top players in baseball, and definitely of the American League. Dave Winfield was probably the greatest athlete I ever played with. It's funny, because Donnie was probably one of the greatest baseball players that I played with. I mean, he knew the game - the fundamentals. He could do a lot of different things - he could hit for power, he could hit for average, he was clutch, he could play first base as well as anybody, he could play the outfield. I think everybody was close to both of them, but Donnie a lot of times I would do things with him after games. I know when I was first with the Yankees, the first year, he got called up, and people would come up and they would know me because of signing as a free agent. Donnie would be with me, and I'd go, "You might want to get his autograph, too. He's with the Yankees and he's going to be a good player." Well, it turns out he's one of the greater players that played in New York. I'm sure those people are going, "I'm glad I got Donnie's autograph. Who gives a shit about Kemp's autograph?" It's just funny. Just the make up that Donnie had, I mean, he wasn't intimidated and threatened by the fact that he was up against one of the top players in baseball. He just went at it and it went down to the last day. It was pretty cool, really.

BOBBY MEACHAM: Going down the stretch, it was so exciting to watch those two guys. We were out of the race obviously - Detroit just ran away with that race [the Tigers finished 17 games ahead of the third place Yankees at 104-58, and would win the World Series]. For us, it was just great to see these two guys going neck-and-neck, trying to win a batting title. Deep down inside, I was good friends with Donnie, but kind of rooting for Winfield, because I'm thinking, "He's a little bit older, he's a power hitter. Donnie has got plenty of chances - he'll win one later on." But I'm thinking, "Maybe this is Winfield's only chance." I was kind of rooting for him deep inside. We were playing Detroit - maybe a week to go in the season - in Detroit, and I was on first and Donnie hit a line drive to left. Basically, it was one of those kind of half-liners - just a fly ball to the left fielder. The left fielder started to run in and I was on first, so I stopped, because obviously, he was going to catch it. I was halfway and then he just stopped, took it on one bounce, and threw me out at second. He had lost it in the lights and all of a sudden, this ball bounced in his glove and he fired it to second. So I was out by like half a step and Donnie didn't get a hit. We only had like a week to go in the season, and I'm like, "Oh man…now I hope *Donnie* wins the batting title! I don't want to be the reason why he didn't win the batting title."

But then that last game, it was real exciting. I remember before the game, Donnie said, "I know I've got to get a bunch of hits tonight. I'm not leaving here until I get all my hits." We took the field and I was excited to see what was going to happen. Then that last inning when we came up, Donnie I think was leading off or hitting second in the last inning. Tim Foli comes down with a calculator out of the clubhouse, and goes, "Hey, I just figured it out. Donnie doesn't have to go up right now. If he goes up and doesn't get a hit and Winfield gets a hit, Winfield wins the batting title. But if Donnie doesn't go up, no matter what Winfield does, he still wins the batting title. He doesn't need to hit right here." I just remember Donnie putting his glove down when he came off the field, ran by me and Foli, and said, "I'm going to go up there and get my hit, and get this batting title." So Donnie already knew he didn't have to hit. That was Don Mattingly at his finest, right there - knowing that he could have won the batting title by sitting that last at-bat, but he went up there and got that last hit. He got a ground ball through the

95 Just Out of Reach: The 1980s New York Yankees

infield and Winfield had no chance after that to win the title. I felt bad for Winny, but I was proud of Donnie for going up there and taking his at-bat, to get that title.

PHIL NIEKRO: They're two of the greatest players I played against or with - no question about that. Dale Murphy was definitely another one. It was just a treat to watch those guys play every day.

TOBY HARRAH: Mattingly has such a nice swing, and a young player at the time just coming up. He hit the ball to all fields and stays in good against left-handed pitchers, so you could tell he was going to be an outstanding major league hitter. And then of course, Dave Winfield playing against him when I was with the Cleveland Indians for a number of years, and how hard he hit the ball. When I played third base, some of the hardest-hit balls I ever had hit at me were by Dave Winfield. He hit the ball as hard as you could possibly hit the ball. He was just a Hall of Fame player - he was great. He finished up with .350 right around, and Mattingly finished three or four points higher [Mattingly finished at .343, and Winfield at .340]. So, both of them had great seasons and played every day. They were winning baseball players.

REX HUDLER: Him and Winfield, the last game of the season, were going for the batting title. That was Winny's opportunity to stick it to George. He wanted to end the year with a title. And I remember Winny, he even shared that a little bit with me, how really he wanted it. Donnie got a hit, Winny got a hit. They exchanged hits - it's all well-documented. But it ends up Donnie won. That was a special moment, where Mattingly and Winny, after Winny made an out, Mattingly was on first base - they hit right behind each other, front and behind - and Winfield went over to Donny at first, they tipped their caps, they grabbed each others hands and they raised it. It was a "Yankee moment." I would love to have a picture of that. That was a Yankee moment that I was proud being at, and I've never been at a game like that since, because I've never seen two teammates at the last game of the season go down for the batting title. And I don't even know if that's happened before. That was a very special moment. I'll never forget sitting in that dugout - I had goosebumps.

MIKE PAGLIARULO: It was the first time I had ever seen anything like that. And to realize that the batting title was on the line between two teammates...it was a great learning experience, of how you handle it. And both guys handled it with class - they're both classy guys, of course. I couldn't stop thinking about, "I wonder if they want one another to lose?" Because you don't really want your teammates to do that. So you think of the emotions that are going on there, that I was wondering - but never asked - about what they were feeling. And I don't know to be honest with you, exactly the feelings. But it was pretty interesting to be around that. And it was the first time I saw Donnie step up to get hits that day, and Dave Winfield. They were both great about it to each other, too. It was a really cool thing to be part of.

STEVE JACOBSON: Winfield felt that the Yankees' corporate affection was with Mattingly when the two of them got down to a batting championship, the two of them went down to the wire. And Winfield thought it was racial, that the Yankees wanted Mattingly.

TOBY HARRAH: I wanted to get back to Texas [after the 1984 season]. I had been in Cleveland for four or five years before that, and I had played for the Rangers for seven or eight years. There's nothing like living in and playing in the same town that you're living in. The opportunity to come back and play for the Rangers was just a blessing for me, and it gave me the chance to finish up my career in Texas, and eventually, work for the Rangers as a coach for a number of years in the big leagues. It really turned out great for me.

chapter 12: 1985

With the arrival of speedster Rickey Henderson, the Yankees hope that finally, they have obtained the missing ingredient that will help them go the distance. But a fast-rising team in their division has other ideas.

BOBBY MEACHAM: I did [think that the arrival of Rickey Henderson to the Yankees was the final piece of the puzzle]. I thought he was a huge piece and thought he was going to put us over-the-top. Of course, for me, it's the beginning of my career, I'm thinking, "Hopefully I can just be a part of it," because I saw all the great players we had - Mattingly coming on the scene the way he did and Winfield already there, and a couple of the older guys. With Rickey added on to that, I thought, "We've got a good shot here." But you could tell, our division was *stacked*. You can go back now and look at both divisions, we almost felt like it wasn't fair. "Why are we in third place with 89 wins, and Kansas City is winning their division with 85?" It's one of those deals.

I heard overall in the '80s, we won more games than anybody [the Yankees won 854 games during the '80s, more than any other team in the American or National Leagues]. So it's kind of one of those odd things that just didn't work in our favor. But it seemed like we were always in second place. Everybody was taking their turns winning the division, except for us...and Cleveland. [Laughs] But I thought with Rickey, we had a chance. He was an unbelievable player. To this day, I tell my son - and my son is 23 now - I got to sit down with or play next to some of the greatest players of my time, on that one team - with Winfield, Mattingly, and all of a sudden, Henderson shows up, stealing his 85 bases a year. And one of the best hitters I've ever seen, Rickey Henderson. Just to witness all that, it was pretty amazing. Rickey, overall, he might be the best player of that whole era right there. I thought we definitely had a chance to win with adding him on.

TOMMY JOHN: The reason why Rickey was traded to the Yankees is Sandy Alderson was brought in to be the general manager of the Oakland A's. Sandy Alderson knew nothing about baseball - Sandy was an attorney. And Sandy's best friend was a guy named Roy Eisenhardt. Roy Eisenhardt was the son-in-law of a guy named Walter Haas. Walter Haas was the guy that owned a little "mom and pop company" called Levi Strauss. [Laughs] So he brought Sandy in to run the thing. And I had talks with Sandy, because I was with the A's for two months in 1985, and I had a great experience out there with Sandy. And we were talking - he traded Rickey to the Yankees for six or seven players. And I asked him, "Why? He was an offensive threat." And he said, "Tommy, when I was given this job, I didn't know baseball. So I went about my job as I would a court case. I put all the facts up on the board - what all the good teams did, what they didn't do. All the facts. And then, I ascertained what good teams had and what bad teams had. The good teams were generally in the top in pitching, defense, runs scored, and runs batted in.

Billy Beane was a disciple of Sandy Alderson - that's where they got 'Moneyball,' that they won the on-base percentage. I remember my agent, Bob Cohen, was Mark McGwire's agent. In fact, I got Mark with Bob. And Mark hit 49 home runs his rookie year [1987]. If you go back and look at Mark's average in the minor leagues, he hit for average, he hit doubles, he hit some home runs - but not a lot of home runs. Bob Watson was his hitting coach with the Oakland A's. And Bob got him to start to pull the ball. Well, Mark hit 49 home runs and drove in a bunch of runs [118 RBI]. And Sandy called my agent and said, "This is terrible. His on-base average dropped from the high-fours to the high-threes." And Bob called me and said, "What do you think?" And I said, "He hit home runs. Yeah, he's going to strikeout, but he hit home runs - he drove runs in." Sandy was big on on-base.

And the other thing that Sandy saw is stolen bases have very little to do with winning ballgames - over the long season. A game, yes. But stolen bases only determine the outcome of the game from the seventh, eighth, and ninth inning. You can steal bases early in the game, but you can have a base hit, a double, a walk, an error, and a home run, and you've wiped out all those stolen bases. So, Sandy saw that, and he said, "We've got Rickey here stealing all these bases, and we aren't winning with him," and he traded for a bunch of pitching as I recall [the A's traded Henderson and Bert Bradley to the Yankees for Tim Birtsas, Jay Howell, Stan Javier, Eric Plunk, and José Rijo]. Sandy was on his way to figuring out that pitching and defense...and Earl Weaver had it right, when he said, "Pitching, defense, and three-run homers. That's what baseball is all about." But Rickey was something else, though.

PHIL NIEKRO: We played a little bit with each other in the Braves organization [Phil and his brother, Joe, were teammates on the Braves from 1973-1974] - he was trying to figure the knuckleball out, then he went to Houston and had some great years. I might have mentioned it to somebody in just baseball talk, "Boy, it would be good to get Joe over here. He throws a knuckleball and we could help each other." The next thing I knew, they traded for Joe - for Jim Deshaies. It was a good fit.

DALE BERRA [Yankees shortstop/third baseman from 1985-1986, son of Yogi Berra]: My arrival was a little different than the normal guy, because my father was the manager. I came over from Pittsburgh, where I played shortstop every day for three years, and came over to a situation where they only had a left-handed third baseman in Pagliarulo, where I was going to play against the left-handers. My dad was the manager, and Mattingly was coming off a great year, where he won the batting title. We had just signed Rickey Henderson. We already had Winfield, already had great players like Randolph and Baylor. Outside of my '79 Pirate team where we won the World Series, that was as good a team as I'd ever seen. And it was a great team - a team that could easily win the pennant.

BRIAN FISHER [Yankees pitcher from 1985-1986]: Yogi was the manager for the first part...in fact, in the winter of '84 I got traded over, so I wasn't in the Yankee organization, I came from the Braves. I didn't really pay them much attention until I got there in spring training. It was a little hard to tell you what was going on, because I was so far removed - I was only 23 years old, and all I thought about was how I was going to figure out to make the big league club. So I wasn't really paying attention to the dynamics. But you had these super power guys - Winfield, Baylor, Randolph. And then you had guys like me, rookies in a sense, without any kind of big league time. I tried not to say anything or do anything - I just tried to go out there and pitch and do my job. So early on, when I was there in spring training, Yogi was the manager, and I didn't get called up until Billy got hired. When Billy got hired, two days later, they called me up out of Triple A. And I went on to have this really good rookie year, and obviously, I didn't have too many stumble periods, so I never got sent down. The best I pitched in the big leagues was probably that year, in '85. Ironically, it was for the Yankees, and ironically, it was for Billy Martin. My time there, I had a blast - I was having a great time. My first time in the big leagues, I was in New York, I was a Yankee - life didn't get a whole lot better than that.

DALE BERRA: As far as dad being fired [Yogi was fired after the team started out 6-10], I remember that the players loved dad. Absolutely loved him. The Mattinglys, the Pagliarulos, the Meachams, the Guidrys - they all loved dad. When he was fired, they were upset. But when Billy took over, dad just told me, "Billy is like an uncle to you. I'm going to go play golf - don't worry about me." Dad being who he is with no ego, obviously, he got mad at that whole thing because Steinbrenner himself didn't fire him, so he got mad at that. But as far as being mad at the players, he took a ride home on the team bus. Which would

101 Just Out of Reach: The 1980s New York Yankees

be unheard of in a situation where a manager or a coach gets fired - they storm out of the locker room and leave. He took a ride home on the team bus, said goodbye to the team, and they all clapped for him when he got off the bus. Told him, "Good luck." Told them, "Billy's a good man," one of his best friends.

That was the whole thing - that was the whole feud [that transpired between Yogi and George]. The entire feud was based upon the fact that dad was not personally told...first of all, George personally told dad that he would be the manager all year, if you remember. That was one of the contentions - "Yogi will manage the club all year." And after he fired him, after 15 games or whatever it was, he didn't do it himself. He didn't get the phone call from George, or George didn't come do it personally. It's very normal for owners not to fire managers - that's a normal thing. But in this case, with George's hands-on approach and his relationship with dad, and dad being a Hall of Famer and the Yankee that he was, he deserved to be told by George. Different than the average situation.

STEVE JACOBSON: When Yogi was the manager, the players liked playing for Yogi. Unlike the Mets of '73 [who Yogi managed, and won the NL Pennant], the players liked Yogi. And when Yogi was fired, that was the source of Yogi's hostility to Steinbrenner, staying away from Yankee Stadium for years and years - not that he was fired, but Steinbrenner didn't have the nerve to tell him to his face. He sent Clyde King as the "messenger." If I recall, Don Baylor kicked a garbage can across the clubhouse and Don Mattingly grumbled out loud, *"Are we never going to have any stability around here?"* It was like torturing Yogi at that time - two weeks into the season. And Steinbrenner was sniping at him all that while. Yogi was among the most beloved of players ever to play for the Yankees and players liked playing for him. Genuinely.

REX HUDLER: This is '85 - Billy calls me up. They wanted me to meet Billy in the hotel bar in Texas. So I flew into Texas, and I think Gene Michael set it up. He said to meet him after the game in a hotel bar. So I did. I meet Billy Martin, and he buys me a light beer from Miller. I was barely old enough to drink. It was pretty cool - I was a little nervous, but he was really friendly. Kind of like Yogi. Managers have a way, they know how to make their guys feel good. So I go to the bathroom with Mark Letendre, at the time, was Gene Monahan's assistant athletic trainer - now he's a Major League Baseball umpire. I go into the bathroom and we're taking a leak, and he looks at me, and goes, "Hey kid, I just want to tell you, the way they're talking about you here is you know how Casey [Stengel] loved Billy? Well, Billy loves you the same way. He knows you're a hard ballplayer, he knows you're feisty, you're a little character. So I just wanted to give you a heads up, and know he's going to be watching you." I was like, "Wow man. *Are you kidding me?"* I had to pinch myself. But here it was, Mr. Steinbrenner drafted me in the first round - 18th pick in the country - gave me a great start. Then, years later, he actually gave me a second chance by promoting me. That's what really kicked me in.

  Billy watched me - he stood behind me during batting practice and when I was out there in the field, taking ground balls. He watched me like a hawk, and I was exhausted, because I tried to make every play like it was a game. I was just nervous as I could be. They didn't really respect me a lot, because they didn't have many rookies on the Yankees. Maybe Scotty Bradley and Don Mattingly - we were like the only "rookies." They weren't real keen on rookies. So we get to New York City, and I get my first big league hit - a double down the right field line, over Bill Buckner's head. Gene Monahan ran down the line and he got the ball out of the stands from the people - I'll never forget that moment. A little bloop double. Stood on the bag at second base, and they put on the scoreboard, "REX HUDLER'S FIRST MAJOR LEAGUE HIT," and the crowd gave me a nice round of applause. It was flattering.

  I would make outs - and I did a lot back then, because I was so young, I couldn't hit a lick - but I flew. I would run and I would hustle. I was a hustlin' guy. So I would run through the base and almost stumble into a somersault past the bag. I would go back to the dugout, and fans would cheer for me. I would go, "What the heck are they doing?" A couple of the older guys [said], "Kid, they're a knowledgeable crowd here. They like your hustle. They like the way you give it up." And so right then, I was like, "This is beautiful. What a place."

I remember Billy Martin pulled me off once - I was on the on-deck circle, and he pulls me off because he was going to pinch hit for me. I get down in the dugout - I put my bat in the rack and my helmet down. The guy ends up getting on first base and I don't think Billy expected that. And he goes, "Kid, get back up there! Can you bunt?" And I said, "What a question...*where do you want it?*" He goes, "Bunt it to the first baseman." OK, so I put my helmet back on. I went up there, and a guy named Ed Núñez was pitching, from Seattle. Hard thrower. He knew the situation, he knew why I was up there. First pitch - fastball inside about 95, right on the inside part of the plate. That is the hardest pitch to get down. I foul it out. I try to get the angle of my bat towards first base to try and bunt it to first base, and I foul it right over the Yankee dugout, over Billy's head. I'm looking at Billy, and he's got his hands in the air, and he's yelling, "Get the 'blanking' ball down!" Now I'm feeling Billy's teeth and I'm feeling what everybody knows about Billy. So the next pitch, the same identical pitch, same spot, same thing - I try and square around and foul it over Billy's head again. Now it's 0-2, and my eyes are following the path of the ball. I made eye contact with Billy again and he goes, "I don't give a 'blank' where you bunt it, just get the 'blanking' ball down!" I stepped out of the box, and instead of getting nervous, I said, "Alright...I'm just going to bunt it to the third baseman."

So 0-2, typically, the bunt's off, because if you foul it off, you're out. Here it comes, three identical pitches. I bunted it down the third base line - I couldn't have caught the ball and *rolled* it any better. It was perfect. So not only did I get the runner over, but I got a clean base hit out of it. There was no play - it was that perfect of a bunt. So I run to the base, and I'm now walking back to first base, and the Yankee dugout is right there to my left. I'm looking at Billy, and Billy is looking at me, and I had chewing tobacco in my mouth, and I took my wad and I spit it at him! Like, "Take that, bitch!" I told myself..."What did you just do? Oh my gosh! You just spit at him! Hud, you're in trouble. That dude, *he's your manager!"* But I couldn't help it - the way he yelled at me, he challenged me. And I responded with a base hit. I took a peek over, and he jumped off the bench and he was pointing to Gene Michael and whoever else his coaches were, saying, "Did you see what he did to me? Did you see him spit at me?" Body language is easy to read out there on the baseball field. The next day, he followed me around. He smiled at me, he said, "Hey kid, how ya doing?" I was in. Billy accepted me. He liked my fire, he liked the fact that I was a bad dude - I was a football player in a baseball player's body, I hustled. And it reminded him of him, when he was a player. So I saw the similarities there.

I'll never forget my first start as a Yankee. My first start was at first base. We were in Oakland, and Donnie was hurt and Don Baylor and Ken Griffey didn't want to play first base, and Billy in the middle of a game the day before on a Saturday, goes, "Hey kid. Can you play first base?" And I jumped up, looked at him, and went, "Put me in there! I'm in! I'm game!" "Alright, tomorrow, you're playing first base." I'm from Fresno, so a lot of my family was there - a three-hour drive from Oakland. And I was telling my family, "I'm playing first base tomorrow. My first big league start." And they're going, "No way." I'm thinking to myself, "Yeah, he'll change his mind." Sure enough, I go in there, and there I am - batting ninth, playing first base. I went, *"Oh shit."* I didn't have a glove. Mattingly's left-handed, so I went over to Don Baylor. He has a first base glove that really...I wouldn't let my cat have its litter in that glove! It was terrible. So I said, "What am I going to do? Well, what about an outfielder's glove?" Baylor had an outfielder's glove - it was floppy and big. I said, "Give it to me. That's all I want. I can catch with it." So I went out there and I did the job. Guidry started and he told me, "Don't you worry about a bunt, kid. Just catch the ball. I'll cover everything." He was a six-time/seven-time Gold Glove winner [Guidry was a five-time winner]. And Billy kept his word and

Just Out of Reach: The 1980s New York Yankees

played me at first base. Man, I'll never forget it. He took me out and pinch hit for me in about the seventh inning. But it was surreal.

DALE BERRA: It's so ridiculous [A bizarre base running gaffe - which involved Berra and Bobby Meacham - in an 11-inning 6-5 loss to the Chicago White Sox at Yankee Stadium, on August 2, 1985]. I'll let you decide. Meacham was on second and I was on first. Rickey Henderson was up and he hit a ball off the left centerfield wall on a fly. I knew that the ball was over the centerfielder's head, but Meacham didn't recognize it and went to tag up instead of scoring on a ball that was over the centerfielder's head. So, because I knew that the ball was over the centerfielder's head, I was literally almost standing on second, next to Meacham, yelling at him to run. The ball hit the wall on a fly, and he decided to run now, and as he was running, he slipped and almost fell down. I was right behind him. From that point on, since he got such a late start and because I was right behind him, Gene Michael waved him on and I mistakenly also went - instead of stopping at third - and got thrown out, too.

Now, if I stopped at third, it would have been fine. But here's the real scenario - you could say it's my fault for sure, because I should not have run through Gene Michael's sign nor the fact that Meacham was tagging up, I should have stayed at first base. So I'm a victim of horrendous base running by him, but I should have looked at the guy in front of me. Rickey would have had to hit a line shot off the left centerfield wall 430 feet away, and based on the way Meacham ran the bases, he would have had a single, and I would have been on second and Meacham would have been on third. Now, obviously, when a ball hits the left centerfield wall on a fly, that shouldn't be the situation, right? It should have been both me and Meacham scored and Rickey on second with a stand-up double. So…he ran the bases wrong and I ran the bases wrong - it was both our faults. But had he done what he was supposed to do, he would have scored easy and so would I.

BOBBY MEACHAM: I went in to pinch run - that didn't work out so well! There were runners on first and second and nobody out, and the rule basically in that situation is a fly ball that's maybe a catch/maybe a double, that type of thing in the gap, if you're on second, you're supposed to be able to be close enough that if he does catch it, you can tag and get to third. But if you're not sure, you just kind of hang around second base and make sure you can at least do that. Well, I did everything right, except for when I saw the ball disappear just over the tip of the guy's glove - Luis Salazar. I went to push off and go towards third, and I slipped. I went down to one knee. Dale was behind me at first, and Dale, obviously, his angle was that the ball wasn't going to be caught. So when I slipped, I knew he was almost to second. As I was getting up, I could hear him coming. So I'm running into third, thinking, "Shoot, I wish I didn't slip. Now it's going to be bases loaded." Well, I see Stick waving me home. I saw the relay man [Ozzie Guillén] with the ball in his hand. I'm like, "I'm going to be out." So I thought to myself, "I guess Dale followed me to third. I know I'm going to be a dead duck, but maybe I can just knock the ball loose and somehow score" - as [Carlton] Fisk is waiting for me with the ball.

So he basically throws me out of the way as I try and knock the ball loose. I hear the crowd groan once, and as I'm getting up, I hear the crowd groan again. I'm like, "What the heck? Oh my gosh...he followed me home too?!" I was like, "Oh boy. *Billy's going to kill us."* I came into the dugout and Billy walked right by me and he didn't say a word to me. But he got Dale, he started yelling at Dale. It was one of those plays where back then, they didn't have everything on film. But that was "Game of the Week," so that's forever. Everyone can watch that. My son used to get teased at school about, "Hey, I saw your dad on 'Bloopers' or whatever." And he'd say, "Dad, they're teasing me about that," and I'd say, "Well, ask them if *their dad* is on any 'Bloopers'." But it's one of those things where you'll see it as a manager in the minor leagues coaching third base, it almost happens a couple of times a year. And even coaching third in the big leagues, I tell the guys the same thing. "You watch. It almost

Just Out of Reach: The 1980s New York Yankees

happens twice a year to every team - that play where two guys are coming in from third." But you usually never see two guys get thrown out at home. That doesn't happen often. [Laughs]

REX HUDLER: Here's another fun thing we did in the dugout while I was there. Marty Bystrom was a right-handed pitcher for the team. And Ken Griffey was kind of older then, he was a little past the "Big Red Machine" days and all that, so he was a veteran player. And we would sit on the bench - and we would spit on each other's shoes. And Griffey didn't chew. He goes, "It ain't fair, man!" So he'd go over to the cooler and get Gatorade, and he would throw it on us! He'd throw orange or red Gatorade on our pinstripes. And Marty Bystrom, he had a gap between his front teeth that was probably a quarter of an inch wide. He would drench my shoelaces with spit and tobacco. I couldn't hang with him because he was too good a spitter.

I'll never forget the word got back to George, that we were having so much fun on the bench grab-assing, that Steinbrenner didn't like it. He had a spy that sat up there with binoculars and watched to see who was messing around. And Billy told us, "Hey, look - the Boss doesn't like what you're doing in the dugout. You'd better take it easy or someone's going to get whacked." I'll never forget that. George was so specific on every little thing that went on. Bystrom got his teeth fixed in the next off-season, and he got that gap taken care of. And man, he was free game - I wore him out on that bench the next year, it was beautiful. He didn't have a way to spit anymore. But those were just kind of the fun things we did in the Yankee Stadium dugout. And then, in '84, when Yogi would come walking through, we would always sit at attention when Yogi came. He was so friendly, so nice - he was gentle. The players loved him. When they fired him, that's why Billy brought Willie Horton in, because he knew there were some players on that team that didn't like Billy, because Yogi was so well-loved.

Yogi would walk by, and they had a drinking fountain machine - they had one of those at the end of the dugout. And Yogi would come down there, and he chewed all the time, so he would rinse and spit, rinse and spit. And I mean [makes an intense throat-clearing noise] - he would choke up *from his bowels.* We got a kick out of that. We were like, "Yogi, are you alright?" We would count how many times he would do that in a game. That was just some of the inside fun stuff we did in the dugout back then. But that will tell you, boys will be boys. We were grown men - or at least those guys were, I was still a young guy. Grown men were just acting like boys in that dugout. It was so fun. It was giddy. It was a regal place to be. We loved every minute of it.

Chris Berman gave me that [Hudler's "Wonder Dog" nickname]. Chris Berman was the ESPN broadcaster, and he'd give guys nicknames when he hosted the show back in the day. I made a few highlight tapes, because I was kind of a radical player. And "Rex" is a dog's name. That was the name that was in all the '50s grade school books. '60s/'70s - "See Rex run." It was fun, I had a lot of fun with it in my career, man. There's another Rex in the big leagues now, he's a pitcher for the Colorado Rockies [Rex Brothers]. The first Rex since me. There ain't many Rex's out there. Anyway, there was "Wonder Dog," and they called me a lot less flattering names in my career, too. The Cardinals, I was "Hurricane Hudler," Jack Buck and Mike Shannon gave me that one. "Headfirst Hudler" - there was a lot of nicknames. But Wonder Dog is the one that stuck.

DALE BERRA: We played good all year long - we just came up short.

MIKE PAGLIARULO: The finish was unbelievable. What I do remember was one of the last series, we were playing against Toronto, and Ron Guidry was pitching for us. The stadium was packed, and Gator had his good stuff that day. I think he struck out the first three batters in a row, and then the next three batters - I'm not positive. I sprinted off that field. It was the coolest thing - I had goosebumps just running off that field. It was so loud. I felt like I was watching the 1978 season or something, when the Yankees won - I remember watching them on TV. It was a great experience. But Toronto had a wonderful club and a really talented team. It was a great battle. Just to be part of that helps you grow, helps you feel like you've done what you can. We expect to win, we always think about winning - we never go to spring training not thinking we're winning. We're working to win - right up until the last day. And there are times when you don't win every year. But the experience really is the fight and the battle, and the way you leave it on the field. I was very satisfied with how that happened, and like I said before, fortunate and grateful to be part of that.

BOBBY MEACHAM: For me, that was kind of a crazy year. I played two months with a wrist that needed surgery at the very end. I got surgery the day after the season ended. And I ended up hitting left-handed against left-handers, just so I could get into the line-up. I remember Billy...I played for *him,* basically. He asked me to play, when I probably shouldn't have, the last two months of the season. He just basically said, "Hey kid, we need you out there. You can bunt every time if you want" - because he knew my wrist was killing me. So I remember playing a ton and my average taking a beating because of it. Just really realized the strength of my game and importance of my game to the team was defense. Defense and moving runners over, and coming up with clutch hits every now and then. I also remember Winfield talking about running the bases right - just to score runs. So my focus was a little bit more than just hitting - it was on the other things and made me a better player, because I saw that I was contributing to us winning games, and winning a lot. We just couldn't quite catch up at the end.

It was the one thing I remember about that last series [against the Toronto Blue Jays] was that we had to win all three to get a tie. We won the first one. I'd never seen a major league centerfielder drop a ball - that was just a fly ball. Lloyd Moseby dropped a fly ball in I guess the ninth inning, after Wynegar's home run, and I got to score the go-ahead run there, to win that game [4-3]. So I thought, "Man, maybe we've got a chance here." All of a sudden, it looked like things were going our way.

We were just given that first game. And I knew game three we had Phil Niekro going, who had won 15 games, and was going in that last game for his 300th win - for win #16. So we felt good about that one. Game two we knew was the tricky one. That was where we just knew we had to score a bunch. Joe Cowley was pitching for us and he had been known to be a little erratic. You didn't know what you were going to get - he might pitch a gem, or he might not. It might just fall apart. So we were hoping. They won the second game to take it all [5-1]. And then game three was fun just because it was Niekro going after his 300th win. Knucksie [Niekro's nickname] was awesome - just a great teammate. Just a class act. It was fun to see him go out there and pitch.

REX HUDLER: We were close with Toronto. I remember Willie had a hamstring problem late in September, and I was in that line-up. And when I saw that line-up, my booty got tight when I got to the ballpark. Because it was September and in New York, when you're two games out late in September, those are *big games.* And I dove and caught a ball. I'll never forget the roar of 56,000 in old Yankee Stadium. As I caught the ball, I got up and threw to Bobby Meacham, who was the shortstop there. I started choking up - I got emotional because of the crowd. I've never heard 56,000 people roar for me before. It was life-changing - it forever changed me into an entertainer, wherever I was in the big leagues with fans. And then when I played in Busch Stadium with the Cardinals, whenever I hit a gapper - which wasn't very often - I was not going to stop at second because of the roar of the crowd.

BRIAN FISHER: We were going into Toronto and we were going to that old stadium which was outside and funky looking and shaped [Exhibition Stadium]. Toronto just had great hitters at that time and a solid pitching staff. They ended up winning 99 and we ended up winning 97. What I really truly remember about that weekend was Phil Niekro getting his 300th win, and thinking to myself, "I wish the season wouldn't end," because I was having a great year - but disappointed that we won 97 and were that close to getting a shot, and not making it.

I just remember Donnie Baseball was at the time - of course, you're talking to a 23-year-old kid at the time - probably the best hitter I'd ever seen. Hitting balls that I didn't think were hittable. You saw him on a daily basis, and then you'd go watch Wade Boggs hit, and had that short porch in left. It sure seemed like every pitch - no matter where you threw it - he had bat control and could hit it off the wall in Boston. Wade's a great hitter, but at that moment in time, I thought Donnie was a little bit better hitter - in terms of being able to spray the ball all over the park. I thought Wade took advantage of the short wall in left field - at least when I was there. It seemed like he was always trying to punch that ball off the short wall in Boston. But Wade was a hell of a great hitter.

At the time, Boston had Steve Lyons, who was just a crazy man. I remember pitching to Wade in a tight game. Wade was up, and Steve tried to steal, and Wade hit a bullet line drive right at the shortstop and a double play. Wade looked at Steve like, *"What are you doing?"* Wade could definitely swing the bat, but I thought Donnie at that time was a little bit better of a hitter.

BOBBY MEACHAM: Oh, absolutely he deserved it [Mattingly was named the 1985 American League MVP]. It just seemed like he drove Rickey in all the time. [Laughs] I think Rickey scored like 145 runs or something like that [146 runs]. It was just crazy - those guys would team up to put points on the board for us. I think that was the year [Mattingly] hit six grand slams [it was actually 1987 that Mattingly set a major league record of hitting six grand slams in a single season], it might have been the year where he hit home runs in eight consecutive games [also 1987]. He was just *a machine.* For the five years I played with him, I used to tease him - "I think you're almost the best hitter I've ever seen." He said, "Well, who's better?" I said, "I played with a kid in college named Tony Gwynn. He might be better." And he's like, "Yeah, but he can't do damage like I do by hitting the ball out of the ballpark." And I said, "Yeah, you're right. Maybe you are better than him!"

Those five years, there was nobody better. Maybe somebody as good somewhere down the road, but for those five years in baseball, there was not a better hitter than Don Mattingly. He was definitely deserving of the MVP that year. The numbers he put up and the situations that he got them, too - it was just phenomenal to watch him, clutch hit after clutch hit. When he was in a streak where he was on fire, you could count on homers in that streak. He was just a phenomenal home run hitter...a phenomenal hitter. And a great defender. Like I said, those five years - and that one in particular - was pretty special to watch.

REX HUDLER: Now, the season's over, and [Martin] wants me to go to Bucky Dent's School of Baseball in Delray Beach. He wants me to play shortstop, so I can be his utility player the next year. I go down to Bucky's Camp - I love Bucky Dent, great friend of mine, super guy - and Clyde King calls me, and says, "Rex, we've traded you son, to the Baltimore Orioles. But we just wanted to tell you thank you. We really appreciate you. Mr. Steinbrenner says that you did a great job. We just want to wish you well." So now, I'm like, "Oh man...*there was my chance.*" Well, they fired Billy and they hired Lou [Piniella] - that's what happened. So Lou said, "Shit, he can't hit. I don't want him. Trade him." So they traded me, and they got Gary Roenicke and Leo Hernández, for me and Rich Bordi.

So now, I'm done with them. I get home from Bucky's Camp, and a couple of weeks later, I get mail on Yankee stationary. I open it up, looked at the bottom, and it said, "George M. Steinbrenner." I went, "Oh man, this ain't just any letter from anybody on the Yankees." I read the letter - "Dear Rex, Just wanted to tell you why I traded you. I believe you're going to be an everyday second baseman. However, I decided to keep Willie Randolph, and I wanted to trade you to my favorite manager - Earl Weaver. I believe they're going to let you play second base and become a regular. You have the ability to

Just Out of Reach: The 1980s New York Yankees

become an everyday second baseman. Thank you for what you did with the pinstripes and how you exemplified wearing the pinstripes - the way you hustled, the way you played the game. I want to say thank you. All my best and good luck, we'll see you down the road, George Steinbrenner." I read that letter and wanted to show my mom right away - "Mom, this is what the boss said!" I was flattered with that. I still have the letter and have it framed.

chapter 13:
#300

One of the all-time great knuckleballers records his 300th win as a Yankee - despite a family illness.

PHIL NIEKRO: When I won my 299th game in New York [on September 8, 1985, vs. the A's], I had five starts left, so me and my brother went back to the hotel, and the phone rang at 11:30 or 12:00. It was my mother on the phone, and she started crying. A young lady that lived across the street from my parents - in the little town of Lansing, Ohio - said, "I'm here at the hospital with your father, and your mother is here. The priest is here, giving him his last rites, and the nuns are here. I think you and Joe better come home as quick as you can, and go ahead and bring your black suits with you." So me and Joe jumped on a plane the next morning - we explained it to George, he said, "Yeah, go." Because I wasn't going to pitch for five more days. I went up there and my dad was in a semi-coma, or comatised. While we were there, he didn't even blink an eye, move, talk, or anything. And then it was time to go my fifth day, to get my 300th win. I was at the hospital with Joe at 9:00 or 10:00 in the morning, not knowing what to do. I said, "I don't know what to do. I can't leave him here. But we're a half a game out of first place - we're in a pennant race."

    Joe and I stayed in that room for four days, just slept in the chairs there, and brought a La-Z-Boy in, and we'd go out to the house and shower. Because it was only six or eight miles from the hospital. And then it was time to go, and I made a decision. I remember Joe saying when we were standing there, "I've heard that people can hear you but can't talk or relate back to you." And I remember telling Joe, "Boy, I don't know if it's good if he heard what you and I have been talking about for the last four days in here." Joe just looked at him, and he said, "Dad, if you can hear me, blink your eye." And my dad blinked his eye. We called the nurses right away. She came in, and we told them he had a little reaction. Then my dad's right hand started moving just a little bit. And Joe says, "Do you think he wants to write something down?" I said, "Joe, he can't even pick his arm up or blink, how can he write something?" So Joe looked at my dad, and said, "Dad, if you want to write something, blink your eye. And my dad blinked his eye again. So we went over to the hospital bed, and we put a pad in his left hand and put a pencil in his right hand. He scribbled on that little pad and dropped the pencil. I picked it up, and finally realized, he wrote two words - "WIN HAPPY" - which told me, "Go up and win that game, your 300th." That made me a happy man. So I said, "OK dad, I know what I've got to do. I'm going." His head kind of just moved to the door, like, "Go ahead and get out of here. Go win that 300th game."

I went up to New York and I kept that piece of paper in my hand. I looked at it I don't know how many times. Even in the bullpen warming up - "I've got to win it, I've got to win it." I ended up losing it - Toronto beat me that night. The next day, we flew back. I stayed there four more days with him - the same thing. Left, I can't remember exactly where we went, Baltimore or Milwaukee, and still had that paper, and I said, "My second start, I'm going to go ahead and win this," and got beat again. Joe was in the spotting rotation [a "spot starter" is a pitcher who is not in the regular rotation, but may start an occasional game], so Joe had to stay back. But I wasn't pitching for five more days, so I flew back to the hospital. I stayed four more days with him, had to leave - can't remember exactly what ball club - but it was my third shot at it. Went there and I got beat my third time. I'm saying, "How is that guy holding on back there? He wants to see me win this 300th game, is really what he's holding on to." My mother said, "You can't keep coming back here. He hasn't changed." I pitched my fourth time, and got beat again. My dad hadn't really changed at all, and my mother said, "Just relax. I'm with him here 24 hours a day."

My fifth one, that's when I was going to pitch in Toronto, the last game of the season [on October 6, 1985]. The end of my two-year contract, didn't know if I was ever going to get a job again - if anyone would sign me. I was 46 at that time, and knowing that if I don't win this game, I may never get another chance at it. And if I did make the rotation, it would have to be next April, and there was no way he was going to hold on in the condition he was in. So I started that ballgame…in fact, me and Joe stayed up until daybreak, to talk about that game. We went in Toronto three games out, and we won on a Friday, we were two games out. Toronto won on Saturday night, they clinched the pennant, and then I had to pitch Sunday. I started that ballgame - a day game - and got a few runs and a few more runs. I remember Willie Randolph came in from second base, and said, "What's going on?" And Butch Wynegar came out. I said, "What do you mean?" "You haven't thrown a knuckleball yet. What's going on?" I said, "Well, I haven't yet and I may not throw one today, Willie." He just looked at me, like, "What is wrong with you? You can't pitch in the big leagues without a knuckleball." I remember Jeff Torborg always telling me, "You've got good enough stuff. You can win in the big leagues without the knuckleball." I never believed him, but I remember him telling me that.

And as the game kept going on, kept going on, we're getting runs and runs and runs, I'm going into the ninth inning and I've got a shutout - not knowing at that time that George had sent some kind of a relay phone play-by-play to my mother in the hospital, next to my father. So she was reporting the game, play-by-play. She was listening on the phone, what Phil Rizzuto and Bill White were reporting on the radio. So she was hearing it and reporting it to my dad as well as she could. Again, he hadn't moved or spoken or nothing. I remember I had two outs in the bottom of the ninth, and I said, "I think I've got a shot at this" - I was winning 8-0. And Jeff Burroughs came up to the plate, I got two strikes on him, and I called time out. Butch came out to the mound and he said, "Do you want to throw a knuckleball?" I said, "I can't think of a better way to win my 300th game," because that's what my dad taught me. If it wasn't for that, I would have never made it to the big leagues. So I struck Burroughs out, the game was over, everyone came out and hugged me and congratulated me.

Joe put his arm around me, and said, "I've got something to tell you about dad." He told me about that relay, that our mother was listening to Phil Rizzuto and Bill White, and reporting it to my dad during the game. And I said, "Well, what happened?" And he said, "Dad opened his eyes and looked at my mom in the eighth inning, and said, 'Well, he's pitching one hell of a game, isn't he'?" That probably is what I remember more about my career in baseball - probably more than anything. We jumped on the plane and went back the next day. He was in a room by himself with a smile on his face, I took the ball and I wrote, "This 300th is as much yours as mine," and handed it to him, put a Yankee hat on him. The doctor came in and said, "You guys have got to leave - he's been up since the game was over last night, waiting for you guys." So I put that baseball in his hand, and he kind of put the ball under his sheet, so no one would see it if he fell asleep. And then we went home, stayed another three or four more days, and a week-and-a-half later, he was out of the hospital and home - like he had never been through that. And my mother took care of him.

Joe got in a World Series with Minnesota [in 1987, and won it], I won my 300th game. I retired, Joe retired, and a month after that, [Niekro's father] passed - I think for the simple reason his only two boys he ever had, he saw one of them win 300 games and he saw one of them pitch in the World Series. That's what he wanted to see, and he hung on for that long. My whole baseball career, that year with the Yankees - that particular game right there - is something I will never, ever forget.

chapter 14: late '80s

An era that saw more managers and players come and go, and the Yankees sag in the standings.

GARY ROENICKE [Yankees left fielder/right fielder in 1986]: First off, I was kind of surprised I got traded. Usually, not too many teams trade within the same division. But being an Oriole for eight years, and we knew New York was a team we had to beat, so to get traded basically to your rival was kind of a shock. But my playing time in Baltimore...I wasn't surprised I was moved somewhere, as my playing time was diminished quite a bit. So maybe a change was due at that time. My first impression was with Baltimore, I got to play in two World Series [1979 and 1983]. But then when I go over to New York, it seemed like the media that was following the Yankees that year was pretty much like it was in the World Series. Just like every day was pretty much the same type of media coverage that we had those two years we were in the World Series. That's the first impression that I had. And then of course, playing in Yankee Stadium for 81 games. That was a little different, too.

MIKE EASLER [Yankees designated hitter from 1986-1987]: I got traded from the Red Sox in spring training of '86, and then in '87...what happened in '87, I got traded to Philadelphia, and then I came back to the Yankees about two months into the season and finished my career off in the United States with the Yankees. I was totally ecstatic about being traded there. Going to the Yankees is like going to baseball heaven. [Laughs] To wear the pinstripes. With the Red Sox, we used to go into town and play the Yankees, and it seemed like I'd always done well when I played against the Yankees. Finally, they traded for me and I really felt good about it. I was happy - I drove almost overnight to get there in time for spring training, because I got traded about the 15th of March. I was in Winter Haven. I drove all the way up to Fort Lauderdale, I don't know how many miles it was [about 200 miles]. But I didn't care, I just wanted to get there as soon as I could.

Well, back in the '80s, I actually enjoyed the National League. Coming up with the Pirates, and playing with no DH, I had to play a position - I played left field and right field at times. It was mostly left field in Pittsburgh. And when I got traded to the American League, it really extended my career by having the DH available. I kind of liked it for that reason - the designated hitter helped me play another five or six years. The strike zones were a little different. In the American League, the strike zone was higher, and in the National League, the strike zone was a little below the knees. They used to joke around and say the National League was the "real league," and the American League was the "little league." But once you got playing in both leagues, let me tell you, both leagues were tough. There were good ballplayers all around.

PHIL NIEKRO: That was the end of my two-year contract, Joe was still contracted with them. Him and I vowed to each other - "Let's get in the best shape we could possibly get in. Let's you and I help this organization win the World Series next year." We roomed together in spring training, and we worked as hard as any two guys could. And then at the end of spring training, I didn't know if I was going to make the ball club or not. I remember Clyde King and Woody Woodward, who was co-general manager that year, one day in spring training called me over to their trailer, and said, "We're going to release you." Boy, that hit me hard, because me and Joe were just going to go out and have the greatest years we could have - that was our mental thinking. I remember in the trailer, when Woody and Clyde axed me, I said, "Does this have anything to do with age? You guys think I'm too old?" And they said, "Well, yeah. We think you are, but we aren't going to admit that. We can't say that. But yeah, age has a factor."

I went back to the club house and told Joe, and Joe just lost it. He went over to the trailer and got in Woody and Clyde's face about that. So I left, and it wasn't a week later, the Cleveland Indians called me and wanted me to come play with them. So I signed a two-year contract with them. Even though I thought I had done good enough with the Yankees - me and Guidry won 32 games a piece in two years, I won 16 one and 16 the next - I felt pretty comfortable. I was doing a fairly good job with them. I made the All-Star team the first year with them. I just thought for sure I was going to make that ball club. So I jumped on a plane, and I went to Phoenix I believe, to work out with Cleveland.

I was very hurt and very sad when I got released in spring training that year, because I was planning on ending my career with the Yankees. But I did have the opportunity to come back and pitch one last game with the Braves, after Toronto released me [in 1987]. Cleveland had me for two years - they traded me to Toronto, because they were in the pennant race. Jimy Williams was the manager. I got out there, pitched one month, didn't do real well, he released me at the midnight hour at the trading deadline, so I had a month left to go in the season. So I talked to the Braves, and said, "That's it. I know my career is over. But I can't leave the game - I have to pitch a game again." They let me come back and pitch one game - they had to clear it with the commissioner to make sure my game didn't have any affect on the standings or anything. So I got to pitch one game, and after that game was over is when I retired. I remember it was September 27th [1987], against the Giants, in Atlanta.

STEVE JACOBSON: [Niekro] was what was left of his career. He was a good player, a good pitcher, and he still baffled people with the knuckleball. He was there, and there wasn't enough around him.

RON KITTLE [Yankees left fielder/designated hitter from 1986-1987]: I got traded mid-season in '86, played there through '87, and then became a free agent in '88. How I got traded was how George got a lot of players - whoever beat him before, they got them on their team!

BRIAN FISHER: Count Montefusco [pitcher John Montefusco] was there - he had just come off hip surgery. So I was the absolute only right-hander in the pen. I haven't looked at the stats in 20 years, but I don't think Count had a lot of games in that time frame, I think I did. It felt like I was up all the damn time. And Rod Scurry was there, Bob Shirley was there, and Dave Righetti was there, and it was me and Count Montefusco. Those were the days where you had five guys in the pen, and I was the only right-hander that year, and I think that had a lot to do with my relationship with Lou, as I felt like I was pitching all the damn time. And then they ended up sending me down for ten days, brought up [Doug] Drabek, and I came back - I didn't pitch great but I didn't pitch terrible. Count had just had his hip replaced or hip surgery and he wasn't healthy. It wasn't truly his fault - he was put in a position I think where he couldn't actually pitch and help us out. But when you've got four guys in the pen, and one guy is not pitching, that puts a lot of pressure on the other guys. And when you've only got one right-hander, that's even more pressure. Ron Guidry was a battler and a gamer all the time. It was a great team and I had a great time - Randolph and Winfield would take me out on these little outings into Harlem. It was my second year and I felt like more of a part of the team my second year. The guys were great. The best two years of my life were playing for the Yankees, because the guys on the field were absolutely the best to be around.

GARY ROENICKE: I was [primarily a utility player]. I played mostly the outfield - left field, right field. And I got to play one game at first base, when Don Mattingly played third base. But I knew what my role was, I wasn't surprised. There were some great superstar players on that club. So I didn't really expect to play any more than I did. I think Pagliarulo was hurt [which is why Mattingly started a game at third] - he was out for a hamstring or something, and they needed some production from that position, and I think maybe a couple of games we weren't getting it. So he decided one particular day...Donnie was a great fielder - there's no doubt there. But it was kind of odd that he played third and not me. And I had played some third base - especially in the minor leagues - and played a couple in the major leagues. He's not the first left-hander to play there, but I'm not sure what the thought was behind that.

BOBBY MEACHAM: I thought it was great [that Randolph and Guidry were named "co-captains" of the Yankees in 1986], because they were both - to me - similar. They were both above the fray there. They were longtime Yankees, they were respected by everybody, they were great players - All-Star players - who stayed out of the controversy, stayed out of the media mess there, and just did their jobs. And really were proud to be Yankees. I was around Willie a lot - even in the off-season - and he just loved being a Yankee. He loved playing for the Yankees. It was something there that told me the same thing - "You should be proud of yourself. You're in the big leagues with the New York Yankees. You should be proud of that and conduct yourself in a way that makes everybody associated with the Yankees proud." That's what I got from Willie. And Gator was just so calm and collected, and just so "regal" almost, is the best way to describe Gator - the way he handled himself in the clubhouse and with his teammates. It just made you proud to be playing behind a guy like that. So I was glad when those guys got that honor. I didn't know it had been that long. I didn't grow up a big Yankee [fan] - I didn't know a lot of stuff about the Yankees. But I learned it quick and knew that was a great honor for those guys. I was glad they were able to get that honor.

RON KITTLE: Willie [who also became the all-time Yankee leader for games played at second base in 1986] just went about his daily business. I was living in New Jersey at the time, so you are teammates, you are friends, and after the season ends, you go on your own merry way - do your own thing - and then come

Just Out of Reach: The 1980s New York Yankees

back and compete. But every team, they want to win. They want to win as good as they possibly can. And I think that's a key for Willie - he played hard, he gave everything he had. There were some great players on the team, it's just unfortunate that it didn't click with the pitching staff that we had. Because we had some good bats, but the pitching was a little bit slack. But Willie played hard, and we expected him every day to be in the line-up.

GARY ROENICKE: Willie was a great player. Playing against him all those years, I know he was one of the hardest guys to take out at a double play. He was very nimble around the bag. He got some clutch hits. He didn't really over-swing. He used the field and sprayed the ball all over - knew what his capabilities were. And very good defensive player. Credit to his work ethic and the person that he was, that he got to play the most games ever in Yankees history [at second base].

BILLY MARTIN JR: I actually worked for the Yankees that summer - 1986. I did an internship. I was in college at Texas Tech University. I got to spend my day working in the public relations department, and I got to spend a little time every day actually working on "Billy Martin Day." August 10, 1986 [was the day the Yankees retired Billy's #1]. I don't know that I really understood the impact of it then, but I think to him it was one of his…maybe the *greatest* moment of his career - other than one of the many World Series. I know what it meant to him. I think only the Hall of Fame would come close to that. [Billy's quote that day, "I may not have been the greatest Yankee to put on the uniform, but I am the proudest"] epitomized my father. Without a doubt.

GARY ROENICKE: I don't [recall Mark McGwire making his major league debut in a game vs. the Yankees on August 22, 1986]. I know the big thing when we played the A's that year, it was pretty much José Canseco - we heard so much about Canseco. That's what sticks out in my mind more than McGwire making his debut.

MIKE EASLER: What we did is when we battled, we battled *hard*. And Lou Piniella [who was the Yankees' manager from 1986-1987, and again for the latter part of 1988] was the type of manager that made you want to play - and play *hard*. Every battle we had against the Red Sox was just a knock-down, drag-out. I don't think we had many brawls or fights, we just played the game hard. We really had something inside to beat them. The media coming at you with all kinds of questions, and people talk about the rival so much that they finally said it was a rivalry. But at that time, we didn't have the pitching staff that they started getting in the '90s. We didn't have a dominant closer in Mariano Rivera. We had a lot of journeymen in the bullpen and in the starting rotation. And Dave Righetti - those guys were young then, they were just coming up. The same thing with the Red Sox in '84. The '84 team was the best offensive ball club in the American League. We had five guys that hit over 20 home runs, I think. But Bruce Hurst, Bobby Ojeda, Roger Clemens, all those guys were young - that was their first for second year in the big leagues. They were just babies. And then finally, it all came together for them in '86, and that's why they won it [the American League Pennant] - because they had the pitching staff, and the Yankees didn't.

GARY ROENICKE: We had a good team - I don't remember how many games we won, but it was in the 90's [the Yankees went 90-72 in 1986]. And then to lose to the Red Sox, who Mr. Steinbrenner thought that was the team we needed to beat, and we didn't do it [the Red Sox finished first in the AL East at 95-66, five-and-a-half games ahead of the second place Yankees]. So that kind of added to the pressure of Piniella trying to overcome that deficit and having the great team that we had, and George wanted to win so bad. Whenever we didn't, he was a little bit upset - especially when he felt like he had the players to win.

BOBBY MEACHAM: That was a bad year for me. I was coming off the injury, so I just never did well. My wrist wasn't

125 Just Out of Reach: The 1980s New York Yankees

the same. Defensively, I could feel it - I was missing something. And offensively, I definitely felt it. I really struggled the early part of that season and I got sent down - I lost my starting job that year. I remember wondering if I was ever going to be the same type of player that I was supposed to be. Just the injury to my wrist really sent me back. So I ended up playing about a third of that year in Triple A. I don't really remember the race that well.

RON KITTLE: I started off [1987] real well. I was sitting on a training table, and one of the assistant trainers came up and popped my neck. When you come back from a broken neck [which Kittle suffered in 1976, playing baseball] - I already had three fusions in there - he twisted my neck so hard, he tore nerves off the back of my skull. From my ear all the way down to my shoulder was black and blue. I mean, I missed three months until I got back to play a little bit. But I was miserable. To this day, I can still feel it. I never complained. It's one of those things - if it's early in your career, if you complain and want to sue somebody…and there were other players in there who saw it happen. They instantly took me to the hospital, that's how bad it was. I couldn't even move for probably two months. So what am I going to do as a young kid? Sue somebody? Then all of a sudden, you're going to be blackballed and out of the game. That's not a good thing. I had more respect for it. It was an unfortunate incident, and it pretty much cost me…it turned my career from…it almost stopped it there, until I began working out again. But to this day, I still can't move my neck.

ANDRE ROBERTSON: After I got hurt, I got traded to Atlanta [in 1986]. I never made it up. We won that International League - it was funny, it was Gerald Perry at first, Paul Runge at second, I was at short, Brad Komminsk was on third. Our infield in Triple A was making more than the Giants - Will Clark, all of those guys. We had a higher salary than they did - we all had big league contracts. But I didn't make it up. The next year, I went to Seattle, I got hurt in spring training. I thought I had a good second half of the year there. They didn't bring me up. I went with Oakland. I ended up getting sent down to Double A. I was through at that point, but I didn't get hired where I wanted to here, so the Rangers called. I went up for a week, then was sent back down. We had a shortstop there - I can't remember his name - that wasn't playing well. My wife had been home, we had a two-year-old, and I said, "I'm not playing. It seems like I'm going backwards." It was not a hard decision to make. I think the last game I didn't even take a shower - I took my [uniform] off, got in my car, and drove home. That was the last time I ever played. That was in 1989.

STEVE JACOBSON: I just remember that that was the guy who could do that [Mattingly set a MLB record for most grand slams in a single season - six - during 1987]. I don't remember any of them specifically, but I do remember he didn't know who Lou Gehrig was - until he got to that streak. And then, he put it on himself to find out who Lou Gehrig had been.

TOMMY JOHN: Terrible [is how John describes the late '80s Yankees teams]. And I'll say this - in all due respect to Tommy John, when a 43/44-year-old pitcher makes your ball club [in 1986], and is one of your five starting pitchers, you're telling me that this is one of the five best pitchers that you can find out there? Now, I'm glad they did, because it gave me more years in the league and I got a chance to win more games and all this. But when a 43-year-old pitcher is one of your prime starters, it tells me that your pitching deteriorated, I think.

So I go back, and my thing was I wanted to retire. I called Clyde King and said, "Clyde, look - I'm done. I'm ready to call it quits. I want to retire as a Yankee. Do you think that George would have any problem with that?" He said, "Let me ask him." And about two or three weeks later, Clyde calls me back, and says, "I talked to Mr. Steinbrenner, and he said you can come back and come to spring training, but you have to keep your mouth shut." And I said, "OK, fine." So I went down there to essentially retire as a Yankee. Y'know, call a press conference, get all the guys there, and say, "Today was my last day in the pinstripes, etc., etc."

I made the ball club! I hurt my back right before my last start, and I wanted to pitch with a bad back, and Clyde King talked me out of it. He said, "No. All you can do is bad. And if you do bad, they won't think, "Well, he's got a bad back." They'll say, "He's 43 years old. He shouldn't be here." So I stayed in Fort Lauderdale, and I pitched a simulated game every other day. And then they brought me up, and in fact, they brought me up to the ballpark, I went in to see Lou Piniella, our manager, and I went, "Hey Lou." And he said, "Hey TJ. What are you doing here?" And I said, "They brought me up to put me on the roster." He said, *"What?!* Let me go check on that." So I pitched a sim game there - it was hard batting practice, basically. So I pitched and we're going on a road trip - we're going to Minnesota and Chicago. Lou said, "Look, I can only give you two starts. And then we'll see what happens from there." I said, "OK. That's a deal." I pitched seven shutout innings against the Twins, I pitched seven shutout innings against the White Sox. And now the writers come in and ask Lou, "What are you going to do with John?" He said, "What am I doing to do? I'm going to pitch him - he's my hottest pitcher right now!" I pitched for the rest of the year.

'87, I think I came back and won thirteen games [John was 13-6]. In '88, it was a tale of two halves. A sportswriter called and asked me, "Did you ever look at your statistics in the first half and second half?" I said, "Well, I know I pitched good in both halves. But the last half I stunk, the first half I was 8-3 or 7-3 at the All-Star break. And he said, "You left the games and you left 21 runners on base in the first half. One runner scored. In the second half, you had 27 runners on base, and 23 runners scored. That's the difference between the first half and second half." I never realized that, so I started looking into it, and I said, *"Son of a gun."* That's when Clyde King told George that we needed a tougher guy to run the ball club. We needed somebody that would kick ass and all that. And Clyde recommended Dallas Green. They brought in Syd Thrift as the general manager, and then he brought in Dallas Green [in 1989], and then that was the beginning of the end for Tommy.

In fact, I saw Al Leiter the other day at an event I did on 9-11 down at Cantor Fitzgerald. We were doing a charity day for them, and I said, "Do you remember that April game? It was colder than heck at the stadium, and Dallas Green left you in." He said, "165 pitches. I pitched one more game, they traded me to Toronto, and it was four years before my arm was healthy again." Dallas wanted to…"Starters got to go longer in the game, starters got to go longer in the game." Dallas was just one of those "kick ass guys." That was good with the Phillies, because he had Mike Schmidt, Greg Luzinski, Larry Bowa, Pete Rose, Bob Boone - he had guys that responded to that. The Yankees had Pagliarulo, Mattingly - guys that were quieter players. They don't need a yeller/screamer/get-in-your-face/curse-you-out [type manager]. That was not their thing. They brought him in, and I think Dallas lasted until August - which might have been about two months too long. I was gone after May. My days were up when Dallas called me before spring training and wanted to know what the hell a 46-year-old guy was doing trying to play baseball. I should "Be out on the golf course or out mowing grass rather than playing baseball." When the manager tells you that, you know your days are numbered.

STEVE JACOBSON: I remember being on vacation and being called by the office and told that Billy had died in an automobile accident [on Christmas Day, 1989], and getting off the ski slope to write my farewell to Billy. Bob Sheppard [the Yankees' long-time public address announcer] read it, and said, *"How unkind."* There was a lot of talk about New York, and George Young [former New York Giants general manager], who was the most astute sports figure that I met in 40-odd years of writing sports, said to me, "What did you do, write the truth about Billy?"

BILLY MARTIN JR: I know Bill Reedy [who was in the car with Martin at the time of his death] would have taken a bullet for my father. They had become very close. That was one of his very best friends - especially there towards the end of his life. I believe Bill. I believe dad was driving and Bill took the hit for him when he initially thought everything was OK. And when he found out that dad had passed, I think he realized there could be problems there and told the truth. And you know what? *I don't care.* It's not going to bring him back. The man loved my father, so who cares about that?

He had a couple of irons in the fire [at the time of his death, regarding possible baseball managerial positions]. But that was I think where he thought he was going to end up [returning to the Yankees for a sixth managerial stint]. He was about to make a trip to Japan, and actually listen to an offer from them. The Colorado Rockies were probably going to give him a shot at being their first manager, which he would have considered. That was his first managerial job, was the 1968 Denver Bears, with Charlie Manuel and Graig Nettles - it was the Twins' Triple A affiliate then. But that would have been his first National League job as a manager. But yes, that was definitely something he was talking about [Martin returning to the Yankees] quite a bit.

chapter 15:
back on track

After not winning a World Series from 1979-1995, the Yankees not only win the Series in 1996, but also begin a "dynasty era" for the team, led by young, homegrown talent. And it turns out the people responsible for assembling these teams had strong ties back to the '80s.

BOB WATSON: Stick got in trouble with George [Gene Michael served as Yankees' GM from 1991-1995]. I don't know, he had some things off the field that got him in trouble. And then he had me come in [as Michael's replacement, in 1995]. But Stick stayed on with me, as my "director of major league scouting" - whatever that is. But we talked on a regular basis, along with Joe [Torre, who served as the Yankees' manager from 1996-2007]. We didn't do anything without checking with each other, and we did pretty good. There was only a couple of things that George overruled us on. We lost David Cone in '96 to an aneurysm, and we wanted to bring in a quality pitcher, because Cone was our #1 starter. But he wanted Darryl Strawberry, and we didn't need Darryl Strawberry. And to this day we didn't need [Strawberry]! We lost *a pitcher.* But he overruled us - he overruled me publicly. That was something that went sideways.

And then I think we wanted to do something else - I want to say we wanted to bring in an infielder, because we didn't have anybody behind Derek Jeter [at shortstop]. Tony Fernández had a broken elbow, and we ended up playing our utility man everyday at second base, and he had one heck of a year - Mariano Duncan. But we wanted to bring in somebody, and he said no. But that part worked out - Strawberry actually worked out, where he got some big hits. He wanted to win as an owner. He wanted to win for New York. New York is the greatest city in the world, and should have the greatest baseball team in the

131 Just Out of Reach: The 1980s New York Yankees

world. He wanted to continue the legacy of winning the pennants and championships.

Derek Jeter, I knew he was going to be a heck of a shortstop. The key thing that allowed him to be the shortstop with no pressure on him and all of the fears of being sent down if he had a bad game and all that, was he had myself, Joe Torre, and Willie Randolph - who worked with him everyday [as a coach], in his corner. And in spring training, the guy that was going to be our "security blanket back-up," if he didn't do well, was Tony Fernández. Well, Fernández broke his elbow, and he was out for the year. And the other guy got hurt, Pat Kelly, who was a second baseman. So our utility man, Duncan, ended up playing second, and Jeter played short with no pressure - other than just catch the ball and get a hit every once in a while. He turned out being Rookie of the Year [in 1996].

One of the reasons why I wanted Joe was because I knew him personally and knew what kind of manager he was, and I got George to back off and stay out of the clubhouse. I took the hit, and that let Joe do his thing. Oh, he was pissed [when Watson told Steinbrenner to stay out of the clubhouse, circa '96/'97]. But I told him if he wanted Joe and I to do the job that he hired us to do, he had to stay out. And he stayed out. What I did - until they tore the place down - was built a side door for him to go and out, to talk to the manager and the coaches, but he could not go into the clubhouse. He respected that and he did that.

The real key…yes, Joe was very instrumental. But the one thing that George let me do was to call two guys out of retirement. One was Don Zimmer. Zim had retired, and I had played for Zim with the Red Sox. I knew Zim over the years and I thought he would be an ideal bench coach for Joe. Joe had been a National League guy all his years, except for the years he was an announcer with the Angels. And Zim knew both leagues and was a gambler and all of those things. And then the other guy he let me bring out of retirement was Mel Stottlemyre. We brought Mel back, and Mel was my pitching coach in Houston. He had just come off of the years with the Mets, and I'd known Mel and his family for a long time. So those two guys, plus Willie Randolph [third base coach], plus José Cardenal [first base coach], and then we had another pitching coach that was in the bullpen - that nobody recognizes, but he was very instrumental - and that was Tony Cloninger. So that staff and my ability to keep George out of the clubhouse, and keep him off of Joe Torre, and keep him from calling the dugout, is the reason why that Yankee run started in '96 and ended in '09 [during that span, the Yankees won five World Series and two AL Pennants].

STEVE JACOBSON: Watson wasn't there that long [he left as Yankees' GM in 1997, and Brian Cashman took over]. He felt that it was very painful working for George, and he moved out. Torre I think was monumental in handling egos at that time. You've got a bunch of guys who've got their own particular pedigree to deal with. And I thought Torre was wonderful in getting them all moving in the same direction. They had a terrific group of people, and I'll give Watson and Cashman credit for putting together the little pieces, finding a place - and I guess that's Steinbrenner's doing - for Darryl Strawberry and Tim Raines and Chili Davis. Really good pieces on the team - guys who had been good players and really knew how to win. I give Torre credit for having those pieces fit together.

Absolutely [in response to being asked if Gene Michael had a major part in the Yankees' success in the late '90s]. Steinbrenner wanted [center fielder] Bernie Williams gone. Steinbrenner's whole thinking at that period of time - he hated young players. Did not like young players. And when they were raising their own talent in the minor leagues - like [third baseman] Mike Lowell - he would like to trade good young talent for players who were still ripe on the vine, instead of waiting for them to ripen. And that's how they got along. Michael had the view for [right fielder] Paul O'Neill, and saw what could be. And Paul was a frustrated player in Cincinnati because they wanted him to hit home runs, and he got to the Yankees, and just the pieces and his effort and the example that he showed other guys on the team…not just the tantrums, that's eye wash. But that flourished under Torre.

chapter 16: the boss

Longtime Yankees owner (and employer of George Costanza), George Steinbrenner.

STEVE JACOBSON: If you remember, Dagwood's boss was Mr. Dithers - threatening to run Bumstead's finger into the pencil sharpener. *That was Steinbrenner all that time.* And torturing Gabe Paul - Gabe left at that point [Paul served as Yankees' GM from 1974-1977], and he was burned out. Steinbrenner burned out *a lot* of people. Public relations men…if you pick up some old media guides, you'll see the succession of PR people that he got rid of. That either walked away…Harvey Greene went to the Miami Dolphins, Jeff Idelson went to the Hall of Fame, Lee MacPhail left the Yankees to go to the American League office - he took Bob Fishel with him, whose life had been the Yankees. It was too much for them. George was constantly writing nasty letters to the league president about the umpires, and every mistake the umpires made that George saw, insisted on replaying on the scoreboard. He was a very difficult person. Ralph Houk knew very quickly when he came back to manage, that he did not want to work for George Steinbrenner.

GOOSE GOSSAGE: I think the key here is if you weren't going to be as demanding on yourself as George was going to be, it wasn't going to work out. But those guys on those Yankee teams, George picked the personalities, because he knew what kind of personality it was going to take to play in New York. And what guy he wanted - that competitor. And I think that's why George and I got along so well - he knew that every time out there, I was going to try and beat your ass. And that attitude - *my* attitude - was no different than most of those guys on those great Yankee teams.

Just Out of Reach: The 1980s New York Yankees

BOB WATSON: He wanted to win. But he went about it in a very different way. I can tell you from a player's standpoint, and then I was his executive VP and general manager. In those years though, as a player, you thought he was a guy who wanted to win, but he was a pain in the rear, because he was in the clubhouse all the time, yelling and screaming if you lost or if you didn't do what he thought you should have done. He was constantly calling the trainer on the carpet if somebody pulled a hamstring or was overweight. He was in the coaches' room, yelling at the coaches. I just thought that was way over-the-top. But then as a general manager, I stopped all of that part of it, and told him if he wanted to yell at somebody, *yell at me*. And we yelled every day, two or three times a day, for two years plus. Until I just had enough and it was affecting my health. And after putting the '98 team together, I told him I was suggesting that he let Brian Cashman take over. And that's where Cashman is to this day.

MIKE EASLER: George was visible. He made it known that he was "the boss," and everybody knew that. I enjoyed the Yankees, I really did, because the pressure was there every single day. The fans demanded more of you in New York, the media hype was really high all the time. So you basically had to be at the top of your game every single day, because if you let down or went into a slump, if the fans don't let you know it, Piniella would let you know it. And if Piniella doesn't let you know it, Steinbrenner would *definitely* let you know it. You knew you were always on the hot seat. But that's what I think Major League Baseball is and is still is today - you're paid to perform. So I enjoyed the challenge.

DAVE RIGHETTI: He was "the hammer." He's what all these franchises need nowadays in all sports. A guy like George, you knew who the boss is. In fact, I'm sure a lot of people used him as an excuse, "Well, *the boss* said it," because the players knew they got no more say after that. You know where the buck stopped, and that was with the man. You know when your manager or coach asks you to do something, and you felt like it was a Yankee thing, you had to do it. And you did it. Nowadays, you don't have that pressure. The player will just blow the coach off. There's no back-up. In fact, a lot of the managers don't have the guts to fight their owners or anything like that. So you've got to do what they say - even if it's not the best baseball decision in the world. George, I thought…there were two things. He was going to treat you like a star - put you in a nice hotel and travel good, and if you ever went to him, he'd take care of you. But he was going to be hard on you too, if you weren't pulling your weight. And that's all you ever really want. There was really no middle ground. He was pretty strong about that. But he gave you plenty of leeway, too. If you earned his trust, that's all you ever wanted. I never got the "handshake" or anything like that, but I could tell he was proud of me. I didn't care to play for anybody else.

Did I know he made mistakes sometimes? Yeah. I was disappointed with some of the stuff that went on. I thought we weren't patient enough with some things. But it wasn't my money. It wasn't me dealing with everything. It was just me as a player…it got to a point, as I said, that guys didn't even want to come to New York. You don't ever want that situation. But the players I played with and the guys that came up in the system - and ended up leaving, unfortunately - you're just proud to be a Yankee. And a lot of it had to do with George. And the coaching we got was incredible throughout the system. It probably still continues. You've got to give him most of that credit - 90% of it. I really believe that. And I know that Gene Michael has been there a long time, and there's been some other people in the background that have been in and out.

But George, he's a Hall of Fame guy, outside of that stupid thing [with] Winfield. Baseball-wise, I know he had some trouble with the Nixon thing [during 1974, Steinbrenner pled guilty to making illegal contributions to US President Richard Nixon's re-election campaign, which led to a 15-month suspension from baseball], but this guy is a Hall of Fame owner. That's the kind of guy you want to play for. Like I said, when he came down in the clubhouse in 1981, I saw him in there one other time I think in all my years. That wasn't something he did. He definitely would go to the press and get you a little bit. But he didn't mind if you fought back. He just didn't like guys that didn't want to fight back. Publicly, you were going to hear about it, and created kind of a tough atmosphere at times.

FRAN HEALY: George Steinbrenner may have been the most important owner in the history of baseball. He had a franchise that people had forgotten about. And when he took it over [in 1973], he took it over with gusto. Now, I'm sure he hurt some toes that he stepped on over the years. But the Yankees became entertaining. When we would go into different cities to play, people would be lined up at 3:00 in the afternoon to get tickets to see the Yankees. When I played against the Yankees when I was with Kansas City, that didn't happen. In fact, you were kind of *happy* that the Yankees were coming in. But once George got a hold of it…I think he had a "three-year plan," he said. Because in '76, he won the pennant. And then he stayed on top. He had no concerns - except the fans coming through those turnstiles. That was his major concern.

That's another thing that's a bunch of bullshit, how "The Yankees told [the broadcasters] to say this and the Yankees told us to say that." Nobody has ever told me to say anything - good or bad. The only thing that George used to say was, "Promote the tickets." And you should! But in the 28 years that I broadcasted baseball games, nobody came up to me and said, "George wants you to do this. Nelson Doubleday wants you to do this." Nobody. That's why I get the biggest kick out of some of this stuff, when they say, "They're told to do this." I don't know if anyone I've ever worked with was told to do anything. What Scooter and I did were birthdays. They would send them in and Scooter would do them on TV, and I would do them on radio - or if Scooter was with me, he'd do them on the radio. And you know what? George encouraged it. George did not discourage that. Never. I think he sent some birthdays in! George Steinbrenner never interfered with me or Scooter, and I don't think he ever interfered with Bill

White or Frank Messer or Mel Allen. Now, did he do it later on? Don't know. He never interfered with it [when Healy was a Yankees broadcaster]. He never said anything about the broadcasters. I kidded him one day, I said, "Are the Steinbrenner ratings more important than the Nielsen ratings?" And he said, *"Absolutely."*

TOBY HARRAH: I just think George is great for the game of baseball and really great to the players. You talk about the salaries that the players are making today, I think a lot of it can be attributed to George Steinbrenner. I know he doubled my salary when I went from the Indians to the Yankees, and I couldn't have been happier at the time. He called me up in his office one time. I thought he was going to hoot on me, but basically, he said, "Hey Toby, keep doing what you're doing. Keep being ready to play, and we're happy to have you in New York. Now get back down there on the field and get to work." That was about the extent of that conversation. But he did call me up in his office once during the season, and I was impressed to say the least.

MIKE PAGLIARULO: I believe he was the most generous guy I've ever met. He demanded a ton, but he treated everybody first class. We had more than any other team - and everybody knew it. Whether it was hotels or buses or whatever accommodations that we needed. I realized that when I first got to the Yankees in '84 - I went over Willie Randolph's house, and he showed me downstairs in the basement, and he had this Nautilus machine. This weight-lifting thing. And I go, "Well, you don't look like you lift a lot of weights, Will." [Laughs] He goes, "After the World Series when we lost, George bought everybody work out equipment - he wanted everyone to get stronger in the off-season." I couldn't believe that. Just things like that, that you never hear.

And there was a game - it might have been that '85 season, when we were coming from Milwaukee or Kansas City - we got in at like 6:00 in the morning. It was a bad flight, and we

Just Out of Reach: The 1980s New York Yankees

had to play Toronto that day in September. And the owner had limousines waiting for everybody, to take us right to the House. He said, "The heck with the buses." He just did it. Stuff like that was much different than how everyone else got treated. It's what made you feel special, made you feel like you were different. And I did feel that way. It was really a special feeling. So when he's critical of a guy making a bad play, well, you know what? I think he deserves to be critical if he wants to be, you know? That's just how it is. The stuff that he does to make sure that everyone can be at their best, well, there's nothing wrong with that. And it certainly never bothered the way I play - I kind of liked it when he showed up, actually, because the guys who were kind of scared ducked out of the way and they didn't play so good. You could always see. He separated people right away.

In the minor leagues, he'd show up for a Triple A game. You could see here comes the blazer and the slacks and the white shirt. All of a sudden, guys would get scared and they just wouldn't do anything - they wouldn't play. And some guys would play. Call that intimidation or whatever you want to call it, but when the owner showed up, that means he's looking - so that's a good thing, not a bad thing. I appreciated that. I felt it helped me and just knowing that he was interested in the way that we played was a great feeling. It didn't change anything that I did really - I made sure I was aware of everything and I just played hard. That's what he expects. That wasn't a hard thing to do for me.

STEVE KEMP: I said this many, many years ago, when my career was over - and I'll say it to anybody and everybody today - George was awesome. George did so much for me. When I got hit in the eye with a line drive [in 1983] and my career was in question, he was at the hospital. He made sure I had the best doctors in Milwaukee. He called my mom, and made sure she knew everything was being taken care of. He flew my wife to Milwaukee and put her up in the hotel in a suite, while I was in the hospital - because I was in intensive care for a day, and was in the hospital for about a week. He made sure that we flew back home on a private jet, because he didn't want me to be there in a regular commercial flight. He just always wanted to make sure everything was fine.

I hurt my shoulder in a collision [with Willie Randolph] the first few weeks of the season, and I kept playing. He would get on Dave Winfield and myself and Don Baylor, for instance. We were hitting in the three/four/five spots. And he goes, "I'm not getting any production out of my three/four/five hitters. I pay them all this money." He'd come out in the papers and say that. It didn't bother me that he said that. It was the truth - we weren't producing like he had hoped we would.

I think George was competitive and so many players in the game today owe him a lot, because if it wasn't for him and maybe people like Ted Turner - some of the owners in those days that were willing to pay money - who knows if salaries would have escalated like they did. But George was willing to do it, because he wanted to bring a winner to New York, and he loved the people in New York. He was just a little bit more "hands-on" than any other owner that was around at that time. I think George had a passion for sports and loved baseball. He was able to be in a position to be an owner and he was going to give it his best shot at producing a winner. George was a gentleman to me and he was a great man. I feel fortunate that I had an opportunity to play for him as an owner.

It would be easy for me to say, "God, I wish I didn't play in New York, I wish I didn't get hurt," but things happen for a reason. I have my faith, and that was meant to be. Again, I look at some of my friendships - Baylor, Winfield, Mattingly, Griffey, Randolph, Cerone, Righetti, Gossage, Nettles, Guidry. Just some great people. Not only were some of those guys I named some of the best players of our time, but they were quality *people,* that were just as good as people as they were players. I guess something that really hit me last night was seeing Mariano [a game during his last season in 2013] - what a class act. He's got to be the classiest guy in baseball and he's got to be the ambassador for baseball. He's just a phenomenal person, and obviously, a great Yankee.

Just Out of Reach: The 1980s New York Yankees

GEORGE FRAZIER: I'll tell you something about George, and this will say everything on how I feel about George. In 1983, we had the Mayor's Cup game at Shea Stadium - I believe it was in May. That's a big game to George obviously - it's the Mets, before interleague, it's the intercity rival thing. The whole deal. And my dad had had a stroke in Springfield, Missouri. They came and got me in the bullpen at about the fourth inning, I went in and I was in the shower, and Bill Kane at the time was our traveling secretary, and he was trying to get me a flight to Springfield. I'm getting phone calls in the locker room - "We don't know if he's going to make it through the night." Of course, it's *your dad.* Anyway, I was coming out of the shower and George was standing there, and he said, "I've already sent the limousine to pick up your wife and two kids at Franklin Lakes. My private jet is waiting for you at Teaneck. And I have a limousine sitting out at Gate C for you right now." I went there and we flew on the airplane to Springfield, Missouri. I got there in the middle of the night, and my dad lived another twelve years. And I never got one bill for the entire Learjet, the travel, or anything - if that tells you anything about my feelings for George.

I know when I got traded, George called me and said, "You're always going to be a Yankee. This is just a trade I had to make." They traded Nettles to San Diego, they traded me to Cleveland for Toby Harrah to play third base. He said, "I really appreciate everything you've done as a Yankee. I want you to know that." That meant a lot to me.

There were things off the field that George and I were intertwined with. The scout that signed Mickey Mantle - Tom Greenwade - lived in Willard, Missouri. And Tom and I were good friends…my dad and Tom were good friends, I should say. And he took care of Tom. When Tom retired, he kept him on the payroll for 20 years, to make sure Tom was OK. I mean, there's little things that George did, even after I got traded, I used to do a Special Olympics Golf Tournament in Springfield, Missouri in my hometown, to raise money for the Special Olympics in our area. What started out to be a banquet and a roast ended up being a $150,000 fundraiser. One year, I had 20 celebrities/ten Hall of Famers - Joe DiMaggio, Yogi Berra, George Brett, Goose Gossage. You name it, they all came for me. And every year, even after I was traded from the Yankees in '83, I continued the golf tournament, and George would send me two-dozen team balls signed by the New York Yankees, and individual balls.

Now, I'm sure George didn't go down there and take the balls around, but he thought enough and had this in his books, to have that done for George Frazier, after I had left and was pitching for the Cubs and Twins. Which I always thought was pretty neat that he would do something like that. One thing that I always admired about him, everybody talked about how he "bought" teams. *He wanted to win baseball games.* If you didn't want to win baseball games, if you didn't fit in, you weren't there very long. I would do anything in the world [for Steinbrenner, who passed away in 2010] - god rest his soul. Even for Hank and Hal [Steinbrenner's sons, who now co-own the Yankees] at this point, I would do anything in the world.

TOMMY JOHN: George was a great owner. He overpaid. Thank god he did - because we all got good money from him. But he was tough. And he should be - if he's paying you the money that he's paying you, he expects a day's work. And that's what George wanted - George wanted you to bust your butt and play hard, and play hard all the time. Every once in a while, he would spout off, but I can say this, George was generous. There are a lot of people, a lot of kids in New York City that needed operations that couldn't afford it, and all of a sudden, a check would show up unannounced, to pay for the operation. And it came from George Steinbrenner. That never got out - George didn't want to be known as a softie. George wanted to be known as a hard-ass. But George had a very, very soft spot in his heart for a lot of people and a lot of things. And he was fun to play for.

STEVE JACOBSON: The good things that he did, he would be very philanthropic and in secret - when he knew that everybody would know. He was anonymous…with his name attached to it.

Just Out of Reach: The 1980s New York Yankees

DALE BERRA: I'm very happy that my dad made amends with George Steinbrenner, because George admitted he made a mistake to my dad, when he came over here and apologized for not firing him in person. George is a great man, with a great heart, and a guy that wanted to win. He wanted to win as much for the fans as he wanted to win personally. My dad would say the same thing - when George said, "I want to win for the fans and for the people of New York," he was not kidding. He didn't want to win for himself, he wanted to win for the fans and for the people of New York. He had a great heart - he helped numerous players and numerous people in the front office that you have no idea about. He was a great owner. My dad and him parted best friends.

GARY ROENICKE: My recollection of that year [1986] is whenever we lost a tough game, we would walk in, and the clubhouse there in old Yankee Stadium is when you walk in the door, the first office on the right was the manager's office. So we would walk in, and we would hear the phone ring and the door shut. We knew what happened is George would yell at Lou for something that he didn't think we should have done for losing that game, and then Lou would come out and get mad at us. That's how pretty much it went during some of those tough games.

BRIAN FISHER: Very few - if any - interaction at all. Again, you're talking about superstars and you're talking about a rookie. No reason to come and find me out. I do remember that he didn't want Tom Seaver to get his 300th win in New York City, against us [on August 4, 1985]. He got his 300th win when he was with the White Sox. I remember Joe Cowley pitched, and every hitter was 3-2, 3-2. I think we were winning 2-1 when I came in, in the fifth. And Ozzie Guillén or somebody popped a ball of the wall that tied the game up. I came out of the game. The only thing that I remember - this is vivid - is at Yankee Stadium, the locker room had double doors. And I was in the first bank of lockers on the right. I'm taking off my hat, and I hear these doors just *explode* open. It's George Steinbrenner, just going crazy - screaming at Joe Cowley, about "How can you pitch backwards all the time? You're always 3-2!" Just going crazy on Joe Cowley. As he's walking back by me, I'm shrinking deep into my locker, because I'm afraid he's going to say, "We're going to send you down, because you just gave up the tying run." He goes, "You're doing great, kid!" And he walked out the door.

RON KITTLE: I'm not a million percent sure, but I was traded [to the Yankees] and we went to Milwaukee, and Teddy Higuera had the Yankees' number. I struck out three times that game - my first game with the Yankees - Winfield struck out three times, I think Mattingly did. I think he struck out like 16. So I wasn't the only culprit when Teddy Higuera was pitching. Then, we come back to New York and we face him again, and I think I had three or four hits. [Steinbrenner] said, "I signed you to be our savior." I said, "[If you wanted to] sign a savior, *you should have signed Jesus Christ.*" After that, I never had any responses from him! But the media knew my personality, they knew I went there to play. But to go from playing every day to not playing at all, that was the hardest thing to do in New York. I mean, I loved the ballpark - I loved playing there, I loved being there and part of the action. It just felt like you were on a field higher than something else.

ANDRE ROBERTSON: What you see is what you got. He was a man in a lot of businesses - I'm in business now. If you did not perform, they were going to get on you. And that's what he did. His belief was, "If I'm paying people all this money, they should be producing." When they weren't, he'd be in there to put his input in. And what you see is what you got. As far as me, I didn't make a lot of money, but I thought I did my job, so I had no issues with Mr. George.

BOBBY MEACHAM: My first experience with him was great - I had a great spring training [in 1983], I was part of a trade that he basically forced. As the story goes, Willie McGee got traded

145 Just Out of Reach: The 1980s New York Yankees

[to the St. Louis Cardinals in 1981] for Bob Sykes. And Sykes never played - he was "damaged goods," so to speak. George asked for a make up trade, and I was part of that. So when I came over in '83, that spring, I did very well. He was real proud of the job I was doing, and proud that he got me over there. I remember him sitting me down and putting his arm around me, and telling me how great I was going to be and all that stuff. As I started to make a few rookie mistakes and the team wasn't winning enough, he got a little frustrated with the team and me in particular, because I was one of the few guys he could move, or try to shake up the team. Everybody else had guaranteed deals and had been around for a while, so I think I frustrated him.

I think I was talented enough to do the things he wanted to see, but still young and making mistakes. Not quite matured in my game to be solid enough to make him feel comfortable with me out there. He kind of knew he needed me, but was frustrated I wasn't doing as well as I should have. I think he came to not really like me very much. [Laughs] At least it seemed so - it seemed like he didn't really care for me and was trying to replace me a lot. But that's OK. That's part of the deal - you try to get better. And that's what he was all about - winning games. Like I told him and everybody else around me, "If you've got somebody better, go ahead and play them. I'm all for winning." He was all about that, that's for sure.

DAVE LaROCHE: One time, he sent word down to me, to quit throwing the lob - but it was after I came in against Texas, and Billy Martin…he and Billy were close. And I threw a lob the last pitch of the game, and struck out Lamar Johnson. It was hilarious - he did a full pirouette and sat down on home plate, facing me. And all I could see was just a mouthful of teeth - he had this big laugh on his face. He's sitting on home plate, the game's over, and I just had to stand on the mound for a second and look at him! I guess Billy got really mad about that. And the next day, someone came down and said, "You've got a message from George. He wants you to quit throwing that lob pitch, because it's embarrassing to the team" - or something. I just said, "Look, as long as it works, I'm going to throw it."

He tried to do things to win. And not everybody agreed with everything he did, but I think he was kind of a catalyst for the players, because he obviously made guys mad over the years. Kind of brought everybody together - "OK, we're going to win despite him...or *in spite* of him." He certainly didn't hurt - he tried to put the best team together he could, and I think over different years, he listened to different people. And sometimes, he listened to people that at least I thought I don't think make good decisions, and sometimes there were some bad decisions. But he had his people that he listened to, and try to sign people and make moves. But again, I can't complain, because he thought he was trying to win. That's what we're all there to do. If I was in charge, I know I wouldn't make all the right decisions, and I'd make decisions that would tick a lot of people off. That's just part of it, but you have to go with your heart. Do what you think is right. I believe with all my heart that's what he was trying to do.

STEVE BALBONI: I don't know him that much - I had very little contact with him. The only time I ever sat down and actually talked to him was in '82, when I didn't play at all in spring training. That's when I was hanging out with Gossage a lot, because he was on that pitcher's program and so was I - they used to send me home. I didn't even stay for the game. I would work out in the morning, and then I would leave, and that's when the pitchers left, too, who weren't pitching. It was weird. And he finally called me into his office, and basically all he said was, "We think you need more time in Triple A," or something like that. I didn't say anything. I kind of understood what it was.

He had just gotten a new guy [Dave Collins], and he didn't want any questions about anything. I don't think he ever played first during the season, but they got him as a first baseman. He was an outfield/first baseman. They wanted more speed, and really, first base was the only spot that was kind of open. I think that was George's idea. He felt the Yankees didn't really have speed, they weren't about speed. But I think he saw that Oakland was all about speed. Because Billy was over there with all these guys that could run. I don't really know why, the only thing I know is he came in, and I played all the time the year before, and I had a great year in Triple A, and I came back, and I wasn't playing at all. It was just kind of strange.

RON DAVIS: I don't have that many memories of George. Except just reading stuff in the paper and all his commercials and stuff. I never really had any true "dealings" with him. The only dealings that I could remember, I asked him if I could bring my first born to LA, and he said sure. Because he said, "No kids on the plane" - this is in '81. And my son at that time was say, six months old. Wives were [allowed], but no kids. I said, "I have a six-month-old baby," and he goes, "Yeah, you can bring him. No problem." Being a young guy and a rookie, so to speak, and with all the old veterans on the team, I never really got to sit down and discuss a lot of things with George - not that I did want to or didn't want to. It just never happened.

BARRY FOOTE: I liked George. George was a tough taskmaster - sometimes you may have looked at it as being unfair, but if you think about it, he treated the players pretty fairly. The people that you'd look at and say he wasn't fair to, maybe a manager here or there. Dick Howser, or somebody like that. But the bottom line is that I really respected George. In '83, I had a back injury that I had for a few years - finally I had to get out of the game. I just couldn't do it anymore. And I worked directly for Steinbrenner as a special assignment scout, and he was always very fair to me, very good to me.

Really, he made the Yankees what they were. And it goes beyond just a lot of the bigger things - small things like the way that they carried themselves. We had rules about uniforms, we had rules about how you dressed. It was all the "Yankee way." That was a big part of the tradition of the Yankees. And you see it in guys like Jeter, as carried on now. It's just something about the Yankee pinstripes that gave you a great advantage. And y'know, George went through some tough times…he and Winfield went through some tough times together on some issues they had. But I liked Steinbrenner. I think he was great for the Yankees. I think he was the one that took the Yankees from an "also-ran" sort of organization, and back to the traditional power that they had become - and they still are.

GOOSE GOSSAGE: I think he felt like I was at the end of my career [in 1989, Gossage rejoined the Yankees for a short time], and I went on to play four more years - I went to Japan the following year, and came back and played for Texas and played in Oakland for two years, and then played at Seattle for another year. And then the strike got me [in 1994, which was the last year Gossage played]. But I think George thought that I was at the end of my career, and he wanted me to retire as a Yankee. I think that's the only reason why he brought me back. But George and I always had a good relationship. We had a couple of run-ins, over the tearing of my ligament in my thumb with the Cliff Johnson fight. There was a love/hate relationship with George. And that was by design - that was by *his* design. You could never relax. You were always on pins [and needles]. But that's kind of New York in a nutshell - it's so competitive there. And George is very competitive.

I always felt that George is the greatest owner that I ever had the privilege of playing for. I've played for some great owners, but I believe George changed the face of the game certainly - money-wise. And he was certainly in a large market. I'm not quite so sure had anyone bought the Yankees, would have kept the Yankees the way George kept the Yankees - in that tradition. He recognized what he had there and I think by now, you've seen what he has built that into. I think he is the greatest owner the game has ever seen and he belongs in the Hall of Fame.

Those were some big shoes to fill, and you couldn't expect Hal or Hank…there was nobody on this planet that was going to fill those shoes. So in regard to the boys taking over, those are big shoes to fill, and I'm not so sure anyone really

Just Out of Reach: The 1980s New York Yankees

knows who's running the Yankees now. I said this spring, "You hated to see George coming, because you knew somebody was going to get read the riot act, or *everybody* was going to get read the riot act - even if we were doing well." And that was the funny thing with George was the more you won, the crazier he got.

The year we won the championship [1978], he goes, "Get ready for next year!" My god George, let us enjoy this for a month. That was just the way he was though. He was so competitive and wanted to win at any cost - whatever it took. And I think he made baseball better, because if you were going to compete with George, let me tell you, you had to get up early in the morning if you were going to compete with him. So, I said, "You hated to see him coming, and now, you miss seeing him coming." That's kind of him in a nutshell. I mean, nobody was safe from George's wrath. We all heard it. We all had our run-ins with him. But at the end of the day, man, you loved playing for him, because you knew he was going to do everything in his power to win.

RUDY MAY: I'm sorry he's gone, because if he wasn't gone, then I would be...I don't know if you know this or not, but I don't participate in any of the Yankees activities - as far as Old Timers Games and activities they have at the new stadium. The Yankees don't want to invite me and I don't know why. I know that Goose and Oscar [Gamble] and Mickey [Rivers] and all those guys call me and say, "Man, you know that Old Timers Game?" They even had an '81 reunion, and I knew nothing of it. Goose and I stay in touch, and Winfield. I don't know...but I do know that one time, I called to - and I don't know who I talked to at the time - but I called them and I asked them if they could send me a uniform, because I was playing every year in an Old Timers Game down in South Florida for the DiMaggio Foundation. And they said no - if I wanted a uniform, I'd have to buy one. So then, I called the Angels, and the Angels said, "OK." They took the necessary information, the uniform was FedEx'd to the house, and I had it the next day.

The Boss 150

  I said that to say this, and I'm going to guess at this - I got traded to the Yankees in '74, I didn't have a relationship with George as a player. I saw him but never talked to him or anything. And then, I was in the airport or someplace in Tampa, at the end of the '79 season [May would be traded from the Yankees to the Baltimore Orioles in 1976, and then played for the Montreal Expos from 1978-1979]. I saw George, he looked at me and I look at him, and I said, "Hey Boss." He goes, "What? What do you want?" I said, "I want to be a Yankee. You don't know who I am. I can do a lot to help your ball club." He looked at me, and said, "OK, OK." When I became a free agent at the end of that season, my agent called me - my agent was Dick Moss - and said, "George wants you, Rudy. And you can't play in a better market than New York." It was amazing, because George told my agent, "Whatever anyone else offers Rudy, *I want him to be a Yankee.* Do you understand?" I had a couple of ball clubs that wanted me, too - including Montreal. When Dick said, "You can be a Yankee," I said, "OK, do it. Get it done." And he did. So I became a Yankee again.

  And the only time I was ever reprimanded by George, it was a funny thing. We were on a plane, flying to or from Milwaukee. There was a writer, Dick Young. Dick Young and I got along, so we're sitting on the plane, and Dick says to me, "Hey Rudy, what happened to the Yankees?" - he's talking about the second half of the [1981] season. So I said, "I'm not really sure. There could have been some complacency there, since we already knew we had won the first half of the season, and we were going to have to play someone in the second half, it didn't matter who it was. But we may have been a little complacent. I don't know." Well, it was probably a three-sentence paragraph at the bottom of his column the next day - "Rudy May says the Yankees were complacent." That's all he said.

  I get to the ballpark that day, and Yogi says, "Hey Rudy, the old man told me to tell you whenever you got here to call him." I said, *"What?!"* He said, "You may want to go up there." I said, "I'm not going up there, I'm in uniform, man! I ain't never been up there!" He said, "Well, use that red phone there," in the

151 Just Out of Reach: The 1980s New York Yankees

manager's office. I picked up the phone, and I said, "Hello, George?" And he says, "WHO IS THIS?" I said, "It's Rudy." He says, "WELL JUST LET ME TELL YOU ONE THING - YOU'RE A YANKEE. YOU PUT ON THAT PINSTRIPE UNIFORM JUST LIKE THE REST OF US. THIS IS *MY* TEAM! I'M THE ONLY ONE WHO CAN CRITICIZE MY TEAM IN THE NEWSPAPER! DO YOU UNDERSTAND THAT, RUDY?" I said, "Boss, I *totally* understand it." He said, "WELL, THANK YOU!" And he hung up. [Laughs] It was funny, because after that, it was like it didn't happen. I mean, it was said, it was done, and it was forgotten. And there weren't any hard feelings on his part that I said that. He didn't even want to know if I said it. What he was saying was, "It was in the paper, it had your name in it, and it shouldn't have been. So whether you said it or not, it doesn't matter. But it's there. And 'I'm the Yankees, I'm the one who does that'." That's what I remember about George Steinbrenner. I loved that guy, and all he ever wanted to do was just win.

REX HUDLER: I ran into Mr. Steinbrenner when I was broadcasting, after my career was over. Mr. Steinbrenner was in the older Yankee Stadium, and he used to sit in his box up there, and now I'm broadcasting for the Angels. I wanted to go say hi to him and see if he remembered me. So in between innings, I went up there, asked the guard if I could go see him, and he let me in the next inning. I walked up to Mr. Steinbrenner, I always carried a baseball in my hand, and I said, "Mr. Steinbrenner, Rex Hudler. I was one of your #1 picks, back in '78." And he looked at me, and goes, "Rex, how ya been? Nice to see ya! Hey, you had a great career." And I went, "Thank you Mr. Steinbrenner...that could be interpreted a lot different from other people, but thank you." He goes, "No, you got ten years in, didn't you? Well, that's a pretty good career if you ask me." "Thank you Mr. Steinbrenner. Would you please sign this ball for me? I'd love to have it for my collection." He wrote on the ball, "To my former #1 pick. Once a Yankee, always a Yankee. All my best, George Steinbrenner." That really made me feel so good that he remembered me.

MIKE PAGLIARULO: It was a really classy organization. It was something the owner wanted, and they built it really nice.

chapter 17: billy

The man that the Boss loved to fire and rehire, Billy Martin.

BILLY MARTIN JR: It would depend on where I was [in response to being asked, "How did Billy Jr. watch games that his father managed?"]. If I was with him, I was either watching the game form the dugout or the family section or the owner's box. I tried to watch all the games when I wasn't at home. He and my mother were basically on the outs then [Billy Jr.'s parents divorced in 1979], but we obviously kept with everything he did. And then I'd spend summers - much of the summer - traveling with him. That was probably when I got the closest with my father, at the age of like 15 up. And spent the most quality time with him and hanging with the teams. It was a lot of fun for me. He was always my dad, but he was gone so much as a young kid, that I never had…our relationship got much better and we spent a lot more time together as I got older.

MIKE PAGLIARULO: I loved Billy Martin. Billy was the kind of guy…"You dumb ass dago," he would say! [Laughs] "One hit today? One play? *Come on.*" He would always give me a hard time. When Billy gave you a hard time, that meant he liked you. But I liked Billy, because Billy was one of the few guys…very much like Tom Kelly with the Twins, only a different demeanor. And I got to know Mike Scioscia a little bit. They could see the field. They could see a lot of things going on in the field at the same time, and they saw the field differently than most. The ball went down the left field line, they know exactly what's going on, on the right field line - they know where everyone has to be. It's just that they saw so many things on the diamond. And that was Billy's gift, I think.

He was a great offensive manager. He pushed guys, he challenged guys. I have so many Billy stories, and I loved him. We didn't always play great for Billy, but he always did whatever he could for us. If I needed extra work on hitting left-handed pitching, he'd make sure that a left-hander goes down there - he didn't care who it was - that I was going to get it. He took care of the players and I felt that. All you had to do was play. Just play your ass off and don't lie to him, and stand up for what you believe in. I know that's a fact with Billy.

Because there was a time I made a play in Anaheim - it was a one-hopper to third base, and I threw it to second. It was a bunt play. And the guy was safe - I pulled off the second baseman a little bit. And Billy was screaming at me - "F this" and "F that." He goes, "What the F was that?" I go, "Billy, it was the right play. I just didn't get my feet set and my throw was off line." "That wasn't the right play." "No, that was the right play." "Get down at the end of the dugout!" So I went down to the end of the dugout, and we ended up losing the game. Clete [Boyer] comes to my locker at the end of the game - "Billy wants to see you." I'm like, "Oh my god. That's it, I'm done. I'm going to Columbus tomorrow."

I walked in there and he's reading the paper. He says, "Listen, dago, where are you going tonight?" I went, "Huh?" He goes, "Are you deaf? Where are you going?" "Nowhere. I'm just going back to my room, why?" "Why did you think you could have gotten him at second base?" "Billy, it's a one-hopper. I was coming in, I was ready for the bunt - I just don't think I had my feet set. It was the right play, I just had to get my footwork better." Because the throw was in time, it just took him off the base. He goes, "Ah...you might be right. I don't know. Get the hell out of here, will you?" That was his way of saying I might be right. But he liked that - he liked guys that stood up for themselves, and when you felt like you did the right thing, you should be able to speak to him. So I did. That's all he wanted to see. Those were the kinds of guys he put on the field. That's who he wanted representing him - that's who he wanted representing

155 Just Out of Reach: The 1980s New York Yankees

New York, which is not a bad thing at all. I'd want the same thing.

RUDY MAY: In regards to Billy being a manager, Billy was a good manager. His record speaks for itself [Billy's all-time managerial record is 1,253-1,013, and he won one World Series and one AL Pennant]. But Billy and I had our differences. The whole thing started when I pitched a ballgame for Billy the first time he managed us. And after the game, I went in the clubhouse, and said, "Skip, I want to do everything I can to help you and everyone win. But when you take me out of a ballgame like that, I wish you would just think about waiting a little bit longer before you replace me." He got all pissed off. He says, "YOU S.O.B.! YOU GET OUT MY FACE! YOU'LL NEVER PITCH FOR ME AGAIN!" And I said, "Now wait a minute. I just feel like I can talk to you about this." He said, "YOU CAN'T TALK TO ME ABOUT IT!" So I left the office.

That was one of the things that really, really hurt me as a human being, because it was some time after that, that we had that big trade to the Orioles [on June 15, 1976, the Yankees traded May, Tippy Martinez, Rick Dempsey, Scott McGregor, and Dave Pagan to the Orioles, in exchange for Doyle Alexander, Jimmy Freeman, Elrod Hendricks, Ken Holtzman, and Grant Jackson]. Well, the fact of the matter was Catfish Hunter and I were really close. When I got traded, we were in Minneapolis, and Catfish knocks on my door. He goes, "Hey man, I've got to tell you...you've been traded." And I said, "What are you doing coming into my room after a game Catfish, telling me I've been traded?" He goes, "Well, I was told to come and tell you." I thought, "Man, how elementary, high school-ish - whatever you want to call it - that is, to have another player come in and tell me that I've been traded." I said, "OK, that's fine," and I never spoke to Billy again. Well, I did - there was a lot of anger between him and I, as to what happened. Later, there was an Oldtimers Game that I played in, and we hugged and said, "Hey man, sorry. It's just a passion for winning." [Laughs]

BILLY MARTIN JR: One of his strengths was learning how to push guys' buttons. And there were certain guys that he didn't need to say a word to. Then there were guys that he did a little "love" every now and then - a little pat on the back. A guy like Rickey Henderson. He'd walk over to Rickey after the trainer told him, "Rickey's hamstring was pretty bad. You should probably sit him." Dad would walk over and put his hand on his back, laying on the training table - "Hey pal, thinking about sitting you tonight. The trainer says your hamstring is pretty bad." "Oh no, skip. I'm your guy, I'm your guy." Dad would say, "Damn right you're my guy, and I need you all year. We've got an off day tomorrow - this way, if I sit you tonight, I'll give you two days rest." "I'm your guy skip. Just let me cruise, let me cruise." "Let me cruise" was "Don't expect me to run 100% to a ball I popped up to the catcher. Don't get on me if it looks like I'm jogging, because I'm trying to conserve what I've got." Dad would say, "Are you sure, pal? Are you sure?" And then Rickey, the one-man-gang that he was, would go out there and walk twice, get on base once, steal two bags - even with his hurt hamstring! It was amazing to watch. And there were guys that he would have to get on. And that pushed their buttons. The classic example, and I don't even want to say his name, because any time you do, you give him more press…he wasn't an '80s guy, anyways. From that '80s teams, I don't remember that many guys that he would just get on.

STEVE BALBONI: As far as the game itself, he was outstanding. I mean, he always got himself in the right position. As far as baseball strategy, he knew what he was doing. He was just a guy that if he liked you, you were OK. If he didn't…that wasn't good. It was good to stay on his good side! [Laughs] Fortunately for me, he did like me. I remember Larry Milbourne missed a squeeze bunt, because they pitched out and he didn't try enough, I guess. It's hard to remember exactly what happened, but I remember he didn't play him much after that. He was a utility guy, and he didn't play much after that. I just remember he wasn't real forgiving about mistakes. You really had to not make

157 Just Out of Reach: The 1980s New York Yankees

mistakes. Mental mistakes...I mean, physical, everybody makes them. But you had to be doing the right thing.

PHIL NIEKRO: I loved to play for Billy. When I wasn't pitching, I was hanging around as close as I could to Billy, and finding out the way he thinks about baseball. I think maybe he was the first manager that looked two or three innings ahead, about situations. I learned he was really good at that. Great guy to be around. I really enjoyed Billy. I didn't have any problems with Billy at all.

TOBY HARRAH: Billy Martin was my favorite manager. I played two years for Billy [with the Texas Rangers] - 162 one year and 161 the next, because we had a rainout - and he was the type of guy that made me believe I was the best shortstop that ever played the game. He just instilled in you a lot of confidence that you didn't know you had. He knew how to play the game of baseball. He taught you how to play *winning* baseball - when to bunt, when to squeeze, when to hit and run, when to take pitches to get a walk, when to hit the ball on the right side of the field, when to try to pull the ball, how to approach the game as far as winning and losing. This guy was all about winning. When you really come to think about it, that's really what it's all about - *and that's winning*. He made you aware of that at a very young age. He made you really focus on what's important, and that's winning and how to win. When he was in Texas, some of the best teams I ever played on was when Billy Martin was their manager.

BRIAN FISHER: Fiery. Under pressure all the time. That's the biggest thing I saw - the pressure, the phone ringing in the bullpen, everyone was a little afraid..."uncomfortable" is probably how I'd put it, in terms of even if you were pitching well, you never knew what was going to happen. Weird stuff would happen. We were playing the Blue Jays and I had a ground ball hit right back at me - I think it was by [George] Bell - and it went between my head and my glove, and I missed it. I came out of the game without any damage or giving up any runs, but I was coming up the tunnel into the clubhouse, and this guy came down and told me that I was to report to the field the following day at 1:00 and take ground balls - until I "learned how to take ground balls." It was just interesting, because of all the pressure to do well - not a whole lot of mistakes were tolerated. From the bullpen, you could see George Steinbrenner's booth, and when things didn't go well, you could see it going crazy and the phone ringing in the dugout, and the phone would ring in the bullpen. The coach I hung around the most with was Jeff Torborg, who I thought was a great guy - but he had to wear a heart monitor for two or three weeks out there, because it was high-pressure.

BOBBY MEACHAM: Billy was the best. I played for Billy three different times, Lou twice, and Yogi once. I find it hard to believe that there was a better manager in baseball. Obviously, everybody knows all the crazy stuff that he did off the field and his temper on the field, but what a great baseball mind. I remember my first spring training, I was the new guy from A Ball, from a different organization, and he took a liking to me and basically just taught me everything he knew. He sat me down, and said, "I'm going to teach you everything I know." I learned so much from that guy. He was - to me - the best. It was maybe the only time I'd been on a team - whether it's coaching or managing in the minor leagues or big leagues, or playing - that I felt we had a distinct advantage, just because he was managing. I can't say enough about Billy. He was awesome.

BILLY MARTIN JR: That's very obvious why [Billy kept agreeing to return to the Yankees to manage]. I'll put it in perspective - I asked him that question one time, when he was going back to the Yankees after Oakland. And Oakland was a really unique experience - especially watching it from my standpoint. I mean, he went there as manager *and* general manager. So obviously, he didn't have to worry about an owner that was ridiculously hands-on, but he called all the shots. That

Just Out of Reach: The 1980s New York Yankees

was his home, that was where he's from - he was born in Berkeley. It was really neat. The billboards just said "BILLYBALL." Giant billboards on the side of the highway - "BILLYBALL. CATCH IT."

When he was going back to the Yankees, I said to him, "Dad, why?" He looked so good - he was so healthy, he had all his color in his face, he had a little gut. It was the healthiest he'd looked in years. He didn't have that stress that the New York area...the press, the stress, the owner, the issues he had to deal with there. He looked great. I said, "Why do you want to go back to that?" And he looked at me like he wanted to smack me - he gave me this look. *"Because I'm a Yankee.* And I'm just not happy anywhere else." That's what he said.

But happy? Happy is probably not the best description of what he meant. He felt like he was a Yankee, and that was all there was to it. Anywhere else to him was just a way to get back to being on the Yankees. And look at his career, look at his life, look at his playing career. He came up a Yankee. He signed in '50, they won a World Series that year. '51 was really technically his rookie year, World Series. World Series in '52, World Series MVP in '53. They don't go in '54 - he's in the Army, '55 they go and lose, '56 they win again, he's traded. And he's never ever the same player. He was in the All-Star game - his only All-Star game - in '56. From then on, he was a vagabond. He was a journeyman. That was who he was - he was a Yankee.

ANDRE ROBERTSON: Billy, he was a good manager - he did things to get in other teams' minds. When he came back [in 1983], I think just my personal opinion, Billy was better for a younger team like when he was with Oakland, he gets that hustle. Some of the things he does, some of the older players didn't really agree with. Billy liked people to go out and run - we had the Lou Piniellas, the Bobby Murcers, some older players that couldn't do that. Dave Winfield could - he did that all the time. As far as me, he let me play. I don't think he wanted to at first, I think we had a bunch of shortstops - Roy Smalley, a couple of guys had come up. I think one thing that convinced him as far as me was Don Zimmer. Don Zimmer, to me, was a great coach. He knew what was going on on the field. He'd been out there. I remember one game out in California, bases loaded, I think Ellis Valentine hit a bullet at me. I picked up the ball, saved a run, I think turned a double play, and he told Billy...I think [Martin] liked Roy Smalley because he hit home runs. I don't hit home runs, but I save three or four runs by making plays like that. I finally got in, and hey, when I was hitting, I was like a second leadoff hitter. So we got things going that year. Unfortunately for me, when we got into August, I had that car wreck. After that, we kind of tailed off.

BILLY MARTIN JR: That term ["Billyball"] wasn't a self-made term. It was a moniker placed on him by others. He believed on putting pressure on his opposition. Any more pressure he could put on them - in an already very pressurized game - the better he felt his chances were. He felt like he could win as long as he understood all his soldiers. He said, "I don't care if they love me or hate me. As long as I know where everybody stands, I'm OK. It's the damn fence-riders that are hard to figure." But he always felt like if a player was about the team, and about doing whatever it took for the team to win, then he felt like he could win. Even if that team wasn't maybe as talented as the team across the field. If the team across the field had a bunch of prima donnas, he was going to beat them. And that's why he didn't want some of those big name/high money guys, because he felt like they were "I/me guys," and not "team guys." He wanted team guys.

STEVE KEMP: Billy Martin was an icon in New York. He played there and was loved by all the people in New York as a player and a manager. It's pretty well documented that him and George had a love/hate relationship. Billy was great to me. My spring training and the first part of the season, everything was fine. And then I had an injury and hurt my shoulder, and continued to play with it - not very many people knew my shoulder was hurt. In those days, if you had injuries, you played.

Just Out of Reach: The 1980s New York Yankees

It is what it is. And I think Billy kind of lost his confidence in me. And then at the end of the year, I had a really serious injury, and got hit in the eye with a line drive during batting practice, which shelved me for the rest of the year and put my career in a position of "What's going to happen from here? He's lost some vision." Billy was bigger than me as a person - as a name. I just tried to go out there and do what I was supposed to do. I think Billy at some point was probably disappointed in my performance.

DAVE LaROCHE: I played against him almost my whole career, and he was always fiery, on top of the game. And you always had to be aware and expect the unexpected, because he could squeeze, steal a base, hit and run, bunt. He managed the game well. He was always on top - he was looking at match-ups before computers. He was very innovative. By this time, he had gotten older, and he was a little bit behind the game. I remember he was late getting guys up in the pen and stuff. He probably had gone a little bit beyond his time I think, to manage. But he still had the fire. I never had a problem with guys that wanted to win. It was like George - I didn't agree with everything, the moves he made or things he did. But I knew in his mind, he was trying everything he could to help the team win. He wanted to win. That's hard to fault.

FRAN HEALY: With his personality, he was always being hired. So maybe there was something to the drinking, because he would get fired most of the time, because he did something off the field that had to do with drinking. He'd get hired by somebody else. He would only last one or two years. When I got to the Yankees, I was told by some players before I even went on the field, I was in Cleveland, they said, "We're just going to give you a thumbnail sketch of this. When you're on the field playing, Billy will rip the guy on the field, but never say anything when he comes in the dugout." And that night, it happened to Roy White. I can't remember what he did in the field - it must have been an error, but I remember he hammered him while he was out there, and when he came in, he didn't say anything.

So Billy kind of outlived his value fast - probably because of that stuff. I heard him talking to an executive one day at Yankee Stadium - they were in an office next to one I was in. He was screaming at this guy. I don't want to tell you who the guy was, but the guy had some juice - he wasn't screaming at George, but somebody that worked for George, who reported to George. I mean, *screaming* at the top of his lungs. I'm assuming he was sober, because it was like 4:30 in the afternoon, before a game. But Billy, he was once defined as having seven or eight different personalities. One of his PR guys said that. I'm sure those personalities were motivated by whether the team was winning or losing. As much stress as he was under in New York, there's nothing like New York, because *everybody* in New York is under stress.

BILLY MARTIN JR: Here's the thing - they like to act like it [Martin's drinking] was something way more than it was. My father drank after the games. Without a doubt. He would go to a bar after the games, sit down - he would sit by himself for his first drink. You could see him going through the game - "I did this differently, I did this right, I did this wrong, I should have pulled my pitcher early, I should have brought in a reliever." You could see him go through the whole game, and then the light would come on - *bing*. He would let it go, he would flush the toilet, it was gone, and have fun. But when people say that he drank during the day, that he drank at lunch, that he drank before a game - that is a bunch of crap. I never saw it, ever. Any player that says that is a liar. And I've heard several players say that, because they want to play it up. Because you know what? Yeah, he did have too much to drink after some games. He did go out at night. Some nights, he just had two. He had a pretty darn good tolerance, and he had a decent feel for...I've heard him say this many times - "Hey, it's time to go." That was his way of saying, "I've probably had enough." He was challenged all the time by people. It was like going out with a gunfighter. But he was damn good to people.

FRAN HEALY: In the dugout, he was serious. If they were winning, he was animated. If they were losing, he was more a "sit-down-on-the-bench-type-of-guy," and probably was trying to keep it inside that he was mad. Off the field, it's been documented some of the problems - and they all went back to drinking. Where Billy came from, I really admire, because he came from a very, very difficult background. I've got to believe that if he didn't drink, he would have had a different life. Because he was a bright, shrewd guy. But when he drank, he became belligerent. I didn't see much of that, because I wasn't really in the bars.

But it goes all the way back to the Minnesota days, when he and Dave Boswell got in a fight in a bar in Detroit [in 1969]. In fact, it's ironic that famous fight in Detroit. I think Boswell [was fighting] Bob Allison, and Billy got a hold of Boswell. He had a chain on - Harmon Killebrew told me this story, Harmon was a good friend of mine with Kansas City, his last year in baseball. Billy got a hold of a chain that Boswell had wrapped around, and he was hitting him. That was one of the big fights. And it's ironic or coincidental that it was called Lindell AC in Detroit - when Billy died in that car accident, the guy in the car accident owned Lindell's. So he was up in New York that day with Billy, hanging out.

TOMMY JOHN: Billy was OK. We were like Venus and Mars - Billy was fiery, he was temperamental, he was hotheaded. And I wasn't. Billy didn't manage by the book - he managed by his gut. When they say, "He manages by the book," they mean the players take the heat, they don't. Because you say, "Oh, I brought in lefty/righty, righty/lefty. They didn't do the job." But Billy would bring in a left-handed pitcher to pitch to a right-handed hitter, because it was his gut instinct. And many times, he was more right than wrong. And Billy would yell and scream and all that, and you would just turn your "hearing aid" off and not listen to him.

If you look back at his history of managing, he was very, very good for the first year, not so good for the second year, and then he was usually gone by the third year. Because of the way he managed and yelled and the pressure and all this, the first year was fine, and the second year guys just got worn down by it and they didn't respond to it. Not saying with the Yankees, but with Oakland, and I remember with the Twins, he lost his job with the Twins in the playoffs...the Twins had a good team. They were going to play the Baltimore Orioles [in the 1969 ALCS], and they had one pitcher, two pitcher, and the third pitcher, instead of pitching Dave Boswell - because Billy didn't like Dave Boswell - he pitched Bob Miller, a guy out of the bullpen, and Calvin Griffith [the Twins' president, majority owner, and de facto general manager] went "outhouse crazy" on him and fired him after the playoffs. But that was Billy.

BILLY MARTIN JR: So did Ferguson Jenkins, though - I agree with exactly what you're saying [in response to the assumption that Martin has been kept out of the Hall of Fame because of his drinking, yet Jenkins is in the Hall of Fame, despite being busted for possession of cocaine, hashish, and marijuana in 1980]. And it is why I think my father is not - because he liked to throw one back every now and then, because he liked to have a little fun. Who didn't that was in the Hall of Fame? Remember this though - the managers don't go in by the same way that the players do. And so, they're committees of guys that are already in. A lot of those guys that are already in have - whether you want to call them "vendettas" or not - issues with my father. A lot of guys didn't like my father's success, a lot of guys didn't like the fact that he was as famous as he was. I mean, he was on the cover of Time Magazine! I don't even know if another baseball player has been on the cover, let alone I can guarantee no other manager has. How many movies he's been mentioned in - he's *still* mentioned in movies. 'Ocean's Eleven' or 'Ocean's Thirteen' referenced him several times, saying, "Oh, he

Just Out of Reach: The 1980s New York Yankees

was Billy Martin" - meaning he got a do-over, he got another chance to do the same job, basically. But he's been mentioned in about seven different movies.

I mean, the Hall of Fame, tell me there was a more famous manager in the '70s and '80s? And his winning percentage alone [.553]. The fact that he never stuck in that one spot for a long time is one of the things that they beat him down for, and it's amazing to me. Whitey Herzog is in the Hall of Fame [as a manager, Herzog had a winning percentage of .532, a record of 1,281-1,125, and he won one World Series and two NL Pennants, while again, Martin's record was 1,253-1,013, and he won one World Series and one AL Pennant]. And should be - I'll say that before I make my next statement. But my father took the same team that Whitey lost over a hundred games with, and almost went to the playoffs - with the '74 Texas Rangers. The very same team - except he called up a guy from A Ball named Mike Hargrove, and a guy from Double A named Jim Sundberg. But it was basically the same exact team. Then he faced Whitey in the playoffs with Kansas City twice and what happened? The Yankees won both times.

Catfish Hunter, Billy Martin, and Brad Gulden meet on the mound - 1979. [Photo by Jim Accordino]

The man who according to Steve Jacobson, once wore a bathroom stall around his head, Chris Chambliss. [Photo by Jim Accordino]

The Yankees' ace pitcher of the late '70s/early '80s, Ron Guidry. [Photo by Jim Accordino]

The swing that launched numerous baseballs and cheers, Reggie Jackson. [Photo by Jim Accordino]

The man with the magic glove and the potent bat, Graig Nettles. [Photo by Jim Accordino]

Nettles swings! [Photo by Jim Accordino]

Another Yankee fan favorite, Bobby Murcer. [Photo by Jim Accordino]

Murcer swings! [Photo by Jim Accordino]

One of the reasons why the Dodgers beat the Yanks in the '81 World Series, Fernando Valenzuela. [Photo by Jim Accordino]

Robert Merrill sings the national anthem, before a battle against the Detroit Tigers. [Photo by Jim Accordino]

The lone homegrown star of the '80s Yankees, Don Mattingly. [Photo by Jim Accordino]

Mattingly shows off a tiny bubble and the beginnings of a mullet hairstyle. [Photo by Jim Accordino]

A view from old Yankee Stadium's right field. [Photo by Jim Accordino]

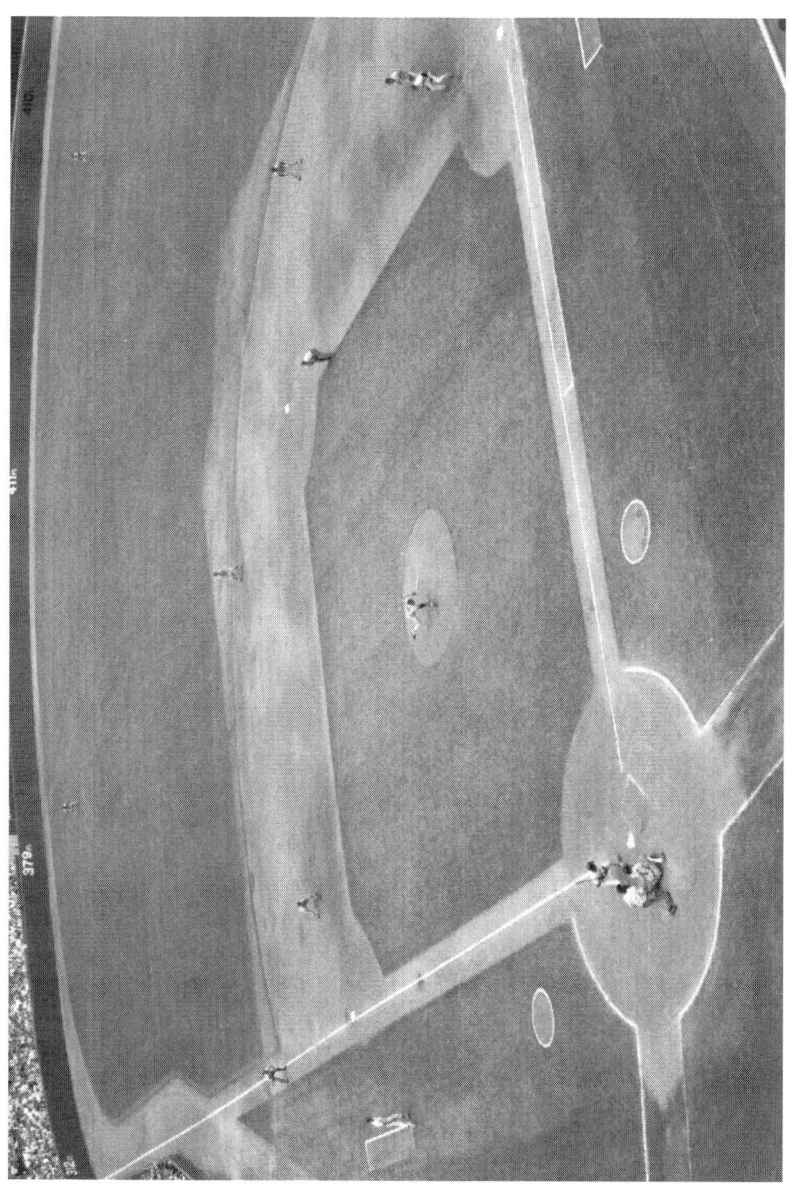

A field on which countless classic moments occurred - a bird's eye view of old Yankee Stadium. [Photo by Jim Accordino]

chapter 18: winny

A player who endured the wrath of the Boss, but continued to thrive nonetheless, Dave Winfield.

TOMMY JOHN: Winny was OK. He got that bad rap - George called him "Mr. May." He said, "I used to have Mr. October, and now, I have Mr. May." Because Dave I think was 1-23 in the World Series or something like that [Winfield went 1-22]. That was just a bad call on George...that was George. George lashed out, and Dave was the guy there - Dave took the whipping. But Dave could do it all - Dave could run bases, he could play the outfield, he had a great arm, he could hit, he could hit with power. You talk about a five-tool player, he had it. Dave was OK.

GEORGE FRAZIER: That's a tough one for me to talk about, because I introduced him to his wife, the twins were born on my birthday. Again, still a very close relationship. I think once you wear pinstripes, that relationship stays forever. With the ball club, with the fans, with your teammates, the front office personnel - even though it's changed over a lot up there. It's still one of those deals where we're all still pretty close, pretty tight. Winfield, what he went through in '81, with not being able to come through in a World Series and playoffs and what Steinbrenner said, all of those things taken into account, Dave was a great baseball player. You're talking about a guy drafted in three sports [the San Diego Padres in baseball, both the Atlanta Hawks (NBA) and the Utah Stars (ABA) in basketball, and the Minnesota Vikings in football]. A mountain of a man. But I always appreciated Dave for what he did in the community. I remember one time going to Minnesota, he did a health check on all the underprivileged kids, and he asked me to go with him. I went with him and sat in the dentist area, where there were seven dentists that he paid to be there that day, to check these kids out. His brother, Steve, was right there with us. It's just the things that he did in his community with his mom, the whole deal. It was pretty special.

BOB WATSON: I saw him the first game he played - he signed on from the college campus [the University of Minnesota], and he played against Houston. You saw this big, tall, rangy guy, that had an excellent arm, a real long swing, but you saw the potential of him really getting it together. He did. And then to play alongside him and sit there and watch him play on a day in and day out basis, you saw a star that was booming. He hit balls, threw balls, caught balls - day in and day out. You just shook your head. For him to be in the Hall of Fame, I think is definitely a right call.

MIKE PAGLIARULO: Dave Winfield, I couldn't believe how big he was when I first met him. I went, "Oh my god!" The first thing I thought is, "If I ever have to get in a fight with this guy, I'm going to need a pipe to knock him out, because I don't think I can take this guy." [Laughs] He was just *so* big. But he was so professional, well-spoken, and my gosh, my first thoughts were how hard he hits that ball and how hard he ran down to first base and played in the outfield and played every day. And to get that big body to play was just amazing. He could be intimidating on the field. It was great to have him on your side. I'd hate to have him on the other team. He was good to play with and always treated me great - he had been around a while. I was actually at the Hall of Fame induction when him and Kirby Puckett went in [in 2001], and he had his great family and all. I enjoyed playing with Dave Winfield - he was a good guy to play with. He's a Hall of Famer, and a lot of people could learn a lot about the game by watching him - the way he played and the way he handled himself in that situation. He was a talented athlete, my gosh.

Just Out of Reach: The 1980s New York Yankees

RUDY MAY: Dave was a great human being. When he joined the team, he bought a house in Teaneck, New Jersey, around the corner from me. And I know he went in and had it remodeled, because all of the counters in the kitchen and the bathroom were all real low - compared to his height. So when my family wasn't there, Dave and I spent a lot of time together. And by that, I mean after ballgames, Dave would come by and we would talk at my house, and we'd go to his house. We could walk from house to house. That happened a lot.

TOBY HARRAH: When I played against him, I didn't like Dave. I just thought he was an arrogant type of player. And there's nothing wrong with that - I think he felt like every time he went out on the field, his team was #1. And that's probably the way to be. But once I became teammates with him...what a super teammate! Pulled for the rest of the guys, interacted with the rest of the guys on the team in a positive way, played hard. You can't really say enough about him. I was so impressed with the way he played the game of baseball, when I was his teammate in '84.

GARY ROENICKE: First off, he was a great teammate. My impression of him was playing against him all those years, he was...this is what the game plan was - try and intimidate. He had a big "intimidating factor." And Dave could do it all - he was a five-tool guy, great athlete. But he had that little confidence/arrogance, and I think that was in his game plan - to psych out the other team, especially the pitcher. But he played hard. I don't know how many times that year he would hit a bouncer up the middle into centerfield and run hard out of the box. Most of us would say, "OK, we got a single." He would end up turning it into a double. He would go hard into second base. He was the first guy I ever saw that did that. He'd hit a ground ball up the middle and it would be a double. The other thing with him is after something would happen, he'd come down and sit next to me and say, "Ah...*I stink.*" I'm thinking, "Whoa! This is the guy after all these years that was kind of the 'intimidating factor' - showing how confident he was." And for him to humble himself, that kind of opened my eyes a little bit.

RON KITTLE: A gamer. He's one of those guys, he's the true factor of what a Hall of Famer should be. He played hard, had some good numbers. I feel bad - he and George battled over some things over the years - but I think George had a unique way to ruffle the feathers and maybe get players to play a little bit better. I think that was his technique. It was pretty much like my dad's - you create a challenge and see if they can fess up to it. But Winny was a good guy, and like I said, they talked baseball, they had fun, but when the bell rang, between the chalk lines, it was a battle.

MIKE EASLER: Dave was a great person - a great individual. Dave was a consummate pro. He played the game hard, he played the game well, he represented the Yankees well. I know he was going through some things with Steinbrenner at the time, but you would never know it, the way he played the game. He played all out, every single game he played. I enjoyed playing with Dave Winfield. I think he was definitely a Hall of Famer and a great ballplayer.

BOBBY MEACHAM: Great player. Obviously a Hall of Fame player. Just one of those guys you looked at and said, "Man, how does he do all these things?" The level of concentration that these guys have every day - these superstars - is unbelievable. No matter whether the owner and he were griping at each other or whether he was having trouble at home, it didn't really matter - they'd get to the field and they'd just…guys like Dave was just the epitome of a professional. He never let anything get in the way of him doing well. He taught the younger players a lot of stuff. He taught me a lot of things.

He'd tell me things like, "Pattern your game after somebody you respected while you were growing up and watched play. Or even now - somebody you see playing right now. See if you can take little things from that person. Say it's

Just Out of Reach: The 1980s New York Yankees

Ozzie Smith, say you can take the way he goes after his defense, or say Rickey, how he runs the bases. Just take something from everybody's game and try to put it to use for your game." And he even taught me about stuff after baseball. He tried to educate a lot of the young guys about, "Hey, you're going to be done - if you're lucky - at 35. What are you going to do after that?" He would try to show us stuff to think about beyond baseball - investing in the right things or just learning another craft as you're playing the game. And diversify your talents. Not just baseball, but other things you can do after you're done playing.

REX HUDLER: The best advice ever given to me by any player, I was 21/22 years old at the time, was Dave Winfield. He said, "Kid, one thing is guaranteed for a ballplayer - you'll be an ex-ballplayer. And I've seen you play - you may be gone next week. So while you're here, you better make sure that you make connections with these people and these fans here that own corporations. You're going to need a job some day. So you make sure to have your eyes open and your ears open. Tell your story wherever you go, because you maybe could use that and find yourself a job when you're done playing, son." And I went, "Winny, I don't want to hear that right now - *I'm only 21/22 years old.* But I hear the wisdom coming out of that. Thank you, man." Winny took me under his wing.

ANDRE ROBERTSON: He's great. He played hard every game. And when you see guys like that, it makes you want to do it. I had a funny little story about him - one time, he asked me to borrow a hundred dollars. And I said, "Wait a minute. You've just signed this big contract, *I'm making the minimum."* Well, he didn't have any cash. A lot of people that have a lot of money don't have cash - I think it's because they don't have to loan it out. [Laughs] But it was just one time. Those are things that get you together as a team. We would go out and eat - that's how you become close. And I think the closer the team is, the better they'll play, the better they learn each other, and how to play together.

DAVE LaROCHE: He was a good guy and easy-going, but intense. He was all business on the field during the game. He was a great talent. Mediocre pitching he wore out.

STEVE BALBONI: He's a great athlete. Nice guy - I go by just how people treated me, and he was great to me. He was a good teammate, he played hard. I liked him, I thought he was great. He was easy to talk to. He's one of the better athletes I've ever seen.

DALE BERRA: One of the best players to ever play the game, Winfield. The best outfielder I ever played with. The best arm, tremendous outfielder, and a great player. Amazing player. A true Hall of Famer. His everyday approach to the game was great, and his hustle was tremendous. His ability was great.

BRIAN FISHER: One of the best athletes I've ever seen in my life - until I saw Bo Jackson. Just a nice man, always there, ready to play. To me, he always had a smile on his face - that's what I remember most about Dave Winfield. Always had a kind word for me. Encouraging. I enjoyed playing with him and being around him. Same thing with Randolph. They were just good guys on that team. It just didn't feel like an exclusive clubhouse, where this guy was going this way, that guy was going that way. It really felt tight-knit - take care of each other and look after each other. But I enjoyed playing with him. I couldn't wait to see him get up to bat, I couldn't wait to see him take batting practice. It was a blast.

BARRY FOOTE: I liked Winfield. I played against him in the National League and I liked him. He played the game hard, he was a good guy. I'll tell you, I was in the game for 24 years, and I can count on one hand the number of guys I would say, "Man, I don't like that guy. He's a jerk." And now that I've gotten into the business world the last 20 years, I know how tough that is. I find five guys a month in the business world I don't like! Overall, baseball players are pretty good guys to get along with. They

Just Out of Reach: The 1980s New York Yankees

might come off as tougher, because this is a tough game. It's a long season. If a writer comes up and talks to a guy, you don't know all the things that are going on, and even teammates don't always know what is going on at home - in the family dynamics - that may have an affect on a ballplayer. But I found in my 24 years in the game that overall, ballplayers are pretty good guys to get along with.

chapter 19: donnie baseball

One of the most popular Yankees of all-time, Don Mattingly.

STEVE JACOBSON: I thought Mattingly was one of the tragic figures of sports, because he was a terrific player and didn't get to ever have the showcase.

STEVE BALBONI: We played together in Triple A. He came up and he played left field, and there was another guy playing first. He kind of alternated DH'ing and playing first. He was an excellent hitter. He used the whole field. Didn't really hit for any power. I think that was the Yankees' drawback with him at first base. They felt like he was going to be a .300 hitter, they just didn't feel like he was going to have the power to be your first baseman in Yankee Stadium. In fact, when I got traded in '84, Roy Smalley was the shortstop in '83, and I had heard that they were moving him to first. The job was Roy Smalley's. And I think he got off to a really bad start in spring training and Donnie was hitting the ball good. And so they decided to just give him a shot, and he did what he needed to do - he learned how to pull the ball and hit the ball down that right field line and ended up hitting some home runs. Plus, he was a .300 hitter and an excellent defensive first baseman. He took the opportunity and ran with it. But it wasn't his job in '84, from what I understood.

REX HUDLER: A Ball, we met each other for the first time in Greensboro, North Carolina. The Yankees sent me to Greensboro in the '81 season, to learn how to play second base. They drafted me as a shortstop, so three years later, they could tell I didn't have the throwing arm or just didn't have the accuracy that they expected from that side of the field, so they moved me to second. They figured there was going to be an

183   Just Out of Reach: The 1980s New York Yankees

opening there with Willie, and they weren't sure. They sent me to Bob Schaefer - Bob Schaefer taught me how to play second base. And I remember I had torn cartilage in my right knee at the time, but it didn't bother me - I still could play on it. It wasn't anything threatening, it was just a little painful. But I went down there and learned how to play second base. And Donnie played left field.

Donnie was enamored and in awe of me, because I was a #1 pick. He was like, I don't know - he was a late pick [the Yankees selected Mattingly in the 19th round of the 1979 MLB Draft]. And he kept saying, "Hud, *you're going to be a big leaguer.*" He would tell me that all the time, and I'm going, "Hey Donnie, I'm not hitting .300 like you are, man. Look at your stroke." And he was a line drive hitter. He didn't hit with any power at all though - he was a spray hitter. He was not Punch and Judy, but he was just a line drive hitter. And I kept telling him, "Hey, don't kid yourself. You've got just as good a chance as I do." And so, we kind of got to know each other, had fun. In '82, '83, '84, I was still in A Ball and he progressed and moved up, and then he got his shot in '84. He was such a good hitter that he could recognize the inside pitch. And when he got in the stadium and saw it was 315 down the right field line, he became a power hitter because of the porch. He could use it, he recognized it. He became a beast.

ANDRE ROBERTSON: I played with Donnie in the minor leagues. I'll tell you what, all I could see him do was flipping the ball over the third baseman's head. He got with Lou Piniella - Lou Piniella made him point his feet backwards. One of the most strangest stances I'd ever seen. But he got him to work through the ball. The next thing I know, he's hitting them in the upper deck in right field. But he always could hit. He worked with Lou Piniella and they got him off to that start.

MIKE PAGLIARULO: One of my closer friends. Our lockers were near each other and we went to war every day. It was a lot of fun, because I can honestly say it was always about trying to win that day and be the best you can that day. Our talks...even when we went out afterwards, you didn't want to dwell on the game, but we always talked about ways we could be better and how we could make ourselves better. And how we were going to play against these guys, and who was going to be the toughest in the division. It was all good talk - it wasn't stuff that we were very worried about. It was always competitive stuff. He was a great athlete, too. Ambidextrous - he could throw right-handed or left-handed. Donnie had a great mind - a presence about him that he wanted to be the man in the spot that wanted to get that hit. There was no doubt about that. He loved that and dwelled on that. It made him better, it made him stronger, it made him tougher - as you can see when he won the batting title, and he almost did it again, when Wade Boggs [won it in 1986, finishing five points higher than Mattingly].

  He had to go four for five or five for five, and in his first two or three at bats, he got hits. I'm like, "Oh my god…he's going to do it again!" And then his next at bat, he lined out to the second baseman. When something was on the line like that, he was going to get it done. You just knew he was going to do it. It's just a shame that he couldn't play in a World Series, because I'm sure that he would have done great. He was a great defensive first baseman, as well as one of the best hitters around. He was always a good teammate - lived by example. A good family man and a good person. He was just a tireless worker, so we spent a lot of time together. They were great days. Learned a lot about life, learned a lot about Yankees and winning. And how to handle things and how to grow up. We talk about raising kids and how you're not supposed to push them into playing baseball - that kind of stuff was really cool stuff to talk about, because there were concerns. We try not to push our kids to play baseball, and let them play what they want to play, because there are so many kids that play too early, and they end up hating it. But that's just the way it works.

MIKE EASLER: I used to watch Don Mattingly play in practice, before the game. There was nobody that took more flips, did more cage work than him. And Mike Pagliarulo. Him

185 Just Out of Reach: The 1980s New York Yankees

and Mike Pagliarulo worked like no tomorrow. I enjoyed it, because I worked right along with them. I just wanted to get better - just like they did. Don Mattingly was one of the hardest workers I've ever seen. That's why he hurt his back I think, because he just never gave up. He was relentless.

TOMMY JOHN: Don Mattingly is in *my* Hall of Fame. But I think Donnie didn't play long enough [Mattingly played for the Yankees from 1982-1995]. If he would have played a few more years, I think Don Mattingly should definitely be in the Hall of Fame. Don Mattingly is one of the best ballplayers I've ever played with. The other one was Don Baylor. Don Baylor is the best teammate - he was outstanding. But Donnie - for the years I was with the Yankees - he was a gentleman on the field and off the field.

He worked his butt off. And this is a Dallas Green-ism - Mattingly and Pagliarulo would go down to the bullpen under the batting cage all the time, and work on tee work and hitting, and Dallas would say, "Jesus Christ! You guys work too much on your hitting! You ought to take the time off!" And I looked at Dallas, and I said, "Dallas, maybe that's one of the reasons why Donnie is .300 hitter, because he works on his hitting all the time." And those guys just shook their head. But that was Dallas - telling those guys they worked *too much* on their hitting. You can't. You work on your hitting. But Donnie was outstanding - he was jewel. Plus, he's from Indiana.

RON KITTLE: Indiana boy. A fellow Hoosier. I watched him battle for a batting title with Wade Boggs in '86 and '87. I'd never seen anything like it. The man was a machine, and you saw him work at it. Thank god he was lefty - it made it a little easier. But he could hit. In game, he was "in it" from the first pitch to the last pitch, all the way. Is he "Hall of Fame caliber"? I don't think so. But if he could get a wild card, he might be one of those guys that you get a wild card in there. I just think the world of him.

PHIL NIEKRO: He's right on that borderline [of deserving to be in the Hall of Fame]. His name is brought up a lot out there. I don't know - you'd have to ask the sportswriters that. For me, he was one of the finest ballplayers I ever played with. The best first baseman - no question about it. I'm just sorry that he had to have back problems...or he'd probably *still* be playing! That's a tough question to ask any ballplayer, especially if you played with him or against him. I know what I would do if I was a sportswriter - I know what decision I would make. But I'm not, so I can't say.

DAVE RIGHETTI: Well, Rickey Henderson said [Mattingly] is the best player he ever played with. I saw him for ten years, and the back thing cursed it, of course, because it was going to be a no-brainer [Mattingly getting into the Hall of Fame]. Him and Keith Hernandez were the two best [first basemen] at that time, in the game. And Donnie ended up playing third base - he was ambidextrous. He was just one of those guys, you never saw him off-balance. And at the plate, he hit all the best pitchers. He took the best guys deep. The Dave Steibs and the Jack Morrises - the guys that were dominating - he hit them. He hit the closers when they came in. He was our "x factor guy," and he always was. What did he drive in, a hundred and forty something runs? [In 1985, Mattingly had 145 RBI] And half that year, he hit second - behind Rickey. Because he could take a pitch. I've never seen somebody take a fastball right down the middle, and he didn't blink an eye. He didn't care.

But he was the best player I ever played with and ever saw over a long period of time. Barry Bonds kind of screws up the mix - he was maybe the greatest athlete I've ever seen on a field. And Rickey, of course. But Donnie was the x factor, so to speak, for us. If he was in the National League, he would have won it already, because they would have bunted all the time, and he would have looked like a star. But they never bunted in the American League. He never got to run in and make those plays that Keith Hernandez did. They make a big deal about that. It spawned a bunch of guys - Keith and Donnie, and the Wally

Just Out of Reach: The 1980s New York Yankees

Joyners. The great first basemen that we've seen since - the JT Snows, and you can go on and on. I think those two guys are the ones that spawned it. Again, it was great to watch both of them. Because Keith, to me, is another one - he's a guy you've got to argue about, a "Hall of Fame guy."

Hernandez and Gary Carter gave the Mets legitimacy, and Hernandez won the MVP with the Cardinals, too [Hernandez was the NL's co-MVP in 1979, along with Willie Stargell]. He drove in the big runs. Plus, he's a San Francisco guy, so I'm kind of partial to him. [Laughs] Who knows, some day they might get in. It might be a veteran's thing or something, but I hope I see it. I hope those kind of guys get in. That's how I look at it - they were the best defenders, and they were the clutchest hitters on the team for years. They hit against lefties and righties and closers, got the big hits, and they were the glue in the line-ups. To me, those guys are Hall of Famers.

BILLY MARTIN JR: You mentioned two of the best fielding first basemen I've ever seen in my life - Keith Hernandez and Donnie Baseball. Hernandez fielded the bunt better than anybody I've ever seen, and Don Mattingly turned the double play better than any first baseman I've ever seen. And to me, they dominated…they were by far two of the best at their position for a good five or six-year period. To me, the Hall of Fame should be that - you should be not only one of the greatest ever at your position, but you should also dominate the league at that position for a while. And Mattingly certainly did that. They let [Kirby] Puckett in because of his eye situation. They said he would have got in had it not happened for that. Well, is Don's back any different than that? Or Thurman Munson's plane crash? [Munson] was maintaining excellence and had no protection in that line-up [during the early-mid '70s]! He was *so* clutch.

GARY ROENICKE: We hung around a lot. I really appreciate Don. To me, he was the best player in baseball - in 1985 to 1986. And I believe he should have won the MVP in 1986. I didn't see Joe DiMaggio play, but they said he was one of the few guys that could hit more home runs than strikeouts, and Mattingly was the same way those two years. He could hit the ball...not many guys can place the ball around, and he could do that. If he saw a left fielder was playing way over in left center, he could hit a ball - just a routine fly ball - down the left field line for a double. He could turn on high fastballs, he could hit low pitches, he could hit left-handers. Gold Glove defense - just a great player. It's too bad that his back acted up a little bit later, otherwise he would have no doubt been a Hall of Famer.

TOBY HARRAH: Class act. Probably the best defensive first baseman I ever played with. He had great range, he would just attack the ball, good arm, and great instincts. You could tell he loved to play the game of baseball. And played every day. What a sweet swing. And the same thing with Dave Winfield - a super teammate. One of the guys in the clubhouse, always in a good frame of mind. Positive all the time. And just played hard - played to win. I think the last few years, him as a manager [of the Los Angeles Dodgers] and the way he finished his career is a testament to the way he played baseball.

MIKE EASLER: Don Mattingly is overall the best hitter I played with. Overall. Average, power, clutch, RBI, defense. Came to play the game hard every single day. I think that's what hurt his career - he just overworked. He was the hardest-working first baseman I've ever seen. I was in the cage a lot, but Don Mattingly was in there every single day, working on his mechanics - day in and day out. I saw him face some of the toughest pitchers in baseball, and he was just fearless.

RON KITTLE: I'm not real sure what happened [regarding a supposed "clubhouse wrestling" incident between Mattingly and Bob Shirley in 1987, that allegedly resulted in Mattingly injuring his back]. Was it something to do with his back, maybe? I know I was injured in '87 really bad - career threatening - myself in the locker room [Kittle's earlier story about his training table accident]. Never said much about it, I just wrote it off as not an

Just Out of Reach: The 1980s New York Yankees

excuse but a "silent mishap." But Donnie, when you work hard and you've got a low stance like he did when he was hitting, you're putting strain on your back. And his back was hurting from working out. I mean, this man would hit for *two hours* before the game. Your body cannot torque and twist that much. And I think it just fatigued. I don't think Bob Shirley had anything to do with it, honestly. I'd blame it on Bob, too. [Laughs]

MIKE PAGLIARULO: Donnie horsed around with lots of guys - with me, as a matter of fact! So there was no incident that went on that he hurt his back. Hell, I remember I think it was in '84 or '85, we were in spring training - me, him, and Bobby Meacham, we were all at Donnie's place because we all stayed there the last week of spring training. We were playing Nerf Basketball, crashing into the wall. That's just how things are done after a day game. It's just the fun players have. Heck, I remember when I played in Baltimore, Cal Ripken was on his streak, and the next thing you know, I'm in the locker room and he comes flying over the couch, tackling Ben McDonald. [Laughs] He dove at him - that's just how guys are. But I don't recall any story about Bob Shirley or anything like that.

MIKE EASLER: I don't know nothing about that. All I know is that when he got hurt, my agent called me and said, "The Yankees want you back." [Easler was playing for the Phillies at the time] I said, "Thank you very much. Get me out of here, *please."* [Laughs] I was happy as hell to come back. But I was at the end of my career then - I was 38 years old, I believe. I still could hit, but they were going in a different direction. I knew the guy got hurt - I didn't know it was something between Bob Shirley and Donnie. Who knows?

DALE BERRA: Great guy. Loved to play the game. Worked hard. Wonderful guy. Consummate modern ballplayer, who lived in the batting cage and prepared himself.

BILLY MARTIN JR: He was one of my all-time favorites. He was really good to me as a kid. He was there early, he epitomized leadership - everything. You could argue he was the best hitter in baseball. My father loved him. He was one of the most respected players - by his peers - that I ever saw. To me, rivaled only by maybe Thurman Munson. The exact opposite of what you'd see with a Reggie or guys like that, that nobody even wanted to be near or talk to. Don was special.

STEVE JACOBSON: They got a pitcher from Kansas City, by the name of Steve Farr. The last two or three days of the season, Mattingly was still taking ground balls at first base in pre-game practice. And Farr asked him, "What is it that you're doing?" And Mattingly said, *"Trying to get better."* To me, that was a very poignant line.

chapter 20: rickey

The fastest man to ever put on a Yankee uniform, Rickey Henderson.

TOMMY JOHN: You want me to talk in third-person? Do you want me to talk like Rickey? [Laughs] Rickey was OK. Rickey had that body on him that was absolutely a Greek god body. And I don't think Rickey ever lifted a weight in his life. I asked Rickey about base running and all that, and I just think it was something when he was born, he was born with the instinct to steal bases. And he was phenomenal.

ANDRE ROBERTSON: Rickey Henderson I think is the best leadoff hitter ever. He's very funny. I think he's street knowledgeable. There are a lot of stories you can tell about him, like he never remembers people's names. Like I was "An-o," there was "Win-o," there was "Wil-o." He'd make up names so he could remember. Like one of those stories was about John Olerud - he asked somebody, "Who's that guy wearing the batting helmet at first?" And he played with him with the Mets before, or Toronto! That's how he was. But, when you put him in that leadoff spot and he wanted to play, there was none better. I remember one day, we were out there and he wasn't warming up. And I said, "Rickey, what's wrong?" He had an incentive, and George hadn't paid him his money yet. So he said, "I'm not playing." We went through batting practice, then infield - he wasn't playing. I think it was like $135,000 or something - twice or three times my whole salary back then. But when the game started, he was out there running. I said, "What happened?" He said, *"He gave me my money."* He went 4-4, stole four bases and scored four runs. When he was happy and on that field, there was nobody better in my estimation. Because he could turn a game upside down by himself.

MIKE PAGLIARULO: Rickey was one of the most talented guys I'd ever seen. He could hit home runs, he was one of the best left fielders in the game. And my gosh, stealing the bases, he could just *go*. And when he turned it on, it didn't matter who was pitching and who was catching - you weren't going to catch him. He was just so talented. Rickey was one of the nicest guys and a harmless guy, that all he wanted to do was just play baseball. At times I thought the media and the press would pick on him a little bit and kind of trap him in some questions. I just felt that he could be gullible that way sometimes and he could be tricked sometimes. I think some guys did that to him, and I felt badly, because some things came out in the paper that he would say, that he didn't really mean to say. And knowing Rickey, he would never talk bad about his teammates. He didn't want to talk bad about anybody. He didn't want to fight anybody, didn't want to talk bad about anybody - he just wanted to play baseball. But it always had to be news, I guess.

The thing that I remember the most is just the way that he played, and as the greatest leadoff hitter in the world - whether it's walking or getting hits or hitting home runs. He was just so exciting to see play. It was really fabulous. And the tougher the competition, the better he got. He could just take over the whole game and create havoc - infielders would have to hurry their throws and the catcher would have to change the pitch sequence just to catch him…and he couldn't catch him. He'd steal second and then third. You just never knew what was going to happen. And of course, Billy loved him, and Lou. They treated him great. He was a great pro and a super guy and great teammate. I played with him for five years, it was great to play with him.

DALE BERRA: Very generous guy. Great guy. Clean-living guy. Didn't drink, didn't smoke, played baseball. Loved it. And that's it. You could mistake a little bit of aloofness for not

Just Out of Reach: The 1980s New York Yankees

hustling - that was always a thing there. But he wanted to win. He was a great guy. And he never had any malice. He would never not hustle because he was mad. If he knew he couldn't catch it, he wouldn't run full speed, so it didn't look like he was giving an effort. But he gave effort 100% of the time. He'd give you anything. He was great with the young kids. He was a great guy, Rickey. He couldn't remember anybody's name! He just played ball.

RON KITTLE: Rickey...that's a whole different story. Rickey Henderson disappointed me. I know he's in the Hall of Fame [Henderson was inducted in 2009]...Rickey Henderson should have been MVP five, six, seven, eight, nine times [Henderson was awarded MVP one time in his career - 1990]. Rickey had more talent than I've seen any baseball player who put on a uniform. But he only did enough for Rickey. It kind of bothered me, because I battled through tons of injuries - a broken neck - to come back into the game. And if I had one quarter of his talent, I would be "Johnny Badass." He just gave enough to get by, where he had the capabilities to do anything he wanted to do. So I don't think he just disappointed me, I think he disappointed a lot of fans and other teammates, too. And he's *still* in the Hall of Fame.

MIKE EASLER: Rickey was great. Rickey was fun-loving. Rickey was nuts! Rickey just played the game and dominated, with his running game. Rickey was a nice, quiet guy. He lockered right next to me, actually. He was just quiet, went out there, and did his job. He knew he was good, he knew he could steal bases any time he'd want, had great personality - everybody loved him on the ball club. He was an igniter - he made everything happen. Rickey was definitely a great player, and I'm glad to see he got voted into the Hall of Fame. He's one of best base runners and base stealers you've ever seen. And I saw Lou Brock, I played with Omar Moreno, but Rickey Henderson was up there with all of them.

    I think so [in response to being asked if Rickey was the fastest ballplayer of that era]. He and Willie Wilson. Willie

Wilson was pretty fast, Vince Coleman, Tim Raines...but Rickey was powerful. He was fast, but he was *powerful* fast. I mean, once he took two or three steps man, he was there. Those guys were fast, but Rickey was fearless on the bases. He was just totally fearless - just like Lou Brock was. He'd steal a base at any time, at any moment. And you knew he was going to steal, and he still used to steal the base.

BRIAN FISHER: Fastest man I've ever seen. The biggest legs on any human being I've ever seen. Just absolute speed. Rickey did stay more to himself than anybody else. I don't think I really did anything with Rickey - went out to lunch or dinner. Rickey definitely stayed a little more to himself. But he was always there, ready to play. He was right there in his prime, hitting leadoff home runs.

GARY ROENICKE: Another good teammate. Everybody on that team, that's the one thing that stands out in my mind of being a Yankee that year - the chemistry was good. Maybe not so much...you hear on the teams that won, how they had fights and all that stuff amongst themselves. We didn't have that that year. There were some great guys on that team, and we're still friendly and give each other a hug when we see each other. Rickey, I saw him a few years ago and he's still in great shape. Talking about talent, this guy could either hit a home run to lead off a game or if you put him on first base, two pitches later, he could be on third. There's not many guys in the history of baseball that could do that.

TOMMY JOHN: I know as a pitcher, you knew he was going to steal second. It was just a matter of time. But then, you had to really work to keep him from stealing third, because he was very adapt at stealing third base after he stoke second. Boom boom. I remember one time with the Yankees, over All-Star break we had a workout, and we were working on all these pick-off moves and fake moves and inside turns to second base - to keep Rickey from stealing. So Tommy John being the wiseass that I am, I

Just Out of Reach: The 1980s New York Yankees

raise my hand, and to the manager - I'm trying to think who it was then - I said, "Why don't we go down in the bullpen, and why don't we work on our pitching, and why don't we work on throwing strikes and changing speeds and getting our curveball over the plate, and don't let Rickey get on first base? If we do that, he can't steal." And that's not Tommy John being a wiseass - that's Tommy John stating the facts. If you work keeping Rickey off the base, he can't steal.

I remember walking out of a game one time. Stan Williams was my pitching coach, and Stan had the knack of saying a negative thought at the right time. It's like, you're playing with somebody in golf, and there's out of bounds on the right, and you say, "Boy, I didn't realize that out of bounds on the right was that close. Wow!" And the guy up there hitting, you start looking at it, and you're either going to pull it left, or you're going to try to keep it from turning right and you'll hit it farther right. It's like you put a negative thought in guys' minds, and the negative thought will come to the front. I'm leaving the bullpen and I've got pretty good stuff that night. Johnny Oates is my catcher - Johnny Oates was a hell of a catcher, I might add. Stan Williams comes out and says, "Whatever you do, *don't walk Rickey.* Oates-y can't throw him out, don't walk Rickey." And I said, "Stan, why would you tell me that, as I'm walking out of the bullpen to start the game?" "Well, I just want to make you aware of it." "Christ, *shut up.*" The first four pitches of the game - ball one, ball two, ball three, ball four. I walk him. I take my hat off, I bow on the mound to our bench, telling him, "Stan, thank you very much." So then I work, and Oates-y throws Rickey out trying to steal second by ten feet. We both did a good job - I held him and Johnny threw it. Boom.

I came in, and I just said, "Stan, please, if you can't say anything positive, just don't say anything to me. I don't want to hear negative thoughts." "Oh geez Tommy, you're really slow to home plate" - OK, that's going to be on my mind. And I know I found that out as a player, and I also found that out when I coached - I would try to tell the guys, "This is what you want to do. This pitch is good, just keep powering this pitch." Don't tell them, "Oh god, your slider sucks," because that's a negative input and as soon as you do it, they'll throw a slider and it will be bad. Just tell them BS, and then you work on it in-between starts. But never put negative thoughts in a guy's mind - the mind doesn't work like that.

REX HUDLER: Oh, what a complete joy Rickey Henderson was! He was beautiful. He would wear leather outfits when we got to Southern California and it was 90 degrees - he'd be in leather pants, leather jacket. We were like, cracking up, going "Rickey, what's up?" And he's like, "Ahhh Rickey! Rickey like his style! Rickey like his style!" His own language was one of a kind, it was beautiful. He was kind of quiet in the clubhouse too, surprisingly. He wasn't a big "yuck-it-up" kind of a guy in the clubhouse - he was a leader on the field. But whenever you could get him loose, it was fun to hear him talk.

My best Rickey Henderson moment, we were in September, and it was when we were in the pennant race and Toronto had a two game lead on us. We're doing the anthem - we're out there standing next to each other in shallow centerfield. I'm playing second and he's playing center and our backs are to home plate. And I'll never forget the lady's name that sang the anthem - Mary O'Dowd. The other thirteen years in the majors, I couldn't tell you one anthem singer. I don't know why she stands out in my mind, but she butchered the anthem.

She butchered the Canadian anthem for Toronto, and the American. She went back to the dugout - she forgot the words - and got the words from the dugout, and walked back to home plate. I'm with Rickey Henderson, and he's going, *"Ohhh! Ohhh! She fucked up! Ohhh! Ohhh no! That's terrible!"* He went on and on. You know what though? I haven't seen too many anthems butchered like that before, either. And he made a spectacle of it. He cracked up, he thought it was the greatest thing ever. I almost had to revive him with oxygen. I wish I had a picture of me and him out there. But he was so entertained by that woman butchering the anthem - maybe that's why I remember her name. And it might be documented somewhere, it was such a butcher-job. But Rickey Henderson, he almost needed oxygen to revive him and I just laughed at Rickey the whole time.

He was so different than any other player that I played with. I played with a little over 600 or 700 teammates. Never ever had anybody like him. Y'know, talked in the third person, he called me "Red" - he didn't even know my name. He didn't know many guys' names. He's a ballplayer, I understand that - I knew some other players that didn't remember names. So now, I'm with the Angels, and he's with Oakland. We get in a brawl. We're out there by the mound, and they're fighting. And some guy grabs me from behind. It's Rickey. I can tell that I was grabbed by somebody that was really strong. So I played possum and went to my knees. I went limp, because no way am I getting out of this one. And he's saying the whole time, *"I GOT YOU RED! I GOT YOU RED! YOU AIN'T GOIN' NOWHERE, RED! I GOT YOU!"* So I played possum, then he let me go, he went around the pile, then I went around and jumped on his back. He saw it was me. He didn't hit me or nothing - we just kind of laughed at each other.

So I had a bond with Rickey Henderson, it was really cool - he knew me and we played together. That's the bond that you hear players talk about one another. Like me and Donnie. Me and Jimmy Deshaies. Jimmy D was a Yankee back in the early days. I remember Dan Pasqua, Willie Randolph, Dave Winfield, Knucksie - all of them, during that short time, were like best friends. It was tough when Joe Niekro died [in 2006] - Phil called me. But the bond goes way deep. Rickey Henderson was the greatest character that I ever played with.

chapter 21: goose

One of the top closers of all-time, Goose Gossage.

BARRY FOOTE: Obviously, Goose was at the top of the heap as a closer in those years with the Yankees.

GOOSE GOSSAGE: You either eat or you get eaten. *And I'm going to eat.* And I hated hitters. I see these guys now hugging each other during batting practice and during pre-game stuff - they're all hugging and loving. We weren't even allowed to *talk* to the opposition. I didn't want to talk to the opposition. I always felt that took the edge away. Here I am trying to beat your ass, you're trying to beat me. If you've got a friend on that other team, take him out to dinner. We used to get fined a hundred bucks if we got caught talking to the opposition. No fraternization. And that's the way it was. Today, it's all lovey-dovey and huggy-huggy. I hate the way the game is going. I hate the way the pitching is going. I was going to say, I don't think they utilized Mariano to his maximum. If you can't save a three-run ballgame one inning, if somebody else can't do that, then something's wrong. Then you shouldn't be in the big leagues. If you can't pitch one inning with a three-run lead, you shouldn't be in the big leagues. And I'm talking about a three-run lead. I just think these closers could go in the eighth inning a little more. They baby starters, they baby closers. The position of closing is easy today compared to what it used to be. It's easy…it's not *easy,* but it is easy compared to what we used to do.

GEORGE FRAZIER: When I came over to the Yankees, he was hurt, Davis was hurt. So basically, I ended up closing games in that first month. 16 innings I think, I gave up one run as the closer. And I remember Goose telling me, "You made nine trips

199 Just Out of Reach: The 1980s New York Yankees

between the big leagues and minor leagues with the St. Louis Cardinals. You're 3-11, you've got a decent ERA, you're throwing 61 games. There's got to be something missing." He watched me pitch a couple of games, and then he jerked me aside one day, and said, "Come over, we're going to talk a minute. When you come out of the bullpen, *I want you to be Muhammad Ali*. I want you to come out of those bullpen gates pissed off - that you're ready to get in a prizefight, and you're going to hit this guy right square in the nose. And you're going to have that attitude every time you walk out of there." As simple as that was said to me, I took that attitude with me, and it really changed my whole career. Because that's the way Goose was. When he started warming up, there was no joking around. If the Yankees had a two-run lead in the sixth inning/seventh inning, it wasn't time to joke around with Goose Gossage - he was getting locked in. And he was a tremendous, tremendous asset. A tremendous person. A heart the size of the Grand Canyon. I mean, just a great guy.

BARRY FOOTE: I loved Goose. Goose was a great guy. He had two personalities - the one that started from the first inning to the seventh inning, and then that one that started in the eighth and ninth. He was just a real competitor, a hard-nosed guy. He was a funny guy. He started gearing up in the sixth and seventh innings for his job in the eighth and ninth - back in those days, you had to pitch in the eighth a lot of times. Today, you've only got the ninth inning. But he was a great guy to be around, and was a real hard-nosed competitor when the bell rang, when it was his time to go out and close the game out.

RON DAVIS: As far as a teammate, he was probably one of the most fantastic guys there is - as far as camaraderie. We lived in the same town together in Jersey, we picked each other up to go to the yard, we went out drinking together, we fished together, we hunted together. That's what teammates do. I don't think the teammates today have that same cross of things we used to do. When we were on the road, there would be eight or ten of us at a local pub, and maybe have some beer and wings after a game to settle down and relax a little bit. Nowadays - as you know, my son [Ike Davis] plays - it's like they've got this and this and this, and then they have to go work out after the game. Since the game is over and there are 25 guys on a team, 25 guys go their separate ways. They don't hang out together.

One of my best all-time friends is Terry Mulholland, and he was still pitching fairly good after about 20 years in the big leagues. And he goes, "I'm just quitting." I'm like, "Man, just go and make a million dollars a year. Who cares if you bounce around, for a million or a million and a half dollars a year?" He goes, "I don't like it anymore. There's just no camaraderie." There's nobody in there drinking - I mean, they've taken out all the beer, they've taken out all the chew in the locker room. We used to sit there and drink ten beers after a tough loss, and there would be three or four guys doing that. But nowadays, they don't even have beer or tobacco. And everyone has their entourage, so one guy has five or six guys and they go with him and this guy has five or six. Everyone has their own personal "bodyguards," so to speak.

FRAN HEALY: Magnificent personality. It's like he was when he pitched - he's going to go on the mound, he's going to rear back, and give you everything. And off the field, his personality was, "Here it is. There's no mystique. There's no, 'I'm going to say one thing and mean the other'." What he says, he means. He's one of the most stand-up guys I've ever been around in baseball. And not afraid of anything. To catch him was a delight, and he had special stuff.

DAVE LaROCHE: He just brought a great fastball and great results. He hardly ever said anything and he was just a good old country boy. Easygoing. Just give him the ball in the ninth and a beer three outs later, and he was fine.

STEVE BALBONI: He was one of the better guys I ever met in baseball. Just a great guy - really down to earth. He was "the guy" - as far as relief pitchers, it was him. But he didn't act like that. And he liked to go out where nobody knew us, and just drink some beer and talk, have fun. It was really nothing about baseball once you got off the field. But on the field, he was all business. It was dead serious/all business. He's one of the best guys I've ever met in baseball.

BRIAN FISHER: Goose and I are from Colorado. I didn't know Goose until after I got to the big leagues and I stole his number! The clubhouse manager said, "Oh, you're from Colorado and you're about the same size as Goose. Here's the number 54." I said, "I'll wear that proudly." So every time I see Goose, I make fun of him, I'm like, "How did they give you back my number? That's *my* number." But Goose and I didn't really know each other until I got to the big leagues and got to the Yankees, because he grew up in Colorado Springs and I think he's eight or nine years older than I am. But after the fact, I see him probably once a year, twice a year, and we make fun of the whole number thing - I'm #54 and so is he, and we're both from Colorado. But you talk about a guy - a legend - who could pitch and throw, and was just a stud…that's Goose Gossage.

STEVE JACOBSON: Dave Kingman could hit titanic home runs, and he hit one off of Gossage, onto the backfield of spring training in Fort Lauderdale. Gossage said that that was one of the proudest moments of his life - that anybody could hit a ball that far.

GOOSE GOSSAGE: I think I was certainly a part of it [in response to being asked if Goose felt that he helped revolutionize relief pitching]. There were guys before me. I look at Sparky Lyle, with the year that he had [in 1977, when he won the AL Cy Young Award with a 2.17 ERA, 13-5 record, and 26 saves], and then I come over and they give me his job on a silver platter? I came over to be the best left-handed/right-handed combination ever. And it didn't work out that way. They talk about Mo's cutter, Sparky had a slider. Every great relief pitcher had one great pitch. And no different than Mo. I saw the total evolution of the bullpen, from what it was when I broke in, where you did not want to be in the bullpen. It was a "junk pile" where old starters went, that could not start anymore, that couldn't go the distance. So they put them in the bullpen. They were still productive, but they couldn't finish a ballgame. And if you couldn't finish a ballgame back then, you were in the bullpen.

When I came to the big leagues in '72, Chuck Tanner and Johnny Sain [the then-Chicago White Sox's manager and pitching coach] had envisioned…right then at that time, is when the evolution of the bullpen really started becoming more of a specialized position. A big position. A big part of the success of your team was in that bullpen. Now, it takes three guys to do what Rollie Fingers, I, and Bruce Sutter used to do. If we could have pitched the ninth inning like Mo, we'd have six hundred and something saves like Mo did. There's no question. I think today, they go overboard. "Closer" was not even a coined phrase - we were "relief pitchers." Closer came about after Dennis Eckersley went to Oakland, and Dave Duncan and Tony La Russa [the then-Oakland A's pitching coach and manager] thought Eck had one foot on a banana peel and the other foot out the door of baseball, and they resurrected his career. They figured that he couldn't withstand the workload of a regular reliever, but they thought, "We'll fill in around him with these other guys, take the workload off him and let him pitch the ninth inning." I set up for Eck out in Oakland for two years and enjoyed every minute of it. So I saw that evolution. Dick Radatz, Lindy McDaniel, Hoyt Wilhelm…I don't know if he went into the Hall of Fame as a reliever or as a starter [Wilhelm was the first-ever relief pitcher elected into the Hall in 1985]. But these guys were all at one point great relievers and started to put relief pitching on the map. Right when I started, that's when it really started to evolve in a more specialized position.

RON DAVIS: That's what they claim [that Davis and Goose were one of MLB's first setup man/closer combos]. I don't know if that's a fact, but yes, they claim the first setup man or eighth inning man [was Davis]. But back in the day, there was no such thing as an "eighth inning man." If you look at relievers today, they're getting 35 to 55 innings in. Well, we were getting 140 in, Goose and I. What these guys pitch in three years, we were getting done in *one year*. Definitely I was a setup man, but the setup man started in the fifth inning back in our era. And then of course, I would go as long as I could, until they got to me, and then Rich Gossage would take over, and Rich is probably one of the greatest relief pitchers there ever was. He was so dominant. If he only had to go one inning today, he might have had a thousand or so saves. I mean, Mariano Rivera is definitely the greatest, and has the numbers to back it. But I think if Goose would have been able to be used like him, I think Goose would have set all kinds of records.

BARRY FOOTE: We had an unbelievable record that year from that seventh inning. With a lead in the seventh, I think we only lost one game all year. When I came over there in '81, I think we were in the fourteenth game of the year, and Davis was just unbelievable the rest of the year. In my time with them, he set a record for most consecutive strikeouts [eight straight strikeouts, against the California Angels on May 4, 1981]. So as we called him, RD, was a great setup guy. I don't know if that was the first time that happened, but it certainly has been part of the setting of the stage of how people run their bullpens nowadays.

TOMMY JOHN: Goose was a great teammate. I used to pick him up and go to the ballpark. Maybe his wife was coming later or my wife wasn't coming in, but I would pick him up and take him in. And I remember some lady cut us off two or three times going onto the George Washington Bridge. If we would have done this now, we'd have been slapped with a lawsuit or whatever, but she cut us off and I had a van then, I jammed on my brakes - I had one of these conversion vans - and jammed on them again. This is like the third time I jammed them. And he gets out and goes up to her window and beats on the window, and goes, "What the…you almost caused us to wreck!" And gets back in the car. Then when we get to the bridge, we're following her and the toll taker, I give him my money, and he says, "Was there a problem with her?" And I said, "She cut me off three times - almost caused me to wreck three times. And my partner her just told her she's gotta learn how to drive." He laughed!

But that was Goose's temperament - go in there. I remember one time, Billy brought him in - bases loaded in the top of the ninth inning. Nobody out and we were up one run. You're going to get a blown save. So Goose could only fail. I remember he was *so* pissed. He threw twelve or thirteen pitches - all fastballs, struck out the side. They didn't have a chance. In fact, one time, Johnny Oates was catching him and Goose was pissed, and he said, "That's the hardest I've ever caught anybody. I've caught a lot of guys that threw hard - Jim Palmer and those guys with the Orioles. But that's the hardest ever." And my kids, we would pick Goose up at the airport, and Goose had this thing of being rough/tough. And my kids called him "Goosie." "Goosie, how are you Goosie?" He said, *"Don't let any of those players hear you call me Goosie."* [Laughs]

RUDY MAY: Goose was the greatest reliever. I do remember this - and I don't know the actual statistics on this - I remember being in Texas during that '80 season, and it was hotter than all get out. I was pitching and the players can see one another go from the bullpen to the dugout or the bullpen to the clubhouse underneath the stands there. I remember it being late in the ballgame, in the sixth or seventh inning, when Goose was coming in. And Goose said, "How do you feel, man? I got your back." I finished that inning and Goose came into the ballgame and saved that game, and he said, "Hey man, do you want to do a little partying? Willie Nelson is [in town]. We'll get in the bus and we'll go to the hotel and party with Willie." So we go over to the hotel and we go up to the top floor of this hotel, and we sat there and had a couple of drinks with him and got to know him. But I really got to know Goose very well. As a matter of fact, there were several times that I went hunting with him in Colorado in the off-season. What a wonderful man he is.

GOOSE GOSSAGE: The game is a totally different game than it used to be. I'd buy into the hundred pitches [limit for starters] if there were less injuries - there are *more* injuries today than there ever have been. Money has changed the game, completely. The whole face of the game. And I don't care what facet of the game you want to bring up - pitching, hitting - you can't even come close to these guys anymore, or you get warned. Or you get kicked out of the game. I've seen guys get kicked out of games with no warning, and he didn't even hit him. The game has gotten soft. I said, "If I see one more fucking cream pie, I'm going to fucking break my fucking TV" [In response to discussing how ridiculous/annoying it is when modern day ballplayers slam "cream pies" into each other's faces after a win].

Baseball is becoming the NBA and the antics you see in football. *Act like professionals.* Act like you've been there, done that. Not like a bunch of college kids. But that's what these kids are. They're all college kids, because they just came out of college, because they're being rushed to the big leagues. You see so many mistakes being made by these kids. They're trying to learn their craft at the big league level, and let me tell you, that is very difficult to do. All kinds of base running mistakes. It's a shame.

The big difference in the game today - money. You can't tell these kids anything. They won't listen to you. There is no one passing the torch. Telling these kids…if we acted like some of these kids act on the mound or at the plate, don't go back in that dugout. Go back out the centerfield gate - don't go back in that dugout because you're going to have to face the shit that's going to hit you. From everybody. Your manager will slam you up against the fucking wall and you won't do that again. Throwing your bat down the third base line, almost hitting the guy coaching third base? Are you fucking kidding me? Sickening. I get sick watching the game anymore.

It's a totally different game. Major League Baseball wanted to put more offense in the game, and they have manipulated the game to the point that the old numbers don't even stack up anymore. And what is baseball? A numbers game. But again, money - they wanted to put more offense in the game to bring a different fan, that doesn't like the 2-1. And how about these games that have been played lately [the 2013 AL and NL MLB Championship Series]? Those are "big league ballgames" - 1-0, 2-1. And baseball manipulated it. The ball is livelier, the strike zone has shrunk down to a postage stamp, it's all been done for the hitter. Ballparks are band boxes - they're small. It's like, 500 home runs does not mean what 500 home runs used to mean. Forget about steroids, it's what Major League Baseball has done. And as far as the steroids, if Bud Selig wanted to have a legacy, he would reinstate those old records - Roger Maris' record and Hank Aaron's record - and not recognize these cheaters. But that will never happen from him.

TOMMY JOHN: I'll say this - if Goose had the rules of the current closers, Goose would have had 600-700 saves, pitching one inning/three outs. He was untouchable for three.

chapter 22:
other '80s yankee greats

Yankee notables of the era that tend to get overlooked.

TOMMY JOHN: Ron Guidry, I never saw Ron pitch in his really, really great years. When I came over, he started having arm problems. But he had one of the best sliders, and if it broke down and in, it was un-hittable. And if he got on top of it too much and pulled down on it, it backed up and if it was a hard sinker, it was un-hittable. When he came in and took Goose's place in '79, you couldn't hit him for one inning. And Ronnie might have been the fastest player on our team - running.

FRAN HEALY: Oh man, was he first class. He threw extremely hard, with good control - which was unusual. And a very nice guy. He had an over-powering fastball and a nasty slider. And rarely bounced the ball - which I was happy about.

GARY ROENICKE: I rode into the ballpark almost every day with Gator. We stayed in the same city. He was a guy that was very tough on me - facing him, very good pitcher. Played hard. Competed hard. Very good athlete - I don't know if people knew that about him. He put everything he had into each and every outing. I'm glad to see him be successful and have a great career with the Yankees.

DAVE LaROCHE: Guidry was a funny guy. Really funny. Good guy and a great pitcher, obviously. We loved to get him going, talking Cajun [Guidry is from Louisiana - hence one of his nicknames, "Louisiana Lightning"]. Especially in spring training, when all the pitchers were doing our drills, there's a lot of time standing in line for your turn. Just get him talking about duck hunting. He was a great storyteller. He was just a funny, down-to-earth, good guy.

BRIAN FISHER: I've never seen a man who could play drums better than him. I used to go down to the basement [of Yankee Stadium] and watch him play drums. That was his workout. He was a gamer - he was the guy that wanted the baseball, he wanted to get on the mound, and wanted to go after hitters. That was the first guy that I watched that I was like, "This guy *attacks.*" He was a gamer. Not very big, but full of fire. The kind of guy I wouldn't want to meet in a dark alley - even as small as he was, he was fiery.

GARY ROENICKE: I actually got to go down [into the basement of Yankee Stadium] to watch him play drums a couple of times. There was a room down the right field line - that's what he would do on the days he pitched, just to kind of release some tension and get himself ready. He would go down and play drums, and guys would come in that had played with musicians and they'd try to keep up with him, and they couldn't do it! He was that good. One particular thing, we had a get-together - I was with the Yankees now - and after one of the day games, we had a get-together out at a club north of Baltimore, where one of the Orioles lived. So I brought out a few Yankees - I think Righetti and Mattingly and a couple of others, and Guidry. So he was going to sit in, Dave was going to go up and sing, and Guidry was going to play the drums. The guy says, "We play on this beat" or whatever, and he says, "You play...*I'll catch up.*" He was that good at it.

GEORGE FRAZIER: Tremendous drummer. I don't know if people know that, but he was an outstanding drummer. I think he played with ZZ Top at a concert in New York one time, as their drummer. People don't know that about Gator. A guy that was really talented. One of the first small left-handers since Whitey Ford to come on and do what he did - to have the record that he did. It was a shame that his career got cut short. But I always just

Just Out of Reach: The 1980s New York Yankees

felt that Gator was one of those guys that I kind of gravitated to. Because in all honesty, I'm a redneck, he's a redneck - we had a good time together. We always talked a lot about baseball. And in his slow, Louisiana drawl, we'd always have a pretty good conversation. Because he'd always came down and sat in the bullpen - he didn't like to sit in the dugout when he didn't pitch. So we'd always end up talking about a lot of different things. But pitching-wise, you sit down and talk to him, you better have small ears, because he's going to teach you a lot of things.

RON KITTLE: I saw him a little bit in his prime. I saw him getting older, but he still knew how to pitch. I'd still throw him on the mound - he gave you every Louisiana little item in his body out on the mound. I had some success against him as an opponent - I think I hit a couple of home runs against him. He was the judge of our "kangaroo court," and one of the funny stories was I hit a home run when I was with the Sox against Tim Stoddard and Bob Shirley. And we had an off day and we had a kangaroo court, and I got fined by him $250 for "Hitting home runs against each of my teammates." So I had to pony up $500 for our team party! A hundred and sixty something pounds of skinny, but he could pitch. He wanted the ball. He knew his stuff was not as good as it used to be, but he was still a true battler on the mound.

BARRY FOOTE: Ron Guidry and I were good friends. I enjoyed Guidry - he had a great slider and good stuff. Just a good guy on the ball club. Tommy John was one of the good producing pitchers that year [1981], and that was the year that Dave Righetti got his start in the big leagues. So there were a lot of good players, a lot of good pitching. I felt like that was the team we should have won the World Series with. It was just one of those things where we didn't get any breaks. We didn't make our breaks and we didn't get any breaks.

DAVE LaROCHE: It was an excellent staff. The Guidrys, the Tommy Johns, and Righetti, that was his rookie year - I think he went up and down a couple of times and finished strong and did a good job for us. Some of the unsung heroes - Rudy May did some starting and did some relieving, and the bullpen, especially when you got late, with Ron Davis and Goose. They were outstanding. It was just well-balanced - offense, defense, and both starting and bullpen. We had a strong team.

TOMMY JOHN: I know what I pitched. I know how well I pitched. And I know I pitched pretty good for a long time. The problem is Tommy John Surgery has been out there since 1974, and I will be dead, I will be in the ground, I will be dust, there will be maggots crawling all over me, and Tommy John Surgery will *still* be out there. So, the surgery will outlive me, unfortunately. But that's the way it is. There are a lot of kids nowadays that think Tommy John was the surgeon that did the surgery! That's truthfully. And I had some players that I coached in the minor leagues - one kid was with the Yankees, and I was managing Staten Island, and we were down at spring training, and one of the kids came up and said, "Hey, that Tommy John Surgery…was that you or your dad?" And I said, "That was my dad that had the surgery." And he said, "God, you must be proud of him." I said, "You better believe it. I am very, very, very proud of my dad." But here's a guy that was in an organization that didn't have any idea what the coach or manager in the organization…but that's just the way it is and it's going to be.

I'm proud that I was the first one to have it, and probably if you look at statistically, the best Tommy John Surgery ever done was the one that Dr. [Frank] Jobe did on me. Because I won 164 games post-surgery, I pitched thirteen years post-surgery, and I never missed a start in thirteen years. So, whatever Dr. Jobe did and whatever I did rehabbing, as archaic as it was, had to be right. And had to be more right than what they're doing now, when guys come back and they get shut down, and they've got this and they've got that, and they've got inflammation. When I came back and I started pitching and I pitched out of the bullpen, I pitched three days rest, I pitched four days rest. I started on a Friday, relieved on a Sunday. I mean, my job was to pitch. And if they needed me, I pitched. But I'll tell you what, the years I had with the Yankees...I had seven with the White Sox, seven with the Dodgers, and two four-year terms with the Yankees. I enjoyed the years I had in the big leagues. And it seemed like every time I got traded or I was a free agent, I always went to an organization or a city that could help me get better. I wouldn't change anything that I did. Even take steroids - I wouldn't even take steroids because then I would get my fastball up to about 55 miles and hour, and that would make it hittable. [Laughs]

REX HUDLER: Willie Randolph was the classiest guy ever, because he wasn't threatened by me one bit. He would let me take ground balls with him in Yankee Stadium. He would say, "Hey kid, watch out for these two guys here, George Brett and Hal McRae." That's when the Royals were big as rivals. "They'll end your career. They won't just come and take you out - *they'll bust your leg.* Be careful." But that type of advice, given to me by Willie, really showed how classy he was and made me feel comfortable. So after that, when they traded me to the Orioles, and then I went to the Expos, the Cardinals, the Angels, the Phillies, and played a year in Japan, that really gave me the background that I needed to endure and to develop mental toughness - through my short little two years of a stint there, in '84 and '85.

ANDRE ROBERTSON: Willie Randolph was awesome. I saw him a couple of years ago when I went up for a show. He's still the same. He was the table-setter. He could do it just as good as anybody. When Rickey got there, there wasn't any animosity - he hit second behind him. He's a team player. Again, if people want to win, we do what we had to do to win. And though he helped me out on the bases, he would "call," when I first went up. The shortstop/second baseman make calls of who's covering. He did it for the most part, because I didn't know everybody up there. That's how I learned to do it, when he wasn't there, and sometimes I'd play second if he was hurt and he'd give me advice. The thing is winning. You want to get that team winning. It doesn't matter who's out there.

MIKE EASLER: Willie Randolph was a quiet pro. He just went about his job every single day. He was a blue collar worker - just did what he had to do. Good hands, would turn the double play. He was just a professional all the way around. You didn't know Willie was there, because he was that quiet. He just went out there and played the game hard every single day.

TOBY HARRAH: Willie is kind of a quiet player. As far as playing against him, he never talked to the opposition very much. And I was kind of the same way, and I think that's the way the game should be played. Once I became his teammate and got around him, he had a presence about him - he carried himself like a Yankee should carry himself. And he was really well-respected by his teammates, the way he went about his business playing every day, and the way he hustled and took the ups and downs, as far as being a major leaguer. He was a great example for the rest of the guys on the ball club. I developed a tremendous amount of respect for Willie, being one of his teammates for the season. He was a class act.

ANDRE ROBERTSON: Yes he was [in response to being asked if Randolph was a clubhouse leader]. He was more of a silent leader, but he could also get on the big stars. He was one of those steady people there throughout the years. They had people in and out, and he would integrate with them and the younger players. With Graig Nettles on the other side of me, how could you not learn to play with a winning attitude, with people like that around you?

GEORGE FRAZIER: Willie was great. Obviously was a very good major league manager [Randolph managed the Mets from 2005-2008], didn't get another opportunity - he's out of baseball now - which is a shame. They need more Willie Randolphs in the game of baseball. I just think Willie as a teammate was all

Just Out of Reach: The 1980s New York Yankees

about winning. When you play with a group like we did with the Yankees, it was all about winning baseball. We didn't care how much money people made, we didn't care about what car they drove, where they lived, or anything else. We cared about putting rings on. And Willie was probably the king leader of that kind of stuff. I mean, Willie was a very good player. But he was also a very good leader in the locker room. A quiet leader. He was good at what he did.

BOB WATSON: The people in New York knew [how good Randolph was], and the people in the clubhouse - he was a Yankee captain [Randolph and Guidry served as co-captains of the Yankees from 1986-1988]. I called him "Houdini at Second Base," because playing first base, you see guys coming down on him as he's turning the double play, and very rarely did he get hit. He was up in the air, he did a sidestep. He was one heck of a player - not only a player, but he was a leader. He showed up every day, he gave you everything he's got. I really am disappointed that he's not on any of these lists to manage. I don't know why. It wasn't his fault that those guys collapsed with the Mets [at the end of the 2007 season], and they let him go. There are guys who have gotten two, three, four chances to manage, and he's not going to get a second chance I think is ridiculous.

GEORGE FRAZIER: Rags was Rags. A phenomenal left-hander. People like him don't come around very often - as far as talent and the ability to pitch. And the command of four pitches. Fresh face out of California. I mean, this was a great, great pitcher. Obviously, with his numbers, you see what I'm talking about with him. But Rags and I are still very close friends - he's the pitching coach with the San Francisco Giants now. So we talk every year and every time we're out, we think of another name to talk to, and find out how they're doing and what's going on with former teammates.

MIKE EASLER: Dave Ragu! Ragu was a good pitcher - he had a great arm, he threw the ball well. And I think once he

Other '80s Yankee Greats   214

made that transition to the bullpen, it really helped his career - just like it did Dennis Eckersley. I faced him a bunch of times when I was with the Red Sox. He came right after you. He had great stuff.

RUDY MAY: I remember [Righetti] as being a great pitcher. He was young and threw very well, and he had good stuff. He came up in '81, won the Rookie of the Year Award, and pitched really well. In '82, he had a mediocre year. Dave and I have a relationship simply because he's from San Jose, he's now the pitching coach for the Giants, and I used to go over all the time when Dusty Baker was managing them, because I do a lot of fishing in the San Francisco Bay. So I'd go and get over there for batting practice and spend some time with them before the game and then leave. And then Rob Gardner - an ex-pitcher - he lives here in Fresno, and he used to have charity events for his wife, who had a liver transplant. She since passed. And Righetti would come here and play in golf tournaments. So Dave and I had an opportunity to talk a lot. I always thought a lot of him. He often times reminded me of Frank Tanana - just in his demeanor...yeah, in his delivery a little bit, too. But his approach on the game. Really a nice man.

PHIL NIEKRO: I probably got closer to Righetti and Guidry - we talked a lot. And Bob Shirley, Ed Whitson. I pitched against Winfield in the National League. Don Baylor I really enjoyed playing with him on the same team. I just made it a point that I was going to get along with everybody, so I didn't have problems over there, and I'm pretty sure no one had problems with me. I just fit in. They help you fit in, they just make you feel comfortable, like you're part of their family there.

TOBY HARRAH: The Yankees had some really outstanding people, and Phil Niekro was one of them. He liked to "polka" the day before he pitched. I would go out with him occasionally, and we'd have a couple of 7 Ups and Coke, and watch everybody dance and have a good time. He would dance a little bit with some friends, because he always felt like his knuckleball was better if he wasn't really too strong, and he had to finesse it more. I remember one time, I had a really fast Porsche, and we went over the George Washington Bridge, going really fast. When we got on the other side, he asked me to stop the car. He got out and kissed the ground, and said, *"I'm never getting in the car with you again."*

GEORGE FRAZIER: Bobby Murcer was a very good friend of mine. We're both from Oklahoma. Kind of a mentor when I went to the Yankees, and showed me how to do some things the Yankee way. Bobby was a great player, a great person. Great ambassador to the Yankees and to the game of baseball. A guy that I always looked up to. Had a quick, dry wit, was great in the locker room with the players when he was a player, and then when he went up to the broadcast booth, it was very similar to that. He was a guy that I missed when he left as a player and went to the broadcast booth, and then I missed him even more obviously on a daily basis now, that he's passed away [Murcer passed away on July 12, 2008, at the age of 62]. He had a great family, and a very good person. Sad to see him leave the Yankees, sad to see him leave baseball, sad to see him leave life.

STEVE JACOBSON: Don Baylor was a first-class mensch. Baylor was a stand-up guy - he was a big, strong man, who was a man in every dimension. And one of the tales that I had heard from the Red Sox is that when he was traded to the Red Sox [from the Yankees, after 1985], the first thing he did was tell Jim Rice to "Get his head out of his ass."

GOOSE GOSSAGE: [Graig Nettles] was a tremendous teammate, a tremendous friend. I think he belongs in the Hall of Fame. I just think that people that don't have to vote for him weren't going to vote for him, because they didn't like him. He was a pretty surly guy with the media. Most of the press didn't like him, because he'd go tell them to fuck off. But I believe he's a Hall of Famer. I don't think he has to take a back seat to any third baseman that's in the Hall of Fame. That's what I think of him. I saw him play every day for six years - just an incredible talent. He was dangerous with the bat, he has almost 400 home runs [390 is Nettles' career total]. Just a tremendous athlete, tremendous competitor, tremendous clutch guy.

That's what the Yankees really consisted of, were great clutch guys - Piniella, Nettles, Reggie was good in the middle of the line-up, Thurman Munson was a great clutch hitter, Chris Chambliss got some big hits, and Bucky Dent of course. Anybody in that line-up could hurt you. Mickey Rivers, let me tell you, if Mickey was playing today, he'd be making 20 million dollars a year. He did so many things - he could beat you in so many ways. He could hit the long ball when you needed it, he could get on base, he could steal a bag, he beat you defensively. So, he was probably, I believe, our greatest weapon. When Mickey wanted to play, we won. And with the rest of that cast, man, it was the greatest machine I ever played for.

REX HUDLER: That set the stage for me in my 21-year baseball career, to be "broken in" by some of the classiest veteran players there could ever have be on a team - Dave Winfield, Willie Randolph, Don Baylor, Ken Griffey, Phil Niekro, Ron Guidry. All of these guys mentored me.

STEVE BALBONI: God, there were so many veteran guys. Lou, Gossage, Guidry. Lou was one of the main guys, Nettles was one of the main guys. They'd tell you stuff you needed to know. But it was such a veteran team, you didn't need a veteran player to take over, because it was a team *full* of veterans. Nobody really had to say anything, except to the young guys. But I think any one of them would say something if it needed to be said.

chapter 23:
the ballad of george and billy

The rollercoaster relationship between owner and manager.

MIKE PAGLIARULO: Billy and George...I can picture them being married - they'd probably beat each other up all the time. They have so much passion about what they want to do and where they want to go...it's just a collision waiting to happen. And it's not a bad collision either, I don't think. You talk about two great minds from two different areas of the sports world, and they're coming together better than most other organizations, really, if you think about it. Look at today - there has to be relationships between executives in the field, somehow. And that was the first real bridge. Whether you want to call it a lot of arguments or a strained relationship - it was a bridge, and they tried to get it right. That's what everything was based on. So for me, that's what I saw in Billy and George.

DAVE LaROCHE: It was like a husband and wife - it was love/hate. They would get so mad at each other, but I think they still loved each other. I say that in a "good love" - not anything wrong with that. Obviously, because he kept hiring him back and Billy kept coming back. And once you put that Yankee uniform on - the pinstripes, especially at home, and play in the stadium - there's nothing like that. Playing baseball is great, and I had great times with every team I was on - and still have respect for all the teams in the game and the Major Leagues. But putting those pinstripes on is like nothing else. And Billy, he was *a Yankee*.

RON DAVIS: I think they were closer than people think. They fed off each other. They made each other famous. They say how love and hate is pretty close together...well, I think they definitely 100% had a love/hate relationship.

The Ballad of George and Billy 218

FRAN HEALY: Impulsive. [Steinbrenner] liked him though - if he didn't like him, he wouldn't hire him. So anybody who says "George didn't like Billy" is crazy - he hired him because he liked him. He could hire any manager. I don't know if George ever told him to bat somebody someplace - I was never privy to those conversations. I know one thing - if I owned a team, I'd certainly have input.

PHIL NIEKRO: I don't know - that was between them and the press. All I knew is Billy was my manager, George was the boss, and he hired Billy to put a winning team together. I read about and heard things, but I just wouldn't let that affect me, because I was so into [focusing on] pitching good for the Yankees.

DALE BERRA: I'm sure he had a fine relationship with Billy, but he would probably get mad at him a lot for doing things that he thought weren't good for the Yankees' image or whatever. But in the long run, I'm sure he loved Billy. George was only going to deal with the people he really liked.

STEVE JACOBSON: George loved Billy's fire. He did not like Billy's inaccountability. Dallas Green he hired to manage the team, and Dallas could have played John Wayne in the movies as a tough ex-Marine, who demanded accountability, and he resented Steinbrenner's intrusion. For the very reasons that Steinbrenner wanted Dallas Green was the reasons why it could not possibly work. It was a marriage that just didn't belong.

BILLY MARTIN JR: My father loved and respected George. There were times he wanted to kill him. [Laughs] There were times that he was so mad at him that he couldn't see straight. But George possessed some qualities that my dad valued - very highly. George was extremely loyal and that in itself was one of my father's most…he felt like maybe one of the key ingredients to winning was loyalty. And George was ridiculously loyal. Very demanding. If you worked for Mr. Steinbrenner, he might call you at 4:00 in the morning. If he had a question, by god, he wanted an answer.

But if something happened, you got in trouble, he'd be there to help you out. He'd give you a good ass-chewing afterwards, he'd tell you "You were a dumb ass" for doing it, but he'd bail you out. He'd keep you in your job. He was a very unique person. His desire to win, his work ethic, his loyalty, those things were things that my father was right on board with. So, did dad think he meddled too much? Sure. But he also respected the fact, and I don't know if my father would have been any different had he been in that same job. I mean, I'm sure he would have given him more raises and never fired himself! I think George is a Hall of Fame owner. I hope the rest of the world does.

chapter 24:
the ballad of george and winny

One of the most strained - yet surprisingly long-lasting - owner/player relationships in sports history.

STEVE JACOBSON: It was the World Series, where he labeled him as "Mr. May." That was a slur - he may as well have called him "Lady May." I thought that was the kind of thing that Steinbrenner did not like - he had paid a lot of money, he had been conned by Winfield's agent, who wrote a contract that Steinbrenner thought was a good contract, and soon found out that he had signed Winfield on for much more money - in the long run - than he thought he had. And he resented Al Frohman [Winfield's agent] and Winfield in that way. Winfield was without personal fire. Boy, he could run from first to third like nobody, and he could catch the ball that was going over the fence. But he did not have "heat" on the team.

[Steinbrenner] wanted Winfield to be Reggie. He wanted Winfield to be the dominant personality on the team, and it wasn't what Winfield was. Winfield was a terrific player. He played good and he played hurt, but I characterize him as a "subcontractor." He did what he did, which was significant, and laid it at the door to the clubhouse, and said, "Here it is. What you do with it is not my problem." I thought there was no fire that went out to the other players on the team, the way the late '90s group did. I thought if there had been somebody like Paul O'Neill on that team, to spur Winfield - he wasn't the "big man" on the team emotionally, just physically - he would have been a much better player.

RUDY MAY: There was trouble with George, and it really, really bothered Dave. Because Dave was really a humanitarian and would help the community, and the Yankees agreed to the contract. But then later, they didn't want to uphold their end of the agreement. And it was all because Dave had a lot of us players participate in clinics that he was doing for inner city youth. I guess George balked on that too, I don't know. But George always thought that there was nothing bigger or better than the Yankees, and that Winfield's organization was getting a little bit too much press without the Yankees getting in there. But that affected Dave, and that affected his play. I know there were times when he was almost in tears when that happened, because Steinbrenner was suing him and the Yankees were suing him. For what? What did he do? He didn't do anything.

REX HUDLER: During that time, George Steinbrenner and Dave Winfield were having problems. We had a clubhouse meeting one day, and Mr. Steinbrenner was in the clubhouse at 3:30 in the afternoon, addressing all the players about some policy that the New York Mets just adopted and that he believed that the Yankees should go along with them. Some drug policy - something like that, I can't remember exactly how it was. And I've never been in a meeting like that with the owner. So Dave Winfield walks in - he's late - he sees what's going on, and he stands up, and says, "Fellas, hey look. We won't do anything. You just come through me - we'll go through the proper channels through the union." We looked at each other. The hair stood up on the back of all the Yankee players' necks, because we could feel the confrontation. *You face the owner of the team, in front of 30 guys!* It took a lot of balls from Winny. It was something. I was so young and naïve, I didn't know what was going on. But that's when George was after Winny. That was during that time when he was trying to get him…he hired that gambler [Howie Spira] to uncover some dirt on him, or something. But that was pretty interesting how that happened.

BOBBY MEACHAM: I remember one time, Dave told me, "Man, this guy's crazy. He's got somebody following me - some private eye following me" and blah blah blah. I'm like, "Come on, man." "He's trying to dig up dirt on me" and this and that. I'm like, "You're being paranoid now. *Come on.*" He goes, "OK, let's go to lunch." I think we were in Kansas City. He goes, "I'll take you to lunch, meet me in the lobby at noon" or whatever. So I meet him in the lobby at noon, and he sees this guy - kind of an older guy - sitting across from us sort of, in the lobby. He's like, "You see that guy over there?" "Yeah." "OK, let's go to lunch, but remember that guy's face." "Alright." So we go from Kansas City to I think Texas, and we meet for lunch again, and he goes, "Remember that guy I was telling you about? Who's that guy over there?" "Oh my gosh, it's the same guy!" He says, "That guy, he's pretty much wherever I go."

Who knows, but it's one of those things where I was like, "This is getting crazy when you've got somebody following you around, trying to dig up dirt." I'd say, "What are you doing? You guys are crazy trying to dig up dirt on each other." He would just say, "He's trying to catch me in something. *But I'm not doing anything wrong."* It was interesting. It was one of those things where I didn't understand it. I said, "I don't get it." Just to myself, I'm thinking, "This guy got a ten-year deal" - which is unheard of at that time - "And it's worked out perfect." I mean, he was overpaid in the beginning, and now, he's perfect. It worked out perfect - in the ten-year span, he probably would have made the same no matter if he went a year at a time. Which was perfect for both sides. I just don't understand why they were fighting at each other. It seemed like it was the perfect thing to happen - "We've got you for ten and you've produced for ten." Or whatever it was - eight or nine that he was there [Winfield was with the Yankees from 1981 through mid-1990]. I just didn't understand the whole fight there. But oh well - maybe they knew something that I didn't.

GOOSE GOSSAGE: Gosh, what would be the word? Probably a rocky…probably a very *uncomfortable* relationship. And it's too bad. I don't even know how that happened. I know that it had something to do with Dave's Foundation and stuff. I'm not quite sure, so I wouldn't be able to talk about it. But I know the relationship there was rocky at best. I think there was more

Just Out of Reach: The 1980s New York Yankees

behind it - I never got into it. There was too much bullshit going on everywhere. There was enough bullshit to go around to cover everybody. But my six years with the Yankees and then going into the Hall of Fame wearing a Yankee cap [in 2008], I didn't choose that, the Hall of Fame chose it. And I was part of a world championship there. So I had a lot of great things happen to me. I didn't want to leave New York but I felt it was time and I needed a change of scenery, basically. And then it was fun going to San Diego and turning that city on for the first time [the Padres made it to the World Series in 1984] - that was really exciting.

MIKE EASLER: What you saw was in the paper, you didn't really know for sure what really was going on. Something about his foundation, something about money that George supposedly paid to his foundation - something, something, something, something...stupid, probably. Probably a breached agreement or it may have been a rollover agreement, I'm not sure. But there's one thing about Dave - you would never know it, he would never bring it into the clubhouse. You could see they riffed and raffed in the newspaper, but never in the clubhouse or anything like that. Dave came to play. Dave was a great teammate, a great player. I played with Dave Parker, Jim Rice - some great players. And Dave Winfield was right up there with all of them.

BARRY FOOTE: It was just beginning [circa 1981] to have some of those little tiffs over I think it was his charitable foundation and things. It wasn't a big deal - you'd see more about it in the paper than anything around the clubhouse. You knew they were having some issues. And George, because he had given Winfield that big contract...at the time it was a big contract. Our guys made as much in a ten-year deal as they get in one year now. But at the time, it was a big, huge contract. And George would have a tendency to come out in the paper and stress some faults about not producing or producing. But Winfield is a Hall of Famer. It's hard to be a whole lot better than that.

The Ballad of George and Winny 224

MIKE PAGLIARULO: The Winfield thing, I just didn't pay attention too much. It was something that was there before I got there, for whatever reason. Dave always played hard. Didn't really talk about it in the clubhouse. I never asked him and not many guys wanted to talk about it with him. Because like I said earlier, what the focus was was winning that game that day. And that was the cool thing about playing - there was none of that bologna when we were playing the game. Because if that ever overshadowed the game, then the manager would step right in and stop it immediately. That would be Billy, Yogi, or anybody - they would not put up with that. Neither would any of the players, the older veteran guys - like Don Baylor and guys like that - just wouldn't put up with that. So that was never around when we played the games. That was more after the games or before the games. And their relationship is what it is…or what it was. It didn't bother me and I don't think it bothered the team. I don't know if it bothered Dave, maybe it did, I don't know. But it certainly didn't affect the way he ran down to first, because he hustled every single day. He never jogged. He played the game all the time. That's an important thing to do, and he never let it show if it did bother him.

FRAN HEALY: That took on a life of its own [Steinbrenner's comment that Winfield was "Mr. May"]. I'm assuming they had a good relationship, because George went out and signed him, he beat everybody out for him, he paid a lot of money, and he was with George's team for many, many years. I'm assuming George respected his ability, he liked him, and George made a statement that, like I said, took on a life of its own. But Dave Winfield is a Hall of Famer, and a magnificent baseball player. And he was obviously magnificent in other sports. He got in one skirmish when Minnesota played Ohio State, and it became a big fight in the basketball game, which didn't make Dave look good. But George had to like him, or he wouldn't have gone after him. And once he got him, how many years was Winfield with the Yankees? [Nine-and-a-half years] It was a long time. Especially

Just Out of Reach: The 1980s New York Yankees

with free agency, you could trade a guy like Winfield, who had a lot of talent. But George kept him.

BARRY FOOTE: Yes, of course it's too harsh [the "Mr. May" tag]. Look, Willie Stargell batted .100 one World Series [Stargell actually batted .208 in the 1971 World Series], and then the next one [1979], he won the MVP. I mean, if you happen to be in a slump at the wrong time of the year, those things happen. And that's what happened with Winfield. And I'm sure Winfield was putting a little more pressure on himself, as well. He went on to win what, two rings - one with Minnesota and one with Toronto? [Winfield was part of one World Series-winning team, the 1992 Toronto Blue Jays] So Winny proved himself. Winny was a great ballplayer, and I liked Winny - he was a really great teammate.

BOBBY MEACHAM: The only thing that I know used to bug - not just Steinbrenner, but people in general - was when you think you have the upper hand, but the other person doesn't really need you. Say, George gave him a ten-year deal - there was no fear there. He couldn't scare him anymore, he had a ten-year contract. He couldn't threaten him. When some people are used to controlling people and they can't all of a sudden, it's kind of like, "Oh my gosh, I can't do anything about this." And I think there may have been some frustration there with George, thinking Dave needed a little nudge to be a better player. Gosh, I don't know what he wanted to see. But he just couldn't nudge Dave, because Dave was his own man. You couldn't scare him or get him worried about what you were thinking - like George liked to do to people. Maybe that was it. It's a stretch, but I don't know, I couldn't understand it, either.

STEVE KEMP: If there would have been [friction between Steinbrenner and Winfield], I would just mind my own business. I know they would banter back and forth. I'm sure it was because George was trying to let it be known to his players that no one was above being chastised. But at the same time, I think

The Ballad of George and Winny

Winfield knew that he was out there playing hard and giving it everything he had. That's all you could ask for. I didn't experience or see anything that was "under the table," or anything like that. It's none of my business, anyway.

RON KITTLE: When George Steinbrenner came down into the locker room, it was like every walkie talkie in the whole place was chirping - *"He's coming! He's coming!"* Everybody was a little scared of what was going on. He compared Winfield to not being Reggie Jackson - "Reggie was Mr. October." He had to get to October to be "Mr. October." If you're not winning in September, you're not going to get to October to do anything. But Winny gave it his all.

DALE BERRA: George wanting to win, if Winfield wasn't performing up to his capabilities with men on base or not hitting in important spots, I'm sure it drove George crazy. But I don't know anything personally about it.

FRAN HEALY: I'm assuming George was frustrated when he said ["Mr. May"], but when you look at the whole thing - when you look at Dave Winfield's career - magnificent athlete.

chapter 25:
the ballad of billy and eddie

Frustration and miscommunication leads to a violent confrontation between manager and pitcher.

BRIAN FISHER: It was weird, because Eddie Whitson came from San Diego and had a lot of success. Big contract guy in New York, he didn't start out too well [in his first eleven starts, Whitson went 1-6 with a 6.23 ERA]. The fans were on him. It was amazing to watch - they were just *vicious*. And they can be in New York when you didn't pitch well. I think that had an affect. And Eddie and Billy did not get off on a good foot. I think it was a combination of the pressure of New York, the pressure of that big contract, and Billy Martin demanding this and [that]. It wasn't pretty. One thing I remember about Eddie is how big his eyes would get when he was upset. It's funny now, but obviously then it wasn't funny - Eddie would just get unbelievably upset and his eyes would get bigger. It was not a good relationship.

MIKE PAGLIARULO: I don't think Eddie Whitson understood Billy at all. As a matter of fact, that incident that happened in Baltimore, the fight there [at the Cross Keys Inn], I know for a fact what happened. And Billy was the kind of guy that wanted the players around him. He liked to have guys around him because he could see what guys are like. The guys would have a beer together, and Billy could see personalities. He wanted to know what guys are like. So they were at I guess that hotel lobby bar, and a couple of guys were there and Eddie Whitson. Eddie was getting a lot of crap from some of the fans, so Billy went over to actually help Eddie Whitson, and to get the fans away, and grabbed Eddie's arm to pull him away. Eddie was offended by that and thought Billy was pissed off at him. He was reading the wrong message - Billy was trying to help him.

Well, then all of a sudden, it pissed off Billy, and then he snapped and all hell broke loose. But Billy was actually trying to help Eddie in that situation in that whole fight thing, and then one thing led to another. But Eddie didn't understand that. Eddie didn't realize that. And I know that, because there were other players that had told me that. Billy didn't want anybody messing with the players. Even if he doesn't like you, he'll protect you. And it's not that Billy didn't like Eddie Whitson...he didn't like him after that, though! That's just how it went, and I think Eddie had problems with some of the fans out there. He thought people were following him home and all this other stuff, and he was telling the press about that. I'm like, "What's the matter with you? What are you doing? *Just play.* That's all you've got to do - is just play." If you can't take a couple of boos, what the hell...you shouldn't be playing baseball then. You shouldn't be playing professional sports if you're going to get booed every once in a while and you can't handle it, for Christ's sakes. When you stink, you stink - that's all. Get better the next day, that's all.

DALE BERRA: I was there. I can't really recount exactly what happened because I don't really remember it that well. But I can tell you that it was something to the effect where Billy was in the bar and literally told Whitson to "Hang in there" or something. And Whitson got mad at him, said, "You're trying to ruin me," at which time Billy told him...Billy was trying to be nice and Whitson was adversarial. I can't get into the conversation. Whitson was not happy with the way Billy was treating him. So I'm not going to say it's right or wrong on Whitson's part to be adversarial. But Billy was not adversarial to start it, I can tell you that. They were in the bar and Billy was actually trying to be nice to the guy.

REX HUDLER: I was with the team when Ed Whitson fought Billy Martin. Oh my gosh, it was something. So, Whitson was a brand new free agent signing. His first four or five starts, he'd get roughed up in the first inning, and Billy wouldn't let him finish his game. He'd yank him - he wouldn't let him settle in. Most of the time, they settle in after the first inning. Whitson would get pulled out of these games, and Whitson would head back to the hotel. Back then, you had to wait until the last out before you left. But Whitson, he would leave the ballpark and he would be at the hotel bar. I remember going in there, Whitson was a good guy from Columbus - I was engaged to a girl from Columbus. So we were friends, we shared a lot. I'd get in there after...I think we were in Milwaukee, and I said, "Hey Ed, how ya doing, bud?" "That greasy MF'er. That greasy bastard." He was mad at Billy. He'd had a few beers, and he was *mad.* Ed was kind of an intense guy. And Billy always had an entourage with him - he always had three different coaches with him. He hired Willie Horton to be his coach/bodyguard. That was his buddy from back in the Tiger days. But Willie ended up being such a good guy - he's such a sweetheart of a guy. Everybody loved him.

But here they come, I can see them coming across the street to the bar. And I'm thinking to myself, "Uh-oh. Something's going to happen here." I could see it. So, Billy comes in, walks by Ed Whitson, and sits down at the end of the bar. And Whitson and I are at a table. Billy sits at an angle where he's looking this way, back towards the bar. And Ed Whitson is looking at Billy, and he's mouthing stuff to him. He's mouthing, "I'm going to kick your ass!" He was probably 40 feet away, so he couldn't hear him, but Billy could see him. Billy gets out of his chair and comes over, and I got up and moved to another table. Billy came over and started talking, and some guy interrupted their conversation, and pulled Billy away from Ed, and then Ed got up and slammed his chair and walked out. Then we take a plane, we go to Baltimore, and now we're at the Cross Keys Inn. The same thing - early inning exit, Billy yanked him, Whitson's at the hotel bar, I had a girlfriend with me in the hotel bar after the game. I went up to Ed, "Ed, how ya doing buddy. What's up?" "I'm gonna kick his ass, Hud." "Ed, come on man. You can't do that. You'll get fired, you'll get blackballed. You can't fight a manager." "I'm sick and tired of him, Hud." I saw

The Ballad of Billy and Eddie

him come in, and that's when I grabbed my girlfriend and said, "Let's go. We're leaving." So we went up to the room.

Sure enough, 11:00 news - "Martin Fights Again." There it was. I didn't hear much about it. We have a day game the next day. We get on the team bus, and Don Baylor and Ken Griffey and all these veteran guys were just talking up a storm. There was a scoop. Telling everybody what happened, how they confronted each other in the bar, how they moved out to the parking lot, they all went out through the door, and then Whitson kicked Billy and broke his arm, and they went down and scrummed and scuffled, it went over to the elevator. It was an old-fashioned melee/brawl. So now, the bus gets to the ballpark in Baltimore, and we're putting on our uniforms. The doors slam, and here comes Billy - there was no Billy or Ed on the bus - running through the clubhouse with his arm in a sling. The doors slam, and five minutes later, here comes a hundred media, running through the clubhouse and banging on Billy's door - *"Let us in! Let us in!"* I've never ever since then seen anything like it. It was a literal soap opera. They sent Whitson home.

Whitson, they did not pitch him in Yankee Stadium, because the fans were so upset with him, because he was messing with Billy - Billy's their boy. The fans took sides, big-time. Whitson had to have a police escort in from the parking lot into Yankee Stadium - at home. Later in the season, they gave Whitson a start at home, and he got the win, he went seven innings. You know how the crowd is in New York - they'll boo one second, and love you the next minute. They cheered for him, and so finally, that all went away, and then they moved Whitson - they traded him [back to the Padres in mid-1986]. But it showed me a lot about that drama in New York. The teeth/fangs that the people can have, the media. It was a really good eye-opener for me being a Yankee early - in the first part of my career.

BILLY MARTIN JR: I believe Ed or somebody - or Ed and the bartender - were having an argument. And dad went over there to back Ed, to have his back. I think Ed thought dad was

231 Just Out of Reach: The 1980s New York Yankees

charging in to jack with him. I don't think dad saw it coming. I wasn't there, but that's how I heard him tell the story. Because he didn't dislike Ed Whitson - not as a person. Ed struggled for that club, and that was a bad call obviously - bringing him from San Diego to New York. But how do you know that until a guy is in that situation?

chapter 26:
some struggle

Why do some free agents who come to the Big Apple fail?

STEVE KEMP: I've seen stuff - or my kids have read stuff - that said that was the start of my downfall, because I went to New York. *I got hurt.* I hurt my shoulder pretty bad the first month into the season [1983] in a collision in Toronto, and I couldn't really have any extension. But I kept playing, and then I got hit in the eye. I don't know if everything that I would read is the truth. It could have been injuries as to why somebody doesn't do well. I don't think New York fans can be any different than if you're playing in Boston or Philadelphia. Detroit fans could be hard - because they're knowledgeable. They know the game, and they're going to let you know if they feel…and they want you to just play hard. For the two years that I had in New York, I'm disappointed, and I wish I could have had the years that I projected myself to have. But I think because of injuries, it didn't happen. I feel like I let people down, but it was what it was. And even though I didn't put up the statistics that were expected of me, I think a lot of people appreciated the way I played the game. At least I had played hard. I think the fans - in some way - would say, "Hey, he's not doing what we wanted him to do. But at least you know he's out there playing his ass off."

I just don't know how you can answer that question or justify it, because there's a lot of different things that come in to the equation. It could have been playing for a different manager, or maybe some guys don't like playing in New York. Maybe it's too much glitter or whatever you want to say - too much exposure. But the funny thing is, these guys that are playing today, they get more exposure than you would have gotten if you were playing in New York 20 years ago. They're on TV every night. When I was playing, we had one "Game of the Week." That was it. Granted, just about every Saturday it was either a New York team, a Chicago team, or an LA team. And granted, because those were the biggest bases - the most people. But you weren't going to put Milwaukee on, unless everybody was excited. And like Detroit, if Mark Fidrych was pitching then yeah, we're going to put that game on. Everybody wants to see the Bird. And I don't think the media can be any more difficult in New York than they can be in Detroit or Philadelphia. Philadelphia can be tough to play there, from what I understood from people. So I don't know why - maybe the way it ends up happening.

TOMMY JOHN: Personalities. John Denny was with St. Louis and the Yankees were courting him. And he called me - John and I were really good friends - and said, "What's it like pitching there?" I said, "John, it's the best. But you've got to be able to withstand the heat and the press when you have a bad game in a crucial series. George will lambaste you. And the heat will be on you and he'll say stuff and all this. If you can stand the heat, this is the greatest place in the world to pitch. But if you can't, then this is not it." So he ended up signing with Philadelphia. [Laughs] Which is *worse* than New York. But it's personalities.

Ed Whitson, Ed was from Tennessee and Ed was a "good old boy" and all that. And Rainbow [Steve Trout's nickname] was the same way. If Steve Trout would have gone to Texas, if he would have gone to Kansas City, if he would have gone to the Dodgers, the Angels - someplace where it was laidback and you could pitch - Trout would have been fine. But he goes to New York and the pressure's on him...I think if you're going to get players to play in New York with the Yankees - I've said this all along - you should do a psychological test on them. OK, the guy can hit, the guy can run, he can do all this stuff. Do a psychological test - some guys can stand it, some can't. And you think you should. "Well, for the amount of money they're paying you, my god, you should be able to play like that." Well, not necessarily. Because you can't overcome what's between your ears...if there's anything between your ears. And a lot of times, that might be best. Find a Gomer Pyle type guy that goes [impersonates Mr. Pyle's voice], *"Oh, golly."* Or a Forrest Gump. *"Fetch Forrest, fetch!"* [Laughs]

STEVE JACOBSON: At some point, some players didn't want just the money. Greg Maddux did not come to the Yankees when he was available [in 1992]. Steinbrenner made him a bigger offer than the Braves did, and he wouldn't come. Part of it was just the scrutiny that New York exerts. And the other part is having the hostility or the pushing that Steinbrenner subjected them to. They were always insecure and always felt unappreciated. Steinbrenner once made a comment to me about Mattingly - he said, *"He's no Jack Armstrong."* Well, Mattingly was as true blue a ballplayer as the city has ever had, and for Steinbrenner to cut him like that was not valid. And a lot of players would not come and subject themselves to it.

Like, we just saw the Red Sox. There were some players on the team that played last year [2012] that did not fit well in the scrutiny that the Boston media subjected them to. It's like some players couldn't put up with the pressure that the New York media put on players here. Some of them, like Tino Martinez, I recall saying, "It was a terrific crowd to play for. They saw how when you played hard, they gave you credit - even when you failed." He replaced Mattingly, and he understood that. It seems that when Steinbrenner was under suspension - twice - that's when both extended periods of success were created. And what I was saying about the Red Sox, when they got rid of those players, they added to what they kept. So they won again this year [the Red Sox won the 2013 World Series].

GEORGE FRAZIER: Because they don't handle the media. They just don't handle that aspect of it. They come there, and the thing that they have to do is understand that when you fail, stand there and answer every single question. When you succeed, answer every question. And the fans will appreciate that. If you come off as a guy who is scared, that you can't handle the media of Yankee Stadium and the news and the press and everything that goes with it, then you're not going to survive in New York City. It just ain't happening.

But if you take the time when you fail, to answer every question, I mean, when I lost three games in the World Series, I could have hid in the trainer's room. I sat there and answered every question until 4:00 in the morning, and then I walked out and went home to Oklahoma. But I answered every single question. And I think that by doing that, obviously, you win fans over, you win the media over, you're a good guy, you're not going to run and hide, you're going to face adversity. But there's guys that can't handle the adversity, they can't handle reading the New York Post - "You suck. Trade me." All that stuff. They can't handle that kind of stuff. And that affects the way they play. And there's been great players that have come there that could not be successful because of that very reason. And a lot of time, it's the pressure of replacing guys - that's the other side of it.

MIKE EASLER: Because of the pressure that the city brings upon you, the pressure that George brings upon you, and just the Yankee organization. Not everybody can handle that. Ed Whitson was having trouble over there. There were a lot of guys that came in that just could not…it's not that they couldn't handle the pressure, it's that the high expectations that were expected of them, they didn't live up to - or they might have had an off-year or something like that. And then the writers are kind of hard on them, and Steinbrenner comes down on you. I don't care how great you are - sometimes, you get to a point where you doubt yourself a little bit, and you cannot play the game with doubt. You cannot play the game reluctantly. You have to go in there with everything in your heart and say, "I'm a warrior. I don't give a shit what anybody says about me. I can care less. I know who I am as a ballplayer. I know what my capabilities are. I'm going to go out there and do it." That's what I felt every single day. Plus, I didn't have to play the field, so I was kind of protected - *I was a DH.* [Laughs]

BOB WATSON: Oh, just like some players can't play in their hometowns. They put a lot of pressure on themselves - along with what you guys [members of the media] do. You don't back off, you don't give people a chance to get their feet under...if a guy struggles the first two games or the first week of the season, you're on him - "He can't play and he's this and he's that." People take that criticism differently than other people. People that don't even read the paper...or back then, listen to the talk shows. Well now, you got guys, god almighty, there's all the social media and all of the other outlets. ESPN wasn't even around. Now, ESPN has got what, fourteen channels? And then the other side of this, they want to live up to the money that they got. And from Mike Schmidt to Don Mattingly, there have been a number of players who wanted to give the money *back*. So again, it's a mental and a psychological thing, and different people react to all of that differently. For me, I was at the end of my career. Hey, I just took it as a challenge - "I'll show you that I can play." I knew what I could and could not do, and I stayed within myself.

STEVE JACOBSON: I give the media *credit* for not letting people off the hook. Accountability was very big in New York - in business and a lot of other things. Including the sports teams.

DALE BERRA: It's not different. I don't know what the difference is. I have no idea. You could say that Whitson's problem was with Billy, but at the same time, it wouldn't have mattered who the manager was.

RON KITTLE: I think it's the pressure of the big city. You hit one home run in New York, it's like five home runs in any other town. So you've got 50 media people instead of four. And if you fail in a bigger venue, it's going to bother you. Steve Trout, I caught him in the minor leagues. To me, that man could have won 600 games. I'd never seen that best stuff out of a lefty. I always explained, he was the best ten-speed bicycle in the world...with no pedals. When he pitched at Yankee Stadium, he was standing on the mound one time with his hat on during the

Just Out of Reach: The 1980s New York Yankees

national anthem. And Lou is yelling at him, *"TAKE YOUR HAT OFF!"* I don't know what happens, but I know playing in New York, either you can or you can't. And there's been a lot of people who can't.

RON DAVIS: I don't think it has so much to do with the player, so to speak. You have good years and bad years. When you have a bad year at Yankee Stadium, it's just multiplied times ten. You can have bad times anytime, and bad games and bad years. It just gets blown out of proportion at Yankee Stadium. So I don't think the players are like, "Oh god, I can't play." I don't think that happens at all. I know all the press wants to write it that way - "He can't handle this." I just think people have bad years, and just because of the media there, it's blown way out of proportion and it's on every paper and every newscast how bad you are, so people start believing it, because that's what y'all write about. And then all of a sudden, the fans won't let you get any better. The way I look at it, if they were playing somewhere else, nobody would really know they had a bad game. And all of a sudden, now, the next game he starts, everybody is booing him when he comes up to bat. That wouldn't happen in Minnesota. So I think it has a tendency to steamroll because of the press.

MIKE PAGLIARULO: I think just maybe their personalities didn't fit. That's a big part of playing in New York. You need to have the right kind of guy - when I say that, I don't mean talent or skill or analytical projections associated with that. People react different to different situations. In an emergency, something happens - a car accident or whatever - people are going to react differently. When you play in New York, people are going to act differently. It's just that way. It makes you either tougher or it breaks you - one or the other. I just think it didn't fit their personalities, their character. And that's something that is a very difficult thing to scout. So you can't blame the scouts, really, because the type of pitcher that was needed, or the type of player that was needed, their personality…there just needs to be a little more research done on that when you acquire a guy. I believe that, and actually, I know it because I saw it with my own eyes - guys that are scared to death. I just couldn't believe how scared they were. I'm like, "What the heck is the matter? We're going to go play *baseball* today. Just play your ass off."

People appreciate when you play your ass off - they appreciate when you put it out and you leave it on the field. They know the difference. Nobody ever remembers your numbers - they remember how you played. And I'm positive of that and living proof. I get that all the time and it's a wonderful feeling to have - not that I intended for that to happen, but it's just what you are supposed to do. Especially in New York. If those guys are unhappy with what they leave on the field, then they're not going to be happy with anything and they're going to be listening to all this jibber-jabber. And you know what? It's going to show up in their game. And it did - it showed up in their game. They were a little tentative or scared or whatever you want to call it. It's too bad, because I played with Eddie Whitson when I was traded to San Diego, and he was a different guy completely. A *completely* different guy - and pitched his butt off there. I'm like, "What the heck? Where were you a couple of years ago? We could have used you!" It was amazing, the difference.

But that's a tough thing, and maybe the organization learned from that too, though. That's part of the stuff that I think the organization learned about and helped build the structure in the '90s and the early 2000's that maintained winning all the time, and having great battles and great teams. It wasn't just about getting free agents - it was about their guys, their core. They have a great core. And that's how you win long-term. That was really the belief in how the things were built. I know what a Yankee looks like. He looks like Derek Jeter, he looks like Donnie Mattingly, he looks like me - because people say that all the time! [Laughs] That's your core and that's how you represent the name on your chest. And you've got to have that flair, and the organization has to be sure about that. And that's not something that a free agent can ever be. A core comes from within your own organization, and the Yankees did that, and they built I believe in the '80s. I know they did, for a fact. And those guys

239 Just Out of Reach: The 1980s New York Yankees

are great guys - they're classy guys, the core that represents the Yankees now. Just look at them - they're great pros, they'll all be Hall of Famers I'm sure. Really, really good people.

BARRY FOOTE: I think a lot of it is the pressure - certain guys just don't react as well under. If you look at that, it's usually the pitchers that don't do as well. I think you've got to be a guy like Catfish Hunter, who just didn't care. Pressure didn't bother him. Some other guys, they're trying to live up to contracts and never made that money maybe before in their life. And just because a guy is getting paid for the number one spot on the rotation doesn't necessarily mean he is a number one starter. But I think that's what happens - rather than just pitching to their potential, they try to pitch *above* their potential.

STEVE BALBONI: I guess you have to come in with a lot of self-confidence, because they'll boo you and they'll yell at you. But they're not hard to turn. So if you hang in there and do well, they'll jump right back on with you, and they'll love you. You need the confidence in yourself and the belief that you could do that. And if you do it, they'll turn. And I think some guys came in and had that confidence and could do it, and some guys, either they didn't have the confidence in themselves or they just felt like it was going to be hopeless and they got nervous. To me, the guys with the self-confidence that hung in there, if they were good players and they got off to a bad start, as soon as they started doing well, everybody jumped right on. It was, "OK. *He's good.*" They were those kind of fans, but I'm sure people like me, going to the Midwest, I could understand - if you're from the Midwest and you played in the Midwest with those fans, it's a shock to your system, to come to Yankee Stadium.

BRIAN FISHER: I guess you can't handle the ups and downs. Because the ups are so high and the downs are so low, and the fans go on both. So, trying to overcome both, it's so difficult, because if you don't understand how to wave that out, I think that part can be really tough. Sometimes, I don't think people handle that too well. Other places, you don't have the same media scrutiny. The Yankees after a game, there's a hundred reporters in there. You go to the Pirates, and there's two. That's a huge, huge difference. That is probably the biggest difference. The scrutiny was a lot tighter. It was a completely different setting. It's not the same anywhere else on the planet - maybe Boston a little bit, but New York is different. And if you don't understand how to handle that, it can be tough.

DAVE LaROCHE: It's a tough city in a lot of ways. And the pressure George puts on and the media and the fans - they expect you to win. And it's the media capitol, so it's not like what you'd find in Milwaukee or Kansas City, where the fans just love to come to the ballpark and they root for you, and they do very little booing. And then, plus, the city never closes, so you can get yourself in a lot of trouble that way, too. It's not good for some people. And there's people that just like to be kind of in the corner - don't want to be interviewed every day or be in the limelight. Just go out, play the game, do their job, go home, and be with their family. And that's fine - there's obviously great players, that's what they like. There's not many players that can play in the New Yorks, Bostons, and Philadelphias, where the fans can be real, real tough.

BILLY MARTIN JR: I think some of them, you can see, you can predict. Kenny Rogers was a guy I predicted. A guy I really like, but he was a guy that was very media sensitive. You don't notice that in the smaller media markets. You don't notice that in Texas, Oakland, Minnesota, places like that, where the press isn't as aggressive, and the competition isn't as great as it is in New York, Boston, and places like that.

FRAN HEALY: That, you'd have to monitor somebody's nervous system. I'll give you an example, with Reggie. They'd have his picture on the back page of one of the newspapers - or two of the newspapers or three of the newspapers on a given day - ripping him. He'd read it, he'd put the paper down, look at me,

Just Out of Reach: The 1980s New York Yankees

and say, "Where do you want to have lunch?" Where somebody else, it would bother for days and would affect them on the field. He didn't care. If he got mad at the media, when they asked him a question, he would answer in Spanish. He didn't care. I don't know Whitson, but from what I understand about that fight in Baltimore, he must have kept *a lot* inside, because it all came out that night. I would dare say when you see New York eat somebody up, it has to do with that individual's nervous system, and you'll never know about it because nobody's going to talk about their nervous system, nobody's going to talk about whether or not it's strong or weak. I guess other people would say the mental part, but I think it's the nervous system, which is connected to their brain.

But some people can struggle and come back - struggle on Tuesday and come back on Wednesday. Some other people struggle on Tuesday and don't come back for three weeks. And you have enough of those funks, you're in trouble. But it never seemed to bother Reggie - he didn't care. In the media, he would deal with the media…I never quite understood this about him or Gary Carter - they would deal with the media, but the rest of the team didn't want to. So they'd go to him. He didn't give a shit, he'd talk - he didn't care. It wasn't, "I'm going to show these guys up." He just talked to the media. Thank god, because we need those guys. It's funny, because I've been on both sides of this - I understand why some players don't want to talk to the media. But on the other side, as a broadcaster - like I just got back from speaking to John Tavares [center for the New York Islanders] up in Toronto - you need these guys to talk. And looking at it as a player, I could see why they'd go into the player's lounge. When you went into the player's lounge, that means you don't want to talk. Reggie didn't care. Thurman didn't want to talk. Certain guys didn't want to talk. I don't know if they didn't want to talk because they didn't feel articulate - I don't know what it was. But I think there's more to it than just disliking the media. Gary Carter was unreal - he was a magnificent interview, and would talk win, lose, or draw. Ray Knight, the same way. And then

Some Struggle 242

other guys wanted to *take on* the media…which was probably a mistake.

chapter 27: managers

Good luck trying to keep track of all the managers the Yankees employed during the '80s. Here's a handy guide...

STEVE BALBONI: It's hard to keep up, because they were firing and hiring!

RUDY MAY: I played for two managers that I would consider the greatest managers that I ever played for, and I played for Billy, Dick Williams, guys like that. But Dick Howser and Earl Weaver were the best. Dick was the kind of manager that just let me do my thing. He said, "Just go out there and play the way I know you can play, and let the rest take care of itself."

RON DAVIS: I played with Billy two or three times. I played with Dick Howser, I played with Gene Michael, Bob Lemon. All those guys were just one year/two year here things, except for Billy of course, and Bob. Billy and Bob would be the ones - Howser and Michael were just Billy's throw-ins at the time. But the true managers were really Billy and Bob - they were outstanding. Billy knew how to control a game, he knew how to control the press. People don't realize how much pressure he took off of all the other people that were playing, by all his so-to-speak "miscues." [Laughs] He would have fights sometimes with George just to keep our team loose. Billy would go out there on the mound and just say, "Hey, where are we eating tonight?" It wasn't about, "We've got this bunt play here or this bunt play here." It was just, "Hey, what bar are we going to tonight?" He would make a joke to make you laugh, to let you relax a little bit. And hopefully, you'd get the job done.

STEVE JACOBSON: I recall Gene Michael managing that team and Steinbrenner liking Michael, but wanting to put pressure on him all the time. Gene, as smart as he was, he wasn't fiery enough for Steinbrenner. I remember Michael standing up and saying to the media toward George, "If you don't like what I'm doing, fire me. *But get off my back."* And that's the way a lot of players around free agency felt about the Yankees. I remember Bob Lemon - who saved their butts in the '70s - saying he couldn't wait to get to the morning newspaper to see what was going on in the Yankees soap opera.

BARRY FOOTE: Gene had been a shortstop [Michael played for the Yankees from 1968-1974] and he went on to have this great analytical career as a scout, and sort of being their "super scout." He was a little different. I think what Bob Lemon brought to the ball club was just this real laidback sort of attitude, and let the guys play. But that's not to say we wouldn't have won it if we'd have had Michael the rest of the way [in 1981]. That was just during that time where George Steinbrenner, his strategy was "move managers around." He'd fire them…he never fired them from the organization, so they were able to pop up again as a manager. But I really liked Lemon - I thought he was a great guy. And I liked Gene - I thought he was a good baseball man. It's just two different styles. But I think it had very little to do with the outcome. It was just one of those things that Steinbrenner thought was it was time to make a move, and he did.

DAVE LaROCHE: Actually, [Michael and Lemon] were similar in a lot of ways. Both were old school - older and had been around for a long time, and been successful in baseball. Lem was very laidback. I think one of the funniest things that nobody knows about - except the players - was when Lem first took over [in 1981], probably within his first week, he brought me into a game…or I was in a game. Anyway, it was second and third and two outs, and he came out to the mound, and I said, "Do you want to walk Gorman Thomas?" And I think Cecil

245   Just Out of Reach: The 1980s New York Yankees

Cooper may have been on deck - either Cooper or Ben Oglivie. They were both left-handed, but were both real tough hitters. Barry Foote was catching, and I said, "I'll just throw him my curveball" - because he was known as a fastball hitter.

So he said, "OK. If we walk him, fine, and if we can get him out, that's the best." So he got back in the dugout - and I didn't see any of this, but the guys in the dugout were laughing and telling me about it - they said that no sooner did he sit down on the bench, and he always sat up on the back of the seat so he could see the whole field. He sat there and I threw the first pitch, and it was a lob, and it went above the roof of the dugout - he couldn't see it! They said he almost fell out of his chair! He said, "What in the world is that?" He didn't know anything about it, he hadn't ever seen it. They said he almost fell down - he stumbled trying to get down to watch it. He was like, "What is that? What's he doing?!" Guys were falling off the bench, laughing. I wish I had seen that…but I didn't. We got him out, so Lem was happy.

BOB WATSON: Gene Michael was a guy who wore a ton of hats. He did everything that George asked him to do. I just think Gene didn't get a real good shake as a manager. I mean, I don't know how long he got to manage - six weeks or whatever, before they fired him. And then they brought in Bob Lemon. Lem just let you play. He said, "Hey, you know how to hit, you know who the pitcher is. If it's hit to you, *catch it."* [Laughs] He was very laidback. I think he made two decisions that "made" his tenure back with the Yankees in '81 - the decision to bunt Bobby Murcer that didn't work out, and then he pinch hit for Tommy John in the fourth inning of the last game [of the 1981 World Series] that didn't go well. Those are the two decisions that backfired on him. But again, you had a veteran group of guys. Probably, if you said, "Nobody was going to manage," we would have done the same.

STEVE BALBONI: Bob Lemon seemed quiet to me, Clyde King [who managed the final 62 games of 1982] just seemed like a nice guy. Gene Michael I had met before - he was very friendly with me. I was very comfortable with him. He's a good baseball guy - he's still in baseball. He was great. It was easy for me, because I didn't know him, and he would joke with me. It was good to have him coming up, because I remember he was up there when I got sent down that first time. I had a triple and a double in my two games, and then I got sent down, and it was just because they had made a trade.

GEORGE FRAZIER: I thought [Lemon] was pretty good. When you get teams like this - I always look back at it now and the Yankee teams - Joe Torre wasn't a very good manager with the St. Louis Cardinals, the New York Mets, and the Atlanta Braves. But he was a genius with the Yankees. It's not that Joe was a bad manager, it was Joe all of a sudden had the horses to go to work with. And when you have the horses to pull the wagon, the wagon's going to go pretty much wherever you want it to. And I think that's where Bob was. We had a good team and everybody knew it. So he just had to make sure that everyone plugged it in, deferred some heat from George and from the newspapers when we didn't play well, and go forward. He did a good job with that.

BOBBY MEACHAM: Yogi was right after Billy got fired the first time I was there, after "Billy III." He was there about a year and the first couple of weeks of the next season. He was great. To me, he was a no-nonsense guy, who wanted you to go out and play. If you didn't play the game hard or made too many mistakes, he'd say, "Hey kid, I'm going to fine you for doing that," and you just keep playing. He just let you go out and play. It was fun to play for Yogi, because he put your name in the line-up if he thought you were going to help him win, and just let it go. I remember him chuckling in the dugout, going, "I'm going to let this guy hit 3-0," and he'd just chuckle about that. But he'd stand up for his players. He asked a lot of us, but he didn't really get in the way - he just let us play. Great guy to be around.

Just Out of Reach: The 1980s New York Yankees

DALE BERRA: Dad could manage with anybody. Dad's rapport with the players was a lot of different. Dad was great. But Billy was great, too. The '84 Yankees, not many managers would have put their jobs on the line to play Mattingly the way my dad did. Behind the scenes, they didn't want Mattingly to play - they wanted Griffey to play, they wanted Smalley at first base, or whoever. And dad said, "I'm playing *him.*" And he ended up winning the batting title, because dad believed in him. Many managers at that time would not have stuck their neck out to play somebody like Don Mattingly at the time.

I think Detroit went 25-3 or something [to start off the 1984 season]. They were literally out of the pennant race before June/July, so even though they wanted to play somebody else, dad said, "I'm playing Mattingly. If you don't like it, fire me" basically. He played Mattingly, and the kid won the batting title and then went off from there. Not many managers would have done that. They would have played who George wanted him to play, they wouldn't have stood up to it. They would have just played whoever he wanted to and kept their job. At that time, he played Mattingly *and* Pagliarulo. He said, "I'm playing who I want. If you don't like it, too bad."

MIKE PAGLIARULO: My impression was how personable he was. How he was so comfortable talking with me. I mean, I didn't feel like he even knew me at all, but he would ask me about how I felt about playing, and he gave me some tips on who I was going to be facing that day, and what they were going to come at me with. First of all, it was hard to imagine that Yogi Berra was even talking to me, but after I got through that, he helped with the actual game itself. And it all boiled down to that - no matter who you talked to, they would all talk about how you played the game that day, and how to win that game that day. All of the talk was around that.

And that's where I learned that no matter what you did or what you said, when you come to the ballpark, it's about the game that day - it's about winning and playing that day. And that's what the focus was - no matter what craziness was around, it was simplified and pretty clear about what was the job at hand and the task that needed to be done for that day. If you keep it simple, that's a great way to play. It helped your focus - being in that environment. For me, playing in New York helped me focus, helped me be aware of all the things around. Just be ready. Be ready to play the first inning, and then play them all. That's encouraged and challenged by your coaches, your teammates, and the fans, because they're educated fans, for sure. They know baseball. That was pretty clear right away, too. It was a good situation, a good place to play for me. I was very comfortable there.

BARRY FOOTE: Yogi is a great guy. He was a great, knowledgeable guy. Heck, he had greater statistics in the playoffs than a lot of players had in their whole careers! He was a good guy and it was great to hear a lot of his stories about the old Yankees. Tough to beat those '48 through the mid '50s teams he was on, that won so many World Series [Berra won ten World Series as a player].

BOBBY MEACHAM: I played with Lou - it was right after playing, going to hitting coach, and then right after that into managing. That was all new to him. Lou had the temperability on the field, but he didn't know as much as Billy. At that time, you could tell Lou was going to be a great manager, but he was learning. That had to be crazy - learning with Steinbrenner in the middle of it all, and trying to figure out how to help us get back to the playoffs and win, with the pressure there. He did a good job, but it was one of those things where you just kind of could tell that down the road, this guy was going to be a great manager.

MIKE EASLER: That was his first year managing [1986]. He was very intense, very..."Lou Piniella." [Laughs] He got very excited about things, he really always stood up for the players, he wanted to win with a passion. Sometimes, he was in overkill, but a lot of times he laid back and let you play the game. He let you play the way you play the game. As long as he knew you were giving 100% and doing the right things fundamentally, you had no problem with Lou Piniella. I really enjoyed playing for him.

RON KITTLE: I saw him as a player - quite aggressive. Played hard. He knew the game of baseball. I don't consider him a great baseball player, but he was a good mind. He did the little things right. And he took that approach as a manager, too. He had Henderson, Randolph, Winfield, Mattingly - there was some pretty good talent on the team that he played with. Now, he has to *manage* them. And I don't know if he really got the players' respect, because he was still playing with those guys earlier. So it might have been a little bit tougher. But he had his meetings, he knew what they were capable of doing. Every major league baseball player knows how to play the game. It's just a little tougher when you're in the New York environment.

GARY ROENICKE: Being a first year manager and never having managed at any level until he came to that level from a hitting coach, he'd really never been in charge. Even though Lou had a lot of years playing - very good hitter and played on some winning teams. A good hitting coach. Just now, he's added the pressure of managing the New York Yankees under George Steinbrenner - with all those great players on that team. So that was a little added pressure for him. Lou managed pretty much the way he played - he was very feisty and pretty much told it like it was.

DALE BERRA: He's a lot like Billy - he was a good man. Many of the guys had played with him, so they had a relationship with Lou. He was good and we were good again.

MIKE PAGLIARULO: Lou is great. Lou is a lot like Billy. In a way, Lou was the best hitting coach I ever had. I wanted him more as a hitting coach, although he was a great manager and took care of the players. A great offensive manager and treated me well. I can't say a bad thing about Lou at all. He played with the Yankees for many years [1974-1984], and so intelligent, as far as the game and offensive strategy. He could tell you what guys couldn't hit on the other team - he was so sharp that way. A great baseball mind. I was very lucky to play and be in his presence - I learned an awful lot from him about hitting.

Many other things today I use - I'm actually coaching now. Just the other day, our manager got thrown out, so I was coaching and we were losing 2-1. There was a situation where guys are on first and second, and we had to get a bunt down. I swear to god, I was coaching third base, and I called the hitter over, and said, "Alright, look. You're going to get one shot to take a whack at this ball. If you don't hit a line drive or put it in play, then you've got to bunt the next one." He said, "Alright," and he winds up hitting a three-run homer, and we win the game. And that experience, that was Lou Piniella/Billy Martin talking to me. That's what they said - "You've got one shot at whacking this ball, and then you've got to get the next bunt down." That's exactly what it was.

And people are going, "Oh, that's so old school." "Old school?! *That's how you play baseball.* That's how you play winning baseball…championship baseball. When you get the chance to seize the day, you do it. And that's just how you play. So that experience certainly helped me, and I didn't realize it at the time. But it changed me. And when I say I'm fortunate and grateful, I really rely on that experience, and that experience is not measured anywhere - but it certainly paid off at the end of the day.

BRIAN FISHER: I'll leave that alone, since Lou released me and got me out of baseball when I was in Seattle [in 1992]. I have to be honest - I didn't like Lou, I don't think Lou liked me. Obviously, Lou was a great manager in terms of his World Series with the Reds [Piniella was the manager of the 1990 World Series-winning Reds]. A great manager and great player, I'm just a mid-level journeyman, who wasn't anything great, wasn't anything special. Again, I have a bad taste in my mouth from Lou - not that I don't think he's a great manager. Obviously,

Just Out of Reach: The 1980s New York Yankees

something I did did not sit well with Lou. He sent me down for ten days. And a great pitcher in Doug Drabek - who turned out to be a Cy Young Award winner for the Pirates [in 1990] - they traded both Doug and I that next year [1987]. So whatever I did with Lou put me in the doghouse. I don't know what it was.

REX HUDLER: Had [Martin] not gotten fired and Lou Piniella took over, I would have been a Yankee and possibly survived that whole thing. Because I was going to be his "utility guy." And then, you go from utility to a starter. But Lou came on, and that's what changed his mind - Lou didn't want me, so I moved on. Here's the beauty of my career - my first year in '84, Yogi. My second year after Yogi, Billy in '85. In '86, they trade me to Earl Weaver. So I played for Yogi, Billy, and Earl my first three years in the majors. And then, I played with Buck Rogers for like three years with the Expos, Whitey Herzog traded for me - I got to play for him, a Hall of Fame manager. And then a guy named Joe Torre took over for the Cardinals, and I got to play for Joe for two-and-a-half years. And then, I played for Terry Francona with the Phillies! So it was really a nice group of managers that I got to play for. But my first three seasons in the majors, those three guys are all Hall of Fame guys. It was really special.

MIKE EASLER: Anybody that took the job with the Yankees - whether it be a player, manager, or coach - you knew what you were getting into. You didn't have to sign a contract, he didn't force you to do it. You knew what you were taking on. A lot of pressure and a lot of demands on you. As a player, it didn't bother me at all, because I would go out there and bust my ass every day, and I knew I could hit so it didn't make a difference. I loved that. I didn't care. I just loved to battle and I loved to go to war. That's why I played Major League Baseball, because I loved the competition.

chapter 28: yankee stadium

What was it like to play inside one of baseball's most hallowed halls?

PHIL NIEKRO: Every pitcher should pitch at least one game in Yankee Stadium. I'm talking about the old one - the new one is nothing like the old one. I've been in the new one, and I don't know, it's not "Yankee Stadium" to me. The monuments out there in left center, just wearing the pinstripes, the Yankee fans, the management, the players, the pride that they carry with them game after game, and George took care of his players very good. It was an honor to play for the Yankees.

RON DAVIS: Yankee Stadium is the greatest stadium in the world to play in. Not the new one - the old one was. The new one is atrocious. It looks like the Taj Mahal from the outside, and then looks like somebody forgot to decorate it inside. To me, it's not very "fan-friendly" - meaning fans that can afford the cheaper seats. The luxury boxes are over-the-top gorgeous and the suites are gorgeous. But just looking at different stadiums since my son started playing, Citi Field is over-the-top compared to Yankee Stadium. Where the Giants play [AT&T Park], that's a gorgeous field. San Diego [PETCO Park], Pittsburgh [PNC Park], the Diamondbacks here have a beautiful field [Chase Field], with the windows opening up. For two billion dollars, I thought the Yankees would have done a little bit better.

GEORGE FRAZIER: I'll never forget it as long as I live. To walk down those stairs - the same stairs that Babe Ruth, Whitey Ford, Mickey Mantle, Lou Gehrig, Joe DiMaggio, the list is forever of great players that walked through there - and to be able to put on the pinstripes…that was the ultimate experience

253 Just Out of Reach: The 1980s New York Yankees

for me. And to be a part of that locker room, to become friends with the late Pete Sheehy [the Yankees' longtime clubhouse attendant], to listen to the stories from the '30s, the '40s, the '50s, the '60s. I considered Yogi a friend and to listen to his stories, and to listen to Mickey, who I became friends with before he passed and played in his golf tournaments and was around him, all of those things, to meet those guys and be around it was unbelievable.

REX HUDLER: No comparison at all. It was *electric*. But back then, there were no other ballparks that had that. It as special. I remember Pete Sheehy, he was really funny. He didn't have any front teeth. He would hang a hanger on the back of your pocket of your pants while you were walking around. He would hand me my check behind his back. [Laughs] Like to say, "Here kid, you didn't earn it. I'm going to give it to you, but don't let anybody see it." And I would come up and stretch in the middle of a game. I would come up the tunnel and stretch in the clubhouse, and he would be sitting on that picnic bench that they had there - a very primitive locker room - and he would go, "What the hell are you doing, kid?" I'd go, "I'm stretching, Pete." "They never used to do that. What are you doing?" Because Sheehy, he was the clubhouse guy when Babe Ruth was there - that's how old he was. I got a kick out of this guy, he was a character. But he was tripping that I was stretching. But that was some of the "new generation" stuff, see? Because even back then, it was coming in. It's all different now too, because the game keeps evolving. I loved that aspect of it.

But when I opened up the clubhouse door, it's like there was a beam of light that came out of that clubhouse door - especially after walking down the dark tunnel and coming in from the parking lot, and listening to fans as I walked into Yankee Stadium as a Yankee, fans yelling, "Yo Hudlah, you're a bum! You'll never take Randolph's job!" And I'm thinking to myself, "Wow...*I'm on your team!* I don't want his job!" But I felt the passion of the people. It was staggering. Of course, it was new to me, because it was the only team I'd ever been with, but never ever any other place was like that. Except the Cardinals came the second closest. So, there's a correlation there - those are the two teams with the most world championships in the world. OK, so there's the passion.

I was very fortunate to play for those two organizations. And it ruined it for every other organization I played for, because obviously, some of the other ones - the Expos...the Angels were pretty good with Gene Autry, but they didn't have that winning tradition. So there was a tradition there. And to go into that locker room after I opened that door and it was like a beam of light, with the pinstripes hanging on the lockers...I actually had a locker spot. I had to pinch myself. I had a locker next to Donnie Mattingly, and I believe it was Ken Griffey on the other side. I couldn't believe that I had a locker space in Yankee Stadium. And you know what? It made me feel good. I developed a small ego. When we would go on the road, there would be hundreds of people in the lobbies. That blew me away. It really felt special to be a New York Yankee. I'll never forget that.

TOBY HARRAH: Well, when I was a kid growing up, Mickey Mantle was my favorite player, and through Billy Martin - who I played for in Texas - I just developed a tremendous respect for the Yankees and the Yankee organization. Playing in Yankee Stadium, where all the great players played in the past, it was just a thrill. I've been living the dream my whole life, it's kind of a young country boy getting a chance to play major league baseball. It's a dream come true. Playing in Yankee Stadium was the ultimate. When you finally played in that ballpark, you'd feel like, *"I've made it to the big leagues."*

BOB WATSON: It's a historic place. Some of the greatest players who have played the game played there. To be, one, in a Yankee uniform, and two, in the place they played, and for me, I hit either third or fourth or fifth in the line-up. Who hit third, fourth, and fifth in Yankee history? To be part of that and be one

Just Out of Reach: The 1980s New York Yankees

of the few right-handers who ever led the team in hitting, that means a whole lot.

MIKE PAGLIARULO: I'm sad it's gone. I certainly loved it. For me, it was the first stadium that I'd ever seen with the upper deck and the lights and stuff like that. Even when I signed, it was the first major league stadium that I walked into, besides the Metrodome, because we came back on the off day - I had to see Yankee Stadium. I drove in, walked in, and I couldn't believe how big it was. How tall it was. You couldn't see the city around you. It was just amazing how big it was. It was an amazing place. I spent many days there and I loved all the days there - the good ones *and* the bad ones. It taught me to grow and be the person that I am. It was a wonderful experience and I was glad to be a part of it. But I certainly do miss it.

STEVE BALBONI: That was the greatest. My first day in there, it was like...it's hard to explain. It's just unbelievable. It was really the only stadium I ever walked in and you kind of felt the history. Playing in Boston, Fenway was close. But it just seemed like there was nothing close to Yankee Stadium. And I would see other players come in, like from the National League who had never been in there, and you could see they were a little bit in awe of it. And then they'd put it on the [video screen] - Babe Ruth, they'd go through all those superstar players that played there. They just kind of threw it in your face, to the other teams.

RON KITTLE: I think in '82 or '83, I walked from downtown all the way to Yankee Stadium. Everybody said, "Hey, *you're alive!*" I just wanted to get to the ballpark, and I walked through the dugout and onto the field, and it's what I expected. I expected that aura to be there at Yankee Stadium - the home runs, the mystique. I loved playing there. It was fun. I just wish I would have stayed healthy, so I could've contributed better and did more for the team. But also, make it more enjoyable, too -

because when you're feeling good and you're healthy, you can do some big things.

TOMMY JOHN: My first year, we're in spring training, and George has a night out for us, at a place called Frankie's, right on the Intracoastal. And I'm sitting down there, and Whitey Ford and his wife come up and they sit down. We're talking and laughing, and I ask him, "Hey, what's it like pitching at the stadium?" He said, "Oh, you'll do well. But remember one thing - Yankee Stadium is made for left-handed hitters. When you pitch at the stadium, make sure your curveball is on, and make sure you can throw it away to left-handers and keep them from turning and pulling into the short porch into right field. Right-handers are easy, because you can just pitch fastball away and you can throw your curveball or whatever and they're hitting it to the big part of the ballpark. But make sure that the left-handers, that you don't make any mistakes on the inside half of the plate." And I took that to heart. I worked on getting my curveball and making sure that I could throw it and keep it away.

I generally pitched left-handers inside - unless I was facing like, a George Brett. I pitched George Brett away, away, away, away. Curveball away, fastball away. And I wanted George Brett to hit me to left centerfield, and I'll take a double off of him rather than hit the ball to right field for a home run. In fact, the first time I ever faced him, George hit a home run off of me in Yankee Stadium. And the writers came over - the big rivalry then was Kansas City/Yankees. And they said, "What do you think of George Brett? He hit the home run off of you." And I said, "Personally, I think George's brother, Ken, had much better power than George." And now, the writers had a scoop. And they ran back over to George, and they said, "Tommy John said he's more impressed with your brother Ken's power than yours." And he said, "Tommy's right - he's got more power than me!" [Laughs] Ken was a pitcher with the Phillies, but he could hit. Ken Brett could absolutely flat-out hit. With power. But George was a better hitter, obviously.

Just Out of Reach: The 1980s New York Yankees

MIKE EASLER: Playing in Yankee Stadium was the greatest time I ever had. I almost turned into a pull hitter, but I wasn't a pull hitter. I was tempted to pull, and my first year there - for the first month or so - I was hitting like .230/.240. I said, "Man, I've got to go back to my inside-out swing. My 'Fenway Park swing'." I loved Fenway Park because of the wall over there. As a left-handed hitter, it made me conscious of staying back and letting the ball travel. Yankee Stadium, I just enjoyed the atmosphere. I hit some home runs to right field mind you, but my game was inside-out, left field. Like a Bernie Carbo-type swing. But I ended up doing well my first year there - I ended up hitting .302.

TOMMY JOHN: They kept bringing right-handed hitters into Yankee Stadium. Yankee Stadium was big left field, big left center, short right field. Yankee Stadium was built for Babe Ruth and left-handed pitching. But they kept bringing right-handers in - they brought in Baylor, Winfield. Then they brought in Steve Kemp, and he was not a pull hitter - he hit the ball to left centerfield. He was a straightaway, good line drive hitter. And then they started shortening up left field to accommodate the right-handed hitters, and all of a sudden, Yankee Stadium is a band box. When I came back in '86, there would be a fly ball in left centerfield and it was iffy if it was going to go out. In the old days, there's no question - there were many games I never saw Mickey Rivers' face. All I saw was his number running around back there, catching fly balls at 420 feet or whatever. But that's the way Yankee Stadium was built. They were reconfiguring Yankee Stadium to fit their trades.

STEVE KEMP: Loved it. Obviously, I got a chance to play in Tiger Stadium, which is probably my favorite...well, that and Fenway, and then New York - all three. I was fortunate to play in those three ballparks. Tiger Stadium is not there anymore, and the old Yankee Stadium is not. I'm sure the new stadium is awesome, but I enjoyed playing in Yankee Stadium. It was exciting, it was a great place to play.

BARRY FOOTE: It was the initial nervousness of just playing in and realizing all the tradition there. But it was a nice ballpark. I haven't even been to the new ballpark - I have been invited many times, haven't gone yet. But it was a great ballpark. Just a lot of tradition. Back then, they were playing the Thurman Munson film almost every game, so you know there was a lot of tragic tradition, and there was also a lot of the great winning tradition there.

RON DAVIS: In '80, I went over and looked at it [Thurman Munson's locker, which was never reassigned after his death - staying that way until old Yankee Stadium closed in 2008]. And then after that, I never really paid attention to it that much. You glanced at it, but you just kind of "moved on," so to speak. In '79, when we got back from the funeral in Ohio, before the game, we looked at it and I shook my head. It was like, "Dang man, *he's gone.*" Then played and finished up that season. '80, you looked at it every once in a while, and then '81, it just kind of got easier - it was like part of the family sitting over there.

STEVE BALBONI: I guess it was just normal [Munson's locker]. I never met him, because I was in A Ball when he was killed. He was a huge person in the Yankee organization. And it was such a tragic thing, that you understood that they wanted to do something special for him. It just kind of made sense.

GARY ROENICKE: Winning the World Series [in 1983 with the Orioles] and clinching the '79 playoffs in Anaheim, that's probably another highlight of mine. Being a Yankee that one year, and got to play 81 games at Yankee Stadium...every time we went in there, just to see the history - I love the history of this game, that's what's unique about baseball. It's got history like no other sport. And then of course, what team do you think about with all the superstars going way back? The New York Yankees. Never got tired of looking at the Jumbotron up there and seeing old Yankee greats and games. That part I enjoyed. Being a visiting player - and even with the Yankees in '86 - I didn't enjoy

259 Just Out of Reach: The 1980s New York Yankees

the dimensions in left field, because you had to hit the ball right down the line. I hit several 400-foot fly ball outs to left center.

BRIAN FISHER: It was awesome. There's no experience like that. Because again, I got traded to the Pirates, I played for the Astros, I played for the Mariners, so I got a different flavor. But Yankee Stadium, Yankee fans, they were into the game, they were crazy, screaming, they knew the game. You couldn't wait to play - at least for me. And it wasn't just at home - because we were so disliked as "the Yankees," wherever we went, there were fans everywhere. Every day was exciting and every day was new. The crowd energized you wherever we went. It's instant energy, because people were so polarized on either direction - they either loved you or they hated you. And Yankee fans, they want to win - they let you know when you did good and they sure let you know when you did bad. The funniest part was walking out after the game, after having a bad game, I'd try to find somebody who had a good game and walk next to them, so they wouldn't yell at me - *"HEY, FISHER!"* It was the greatest place to play baseball - especially for a rookie having never been in the big leagues and landing that spot in that situation, I was blessed. I couldn't ask for a better situation. Anything better would have been to go to the playoffs or go to a World Series. That would have been icing on the cake. But it was still an awesome experience.

ANDRE ROBERTSON: I come from a small town, so for me, the people are knowledgeable. When you're playing well, they're on your side. When you aren't, they're going to get on you. There were times I was struggling hitting, but hey, that's going to happen with everybody. My constant was, "Hit the ball to me, take a right turn to first base," that's what I wanted everybody to do. Hit it to me, right turn - that means you're going back to the dugout. I think the fans appreciated that. I played hard every day. I still get letters every once in a while to that affect. Like, "I wish you could have played longer." It makes it kind of sad, but hey, I got to play with the team everybody loves to hate. I was in a

World Series. I think I pinch ran one time and that was it, but there are a lot of people - Hall of Fame-type people - who have never been in one. I appreciate the time I had there and trying to get back in it - these golf tournaments and stuff like that, to get back in touch with some of my old buddies. That's kind of what I'm doing now. My kids are grown and I have a little more time to do that.

STEVE BALBONI: They were very knowledgeable fans. They were tough fans. If you do well, they love you. If you play well there, they're outstanding. And if you don't, they're on you - it's difficult. But that's that whole "northeast mentality" - Boston, Philly. They're all pretty much the same. Great fans though - loyal, dedicated. And like I said, very knowledgeable fans.

BILLY MARTIN JR: [Billy Martin] was very much into anything Yankees, obviously. The tradition, the history, the commitment to excellence that that organization has. That was what did it for him. To walk around New York with my father was a blast. Somebody would yell from the fifth story of a building that was washing the window - *"GIVE THEM HELL TODAY, BILLY!"* A cabbie driving by - *"TAKE IT THEM, SKIPPER!"* It was awesome. It was really neat to be there with him. And to this day, I still have people approach me in the city. Elevator operators - "Are you Billy's son? You look just like him. Your father was so good to me. He always said hello."

But to answer your question, yeah, he spoke with the utmost admiration and respect for the whole…what he called the "Yankee way." But he was very historically minded. Just driving around the city, he would point out, "Here's where the old Polo Grounds was. That's where Ebbets Field used to be." But nothing was Yankee Stadium to him. Nothing compared to the Yankees to him.

To give you a goofy example, sitting with him, watching the '78 World Series. He had been fired from that team, after a hundred games. We were watching the game in Texas at our home, and about the third inning, he realizes, "Who are you

Just Out of Reach: The 1980s New York Yankees

cheering for?" And I said, "Not the team that fired you, dad." And he looked at me, with this befuddled look on his face. It was tearing at me, because I loved those players - I knew every one of them. They were all really good to me. So I wanted them to hit line drives right at people, because the way baseball is, it's a game of individual performances. I wanted the pitchers to throw quality pitches, but I wanted the team to lose. I did not want them to win without him being the manager. And he said, "Pal, those are my guys. That's my team. *We want them to win."* It was very hard for it to sit with me - to this day. To me, that was saying that George was right for firing him. And that was never right in my opinion.

GOOSE GOSSAGE: Oh my god - out of body experience. That's as close as I can describe it. I grew up here in Colorado a Yankee fan. My mom and dad were huge Yankee fans - through the '40s, '50s. So my whole family were Yankee fans growing up here. We didn't have the Rockies. Denver was a farm team of the Yankees way back when - I believe in the '40s or '50s. Growing up a Yankee fan and then getting to play for them, Mickey Mantle was my idol. Getting to play for them was…the first time I stepped foot into Yankee Stadium was the old Yankee Stadium, when I was a member of the Chicago White Sox in 1972, before it was refurbished. So I got to see it in all its grandeur. I didn't even want to step on the field - it was like, *"Oh my god."*

And every time that I walked back into that stadium - whether it would be a year since I'd been there last or the day before - I got chills every time I walked into that stadium. It was incredible. I have no connection with this new one. It's alright. But it's not where Babe Ruth played and all the boys - Lou Gehrig and all the guys. If they could have built this stadium and rolled it over and plopped it down right where home plate used to be, then they'd have something. But they could have built this stadium out here in Colorado - it wouldn't have mattered. Just so many things and so many events and so many big games - football, and the characters that played there.

Yankee Stadium

It was just an incredible, incredible place to play. As are all the old stadiums - the Old Comiskey Park where I broke in was tremendous. That was a grand old stadium. I cried when they tore that down. That's where I cut my teeth in the big leagues. Fenway Park. Tiger Stadium was one of my favorite stadiums. It took you back to way back when, in the early 1900's. All the great players that played in these stadiums - it was just unbelievable. And I really miss Tiger Stadium. I loved that stadium, as I did all the old stadiums. Fenway Park is awesome. But yeah, Yankee Stadium, man, I think it's the grandest of all the old stadiums. It's too bad they couldn't have done something to renovate it. But nothing stands in the way of money.

chapter 29: inside the broadcast booth and the press box

Take a peek into the world of the sportscaster and sportswriter, while following the '80s Yankees.

FRAN HEALY: Channel 11 [WPIX] did TV when I initially went into the booth. Then shortly thereafter, SportsChannel came into existence. I did radio when I was with Channel 11, and then when SportsChannel came into existence, I did television with Phil Rizzuto - who I had a magnificent relationship with - Mel Allen, and I think Bill White, and Frank Messer did some too. But Mel Allen was the guy I worked with the most, on SportsChannel. On radio, I worked with Rizzuto, White, and Messer, and TV, it was Scooter, White, and Messer. It was terrific, I really enjoyed it. I enjoyed Scooter on and off the air. In fact, I was just in Toronto telling a story, that I drove from Detroit to Toronto - Scooter didn't like to fly - after a game, because the Yankees were going to Toronto for a game. Scooter and I drove that night, and we beat the plane, and plus, the stories that Scooter was telling me about the old Yankees - DiMaggio and all those guys, Marilyn Monroe [DiMaggio and Monroe were briefly married in 1954], everything. It was fascinating. And Mel Allen had great stories, also.

Scooter was magnificent to work with. When Scooter and I worked together, what happened was I went into the booth...quite honestly, at that time, when I was a kid, prior to going to pro ball, radio was on in my house. And my grandfather used to listen to the games, and later on, I would hear my father listening to the games - he played minor league ball, and my uncle [Francis Xavier Paul Healy] played in the big leagues. So the radio was on. And I used to think, because I was a kid, "Boy, this is boring on radio." So when I went into the booth, that was on my mind. And again, what happened was I ended up working with Phil Rizzuto, who had a great sense of humor. You'd have to get some tapes to listen to it, because it was pretty good. We talked baseball, as well as a lot of other stuff - for three innings, not for nine. Nine innings, they would have had us committed as a couple of buffoons! But for three innings, it went over. And when Bill White and Frank Messer came in, it was more of a "baseball broadcast."

But with Scooter, it was a baseball broadcast. And I think the greatest compliment we ever heard - I ran into Joe Cronin, who had retired from baseball, as the President of the American League. And when I was introduced to him, I thought, "This guy is going to say, 'You guys have got to talk baseball'." And he said to me and Scooter, "I live on Cape Cod and I listen to you guys every night. *I love it.*" This is a conservative baseball guy. But we used to talk about the game, we talked about the old timers, and we talked about stuff that had nothing to do with baseball. But the relationship - to me - was precious. Scooter enjoyed it, and it wasn't serious. We hoped it was entertaining. I'm sure some people who wanted to hear "Ball one/strike one" found it offensive. But I would say 80% of the people found it entertaining.

Mel Allen was different. I wouldn't do with Mel what I did with Scooter, because Mel didn't play, but he was a legend - an absolute legend. There was a certain way I would handle Mel different then I would handle Scooter. Scooter was entertaining, extremely funny, off-the-wall. Where Mel Allen was the consummate professional...but would bend from my style. One day I worked a game, and I can't remember the year - I want to say early '80s - but in the booth, I was doing the play-by-play, and on my left I had Mel Allen and on my right I had Joe DiMaggio. And Joe did nine innings with us that night, out in Oakland, California. Fortunately, Stan Isaacs wrote a nice article about it in Newsday. Unfortunately, I'm sure it wasn't seen by as many people as usual, because the game started at 10:00 back here. So that was a big thrill - DiMaggio on one side, Mel Allen on the other, and I was in the middle. It was a terrific night. But Scooter was *the guy*. And then I went over and worked with Ralph Kiner [with the Mets], and he's the same type of guy as Scooter.

No [in response to being asked if Rizzuto ever mentioned being disappointed about not getting into the Baseball Hall of Fame sooner than he did in 1994]. I used to kid him, I'd say, "If they put you in posthumously, would you come back?" And he said, *"Absolutely!"* I think I said that to him on the air. The other thing is he never complained about it. Every year, when the Hall of Fame came up, the Hall of Fame voting, it was written all over the place - "Phil Rizzuto, Phil Rizzuto, Phil Rizzuto." When he got in, they never did it again. In fact, I interviewed Oscar Robertson for a 'Halls of Fame' show in Cincinnati in a hotel room, and I asked him, "What does it mean to you, the Basketball Hall of Fame?" And he went on to say, "Well, the Basketball Hall of Fame is different than most, because you need the four other guys" - and he didn't even know my relationship with Scooter, he goes - "How can Phil Rizzuto not be in the Hall of Fame?" So nobody's saying it anymore.

It's interesting, because SportsChannel did both teams. I wasn't hired by the Yankees or the Mets - I was hired by SportsChannel. SportsChannel at that time talked to me about doing both teams. And Frank Cashen [then-Mets general manager] said no, because he explained it to me, "If I took you, while you were broadcasting the Yankees, and let you do our games too, it looks like the perception is I need you - as a Yankee broadcaster - to help our broadcast team." But then when it was proposed a while later, Frank said OK, thinking that I was going to do both teams, but I wasn't. What happened was SportsChannel had one representative on the Yankees and one representative on the Mets - at that time. So they said to me, "We're changing broadcasters every year. Why don't you switch over to the Mets?" I said OK…forgetting that George didn't like the Mets.

So, I went over to the Mets, and that's how I ended up with the Mets. It was as simple as that. I didn't even think about it, but years later, people were saying I must have been fired off of the SportsChannel broadcast. But it didn't happen like that. It was just, "Why don't you go to the Mets? We're switching broadcasters almost every year, we'd like to get a constant." I said OK. It was as simple as that. And then I heard all these complicated scenarios after that. The complicated part was Frank - at the time when I went over there - thought I was doing both teams. And he said, "How are you going to do both teams?" And I said, "I'm not. I'm only going to do the Mets." "Oh, OK." So they said, "Let's do a press release, so people don't think he was fired off the Yankees and came over here."

TOMMY JOHN: The thing with New York press, the press is looking for things to write about. And you just have to make sure that you don't give them ammo. And the thing that I told the press, I told them, "Look, you treat me with respect that my job deserves and I'll treat you guys with the respect that your job deserves. And when we both do that, we'll be fine." And that's what I did - I treated them with respect, and they treated me with respect. Some of my best friends are sportswriters - Murray Chass, Steve Jacobson, Moss Klein, Billy Madden. Those guys are really good friends and they had their job to do and I had my job to do.

STEVE JACOBSON: If you were a PM newspaper - which we [Newsday] were at that time - it was getting to the ballpark at about 5:00 and talking to players on both sides. And writing essentially an early story, and then subbing it late. But always, being on the lookout for Steinbrenner to be cracking the whip someplace. You had to write it and give it to somebody who transmitted copy. First it was Western Union, and then it went to something called CanFax, that transmitted it. Newsday, for one, broke in some kind of fancy dictation service…not a service, somebody who was a high-speed stenographer, and you dictated your story into the phone. It was not very pleasant, because some of the mistakes that words sounded like…like I wrote something about, "According to league rules," and it came up, "According

Just Out of Reach: The 1980s New York Yankees

to Lee Gruels." And if the desk didn't get that, you saw that in the paper.

[The press box at old Yankee Stadium] was just a long, single row of seats. There was a back row also, but there was a long front row. Each newspaper had essentially its place. And the second row was for non-regulars who were there - probably some other papers and columnists who weren't working the game in the sense of covering it. Typewriters were being phased out in the '80s. The classic story was the Dodgers were in town in the World Series, and the old pressroom there was jammed with multiples at desks that were made for one. But there wasn't enough electricity. So Dick Young, who was the "Grand Poobah" of the New York press corp, set up his computer - which he was new at, also - before the game, and couldn't find an electric outlet. So what he did is take out the plug from the cigarette machine and plugged in his computer there. The game was over, and some of the people wrote in the press box.

And George Kimball - a big, blustery Irishman from Boston, who had only one eye - came down, and he wanted cigarettes. He put his money in the machine, pulled the plunger, and the money came back. He did it again, and again, it came back. He smacked the side of the machine, and realized that the plug wasn't in - somebody else's plug was in. He went in the back of the machine and took out the plug that was filling the outlet, and plugged in his. And in the meanwhile, he vaporized what 750 words that Young was about to transmit! I'm surprised you didn't hear the shrieks and complaint of Young when that happened. [Computers back then] were very sensitive to electricity and they were designed to be used in air-conditioned circumstances, and quiet. And everybody knew that that wasn't what we had to work with - computers got activated by crowd noise and things like that.

Some [in response to being asked if there was competition between the local sportswriters]. There was a much more collegial group than there is now. People were around and respected each other. Sometimes there would be a phone call to Steinbrenner in Cleveland, and somebody else would think the same idea also - an hour later - and call him. And he would be miffed at you that you copied him or something like that. But Murray Chass and I occasionally had some irritation. I remember going to play tennis with Chass in Baltimore - the hotel there had tennis courts and we went out to play - and we passed Munson in the corridor. And the two of us interviewed Munson, with the promise not to use his name, which was probably obvious at the time. And he was bitching about the way Steinbrenner was interfering with Billy. Munson was just railing, "Leave him alone! Let him manage!" And George, of course, couldn't.

The group now is more competitive. I think some of us that were known as "chipmunks" in the earlier phase liked to look for personality and some humor, and some humanity in the people that we were covering. And the guys that came afterward are hard, hard people. That's a different wave of covering. You're always taking the temperature of the team, and the game plays out over the course of the season. There was some of that in baseball. But there was more acknowledgement that it's a marathon, not a sprint. And there's a layer of "gotcha journalism" in covering the teams now, that I didn't think was there [back in the '70s and '80s].

chapter 30: a fan's perspective

One man looks back on what it was like to be a Yankee fan in the '80s.

MARC "THE HERSCH" HERSCHMANN [Yankees fan, stand-up comedian]: Essentially, I started to become a real hardcore Yankee fan when I was a little kid, which was when I was seven or eight - you're talking like the late '70s. But I probably didn't start really going to games until the '80s. I'd say the most amount of games I ever went to started when I was able to drive, which was 1987, when me and my buddies started to get our driver's licenses. So you've got to figure the late '80s is my real formative years in the stadium, where I would go. Our real "hardcore times" in the bleachers - when we became real Bleacher Creatures - was say, the late '80s into the '90s. We went maybe as many as 30-40 times per year. That was a little unfortunate for us, because that was when the Yankees' fortunes started to take a turn for the worse. But it was a lot more than that for us - it was the camaraderie. Our love for the Yankees was unrelenting. It was an opportunity for us to go ahead and have a lot of fun, bond, and root for our heroes. It was an experience for us, where we would spend $6.00 round trip for the Throgs Neck Bridge, maybe $5.00 to park, and $4.50 to sit in the bleachers. So if you add it up, it wasn't really that much money. It was kind of a no-holds-barred atmosphere in the bleachers, which definitely was not the same as it was in the stands. Life in the bleachers was a lot different. We were kind of like an "ungoverned island" it felt like, and we got away with a lot of stuff. It was an experience that I'll never ever match anything like that for as long as I live. I have memories that are endless.

A Fan's Perspective 270

Frankly, I don't remember purchasing any food in the bleachers. Being that we had this family atmosphere out there, and again, when I say the "Bleacher Creatures," there was a crew of figure, 30 or 40 hardcore people who were there pretty much every game, or close to it. We got to know who they were personally and their names and their nicknames. I always remember this one lady; we called her "Momma." And Momma was in charge of ruling the roost. She would have buckets of chicken and we would bring in other things to eat. So I don't remember ever purchasing anything inside the stadium, because we'd always bring in sandwiches and heroes and wings and beer. Forget it, it was ridiculous. The one thing that I do remember as far as purchasing food at the stadium, outside of the stadium there was a guy right down River Avenue, not too far, and we called him the "Buck-A-Beer/Buck-A-Dog Guy." For a buck, you'd buy a can of Budweiser beer and for a buck you'd buy a hotdog. We'd stuff up right before the game and maybe after the game, or maybe even smuggle in some. But again, being teenagers, I guess we were 15/16/17/18 years old, we weren't looking to spend big bucks at the stadium. So we would go ahead and go that route.

There's a couple of different opinions on this, but I think the real hardcore Bleacher Creatures probably started in the late '70s/early '80s, is my guess. There were a couple of characters that get some credit for it. There was a guy, his name was Ali [Ramirez], who after he passed away, they made a bleacher seat in his honor. He was in charge of the cowbell. And the cowbell was a big thing where he would go ahead and start chants and get the fans all wilded up. So Ali sometimes was given some credit. There were some unbelievable characters out there. This guy Ali, I'd imagine when he passed away in the mid-'90s, was probably well into his eighties. There was another guy, who used to run this little game, where for a dollar, you could bet on the big screen, they had something called the "Subway Game." Not unlike a lot of stadiums, where they have "pick which cup the ball is in" or whatever, this was the subway race, where you'd either pick the 4 train, the D train, the A train, the C train, or

Just Out of Reach: The 1980s New York Yankees

whatever it was. And you had to go ahead and pick which train was going to win the race on the big screen. You'd give the guy a dollar, and he'd go ahead and collect all the money, and he was running a little miniature gambling ring over there, but not for a lot of money, obviously. These are the guys that I remember as being the real linchpins of the bleachers.

But for me, when it really started, when I was a kid going to games when I was seven/eight/nine/ten/eleven/twelve, I didn't go to the bleachers. I would go and sit in the regular stands. It wasn't until we became 16/17/18 and we were able to go out on our own, that we said, "Wait a second...these bleachers look like an unbelievable experience." That's what we started to do. There would be times where we would be out there and three or four innings would go by and we wouldn't even know there was a game on! That's what the dynamic was like. There would certainly be the jeering of the opposing players. I remember there was once a nasty song they would sing to an outfielder for the Red Sox and Minnesota Twins, named Tom Brunansky. "Tom Brunansky is a Horse's Ass" was the name of the song - you can only imagine what the lyrics were like. So there was like a ferocious element to these people, but in a good way - we were all one big happy Yankee family. But let me tell you, if someone came in with a Red Sox jersey, forget it. They would be *minced* - not physically, but verbally. Or if there was a hot looking broad in the stands, which you have to remember, when the bleachers come to an end, there were the box seats over there. I can't tell you how many times we would get a "Show us your tits" chant going. I remember when a girl actually did it only once, where she actually pulled up her shirt and bra, and you saw bare bosoms. And for me, as a 17-year-old kid, it was like Christmas morning. I'm talking about it 25 years later, so you can imagine what kind of an imprint it left on me.

There was the big "Box seats suck" chant we used to do, where we would just rip apart the people in the box seats. My personal favorite was "We pay four-fifty, you pay twelve dollars," because they were paying $12.00 a seat to sit there, where we were paying a lot less than that. And the seats certainly

A Fan's Perspective 272

weren't that far apart from each other. The crew of people, you'd get celebrities sometimes coming in. My personal favorite was a guy named Melle Mel, who was one of the forefathers of hip-hop and rap [as a member of Grandmaster Flash and the Furious Five]. Melle Mel was out there pretty frequently - he was from the Bronx and he was a huge Yankee fan. He'd come out and he'd sing with us. I remember he used to put on dark sunglasses and he would make believe he was Stevie Wonder - because he had the long braids just like Stevie Wonder did, and he would get a rendition of "I Just Called to Say I Love You" going in the whole bleacher area. There was also a soap opera actor that used to hang out in the bleachers all the time, Larry Pine. He used to have a pretty big role on the show 'One Life to Live,' then just out of nowhere - after not seeing the guy on TV in years - I recognized him in this new show, 'Hostages,' with Dylan McDermott.

Be mindful of the fact that the area we were in - which was the right field bleachers - did not make up the whole bleachers. So you had your Bleacher Creatures pretty much in one area in the right field - right directly behind Dave Winfield, mostly. But closer to the left field side, they weren't really part of any of this stuff, so it was mostly that hardcore crew of people in the right field bleachers. And one of my personal favorites, Jesse Barfield. One memory was how during the seventh inning stretch, the Bleacher Creatures would always scream like maniacs, *"JESSE! JESSEEE!!!"* And he would always throw a ball to us. Only to us. Every single time he was out there in the seventh inning, he did it. It was chaotic. It was like he was throwing a pot of gold to us - people would go crazy. I often think about the time he threw a ball to us, and my cousin, Al, was in the middle of the scrum, and came out with the "Jesse ball," as we called it. It was an incredible day.

There's a lot of differences between the old stadium and the new stadium. I prefer the old stadium by far. To me, we lost a lot of the great fan interaction. In the old stadium, this is something that we would do - if we went to 30 or 40 games a summer, maybe for 20 of them, we'd go outside the player

Just Out of Reach: The 1980s New York Yankees

entrance/exit after the game, where you could watch the players come out dressed in their regular clothing, usually holding a kid or a baby. You could scream and yell and try to run up to get their autograph, and usually get swatted away from security. But we were successful many, many times getting autographs. I remember one time, Lou Piniella came out, and he signed something for me, and he put his hands on my shoulders, which was like, forget it. It was a miraculous experience for me. One of our favorite guys was Rickey Henderson. And he was dressed with these tight pants and a silky white shirt, buttoned down halfway. Rickey was so damn cool, boy. In the '80s, he was the coolest thing around. I remember security was so lacking - where these guys would pull their cars out of the lot, ready to go back on the Major Deegan or wherever they were going - that you could literally just walk right up to their cars. One time, I stuck my hat in Dave Righetti's car, to get him to sign an autograph for me. My hat actually dropped in his car and he closed the window in all the hubbub of everyone else clamoring at him, and he drove off with my hat. I don't know if Dave Righetti is still wearing it...

    Mattingly, you have to realize, when Mattingly came out...here's what would happen - the area where the players walked out with their families was about I'd say, 15 or 18 feet wide. And you'd have security on either side, usually. And a lot of the players would walk out and people wouldn't even know who they were. You wouldn't even recognize them. For me, I would always know who they were, because I'm a nut cake when it comes to knowing what people's faces look like from their baseball cards. So I'd go, "Oh, that's Paul Zuvella." And someone would go, *"Who the hell is Paul Zuvella?"* I would always know who the players were. But when Mattingly came out, it was bedlam. Everybody there would go crazy, and security would cover him up pretty good. So you couldn't get near Mattingly - you couldn't get near him at all. And the way the thing happened with Piniella, is you kind of had to be a little sneaky. They would let you walk from one side of where the gates were to the other. And if you happened to walk past where a player was coming out, you potentially had a chance to try and go ahead and say hello, get a handshake or something, without being swatted out of the way by a security guard. So it really wasn't always the best-laid plan they had. But how the Piniella thing happened, I just was going across, I saw him coming out from the tunnel, and I got a chance to meet him.

One guy who I used to scream his name relentlessly, he was an old Washington Senator player and then became a Yankee coach, named Frank Howard. His nickname was "Hondo." It got to a point where these guys would know who we were, because we were there so often. And I used to scream to him - to the point where my voice would be gone - "HONDOOO! I LOVE YA, HONDOOO!" One time, he turned to me and my buddy Dave, and he goes, "Kid…I got ya, kid. *Enough already."* He shutted me up, which was certainly one of the greatest things ever, that I got acknowledged by Frank Howard, simply because I was being a moron. I remember Stump Merrill was a good guy - he would be friendly and say hello. Spike Owen was a shortstop with the Yankees, and he was a super-swell dude, also. I remember once walking past a limousine, and Willie Wilson, who was a superstar for the Kansas City Royals, was in there. He was kind of peeking into the limousine, and I walked up behind him, and he was pretty pissed off. He pretty much gave me, "Dude, this is my space. *Back up."* And I did. Quickly. He was not pleased. Listen, you get your level of people who wanted to talk to you and entertain you, and other guys just wanted to be left alone.

Certainly, the old stadium…yeah, you tore down the old stadium, there was the mystique of the House That Ruth Built. Babe Ruth played there and Joe DiMaggio played there, and Lou Gehrig, and Mickey Mantle. Then you tore that down, and obviously, you tore a lot of memories down with it. But certainly, the affordability of the place I think…the bleachers are still somewhat reasonably priced, but as far as the regular man, the everyday man, now all of a sudden can't really afford the new stadium as much as they nearly could the old stadium. And obviously, it's all corporate, and you can go in there and watch

Just Out of Reach: The 1980s New York Yankees

the game with 50,000 at this stadium as opposed to the other stadium, and it's a totally different tenor. The crowd is remarkably different. The acoustics, just the mystique - it's hard to put a definitive word on how to explain the difference. But if you're a real hardcore Yankee fan, you feel it in your belly. When you're in the old stadium versus the new stadium, it's not even comparable. I was there for the last out of the 2009 World Series in the new stadium, and yes, it was unbelievable, but I can tell you right now, if that happened in the old stadium, the roof would have blown off. So that to me is a regret, that they actually did that. I would have preferred that they would have kept the old stadium and just did a major renovation on it. But listen, this is the corporate world nowadays, that's what baseball does and so be it.

The Righetti no-hitter I was not at, but as far as a childhood memory of watching, the July 4th no-hitter for Righetti was huge. The race between Mattingly and Winfield, that was something that I remember - the batting title race they had in the mid-'80s was pretty neat as a kid growing up as a Mattingly junkie. To watch him go toe-to-toe with Winfield, who, for me, Winfield never really grabbed the hearts of the fans the way they expected him to, when they went ahead and paid him that humongous contract in '81. Whereas, Mattingly came in, and he was a homegrown talent. To this day, he's probably still one of the top three or four most popular Yankees in history, even though he never won a championship for them.

Another character was a beer vendor; his name was "Cousin Brewski." He's actually still there at the new stadium. And Cousin Brewski eventually got moved from the bleachers into the stands, because he was considered too much of a rebel rouser. He would sing "Proud Mary," and would get the fans all crazy. He was a super guy. When I see him now at the stadium once in a while, I bring it up, and he's almost emotional/very nostalgic when he talks about the old days. Again, it almost felt like we were an ungoverned island out there, where they left you alone, and you'd see someone passing a joint along. You would see their own beer bottles coming in. Eventually, that stopped. I think once the turn took, where the Yankees started to get more popular again and more non-diehards were there but regular fans, I think they started to get rid of that. But you have to remember that for a while, when the Yankees got to be a pretty bad team in the late '80s and then early '90s, there weren't really those many people in the stands. So the people that were coming were the super-hardcore, diehard Yankee fans. They essentially left us alone out there.

It's interesting, as a kid, I had gone to a lot of Mets games. My best friend - who actually was my partner-in-crime for all those Yankees games - his dad was a very successful restaurateur in Manhattan for many years. And he would have season tickets for both the Mets and the Yankees. So we used to go to some Mets games when we were kids, because he had season tickets eight rows behind the Mets' dugout. For us, there definitely wasn't that hatred towards the Mets. I don't think that the real diehard Yankee fans were ever bothered by it. I think their attitude was still, "The Mets suck." Even when they won the World Series [in 1986], their attitude was, "The Mets *still* suck." You have to realize, the Mets were bad for so many years that them going ahead and being successful for a little blip on the radar and then fading away again for a while, I never really felt like it bothered anyone too much at all. The real hatred out there was always for the Red Sox. You could get away with coming out to the bleachers back in the day with a Mets hat on. But if you came out with a Red Sox hat on, you were gone. Literally, eventually security would come up to you and say, "You might want to take that hat off." I saw that happen many, many times, because people would just be obliterated out there. Really beaten up verbally, in a not pleasant way. So, the Mets thing, you'd get a couple of "Mets suck" and "You're a jerk," but after that, it pretty much died down.

It was an experience for us - they used to have a parking lot right next to the stadium. It used to be called "Parking Lot #8," I believe. And on the top of it, we would park our cars, and we would go rollerblading, we would barbeque, and we would be there for as many as two or three hours sometimes. Because

Just Out of Reach: The 1980s New York Yankees

again, when you're 17/18 years old, other than school, you don't have a lot of responsibilities. So, we spent so much of our time being around the stadium, because it was just a happy place for us. The friendship, meeting new friends - some of them I still search for on Facebook all these years later. But a lot of them we just knew from first name. There was a guy named Ike that we used to love, I mentioned Momma, there was a guy named Joe, but again, how do you go about searching for a guy named "Joe" on Facebook? It's not that easy to find.

I don't remember exactly when it changed, but when we were in the bleachers as Bleacher Creatures in the '80s, you could just sit wherever you wanted. There was no assigned seats - you'd just sit. And then eventually, once things started to change maybe later on in the '90s, you had to actually get an assigned seat with a ticket number, assigned to where you were going to sit. Again, as the Yankees got better and the things changed in the stadium, things kind of changed for the worse, a little bit. It was certainly formative years for me. It's actually when my best friendship formed with my buddy Dave - who's my best friend 25 years later. I don't think there's a price I could ever put on what those days meant to us, and what it meant to our friendship being formed. Driving from Valley Stream to the stadium back and forth each way, every 30-40 times a summer, eating before the game, hanging out in the middle of the game, just the bonding that was formed is something that has obviously lasted us 25 years, and it's going to last us a lifetime. That's something that I'll never forget. And my passion for the Yankees is incredibly strong to this day. I have three children that I'm passing all my passion for the Yankees to them - whether they like it or not. And so far, they do. For me, when people go, "Oh, you're a Yankee fan because they won a lot," it really has nothing to do with that for me. They've won a lot well after the fact I became a rabid fan. But I became a rabid fan because it changed me as a person. It really was a big part of my life.

chapter 31: booming baseball card biz

The '80s is also when the popularity of baseball card collecting began to truly skyrocket. An expert of sports cards and memorabilia helps break down the collecting craze.

SCOTT STIMELL [Sports memorabilia dealer/owner of Cardboard Memories store]: Just so you have my background, I've had the Cardboard Memories store [cardboardmemories.com] for 21 years in the East Northport area [of Long Island, New York], and now in Commack. If I did focus solely on baseball cards, I probably would have been out of business a number of years ago - I've moved into memorabilia. But I have a tremendous amount of cards.

The '80s cards were filled with a tremendous amount of would-be Hall of Famers, because it was a crossover period of time. You could go back into the '60s when guys came up - like Nolan Ryan, Reggie Jackson. *A lot* of Hall of Famers, that played in the '70s also, until '86/'87/'88. You've got Mike Schmidt, George Brett, Carlton Fisk…so if you want to look at it from the aspect of just looking at the tremendous ballplayers, those years are filled. You still had the guys that were coming up that *won't* be Hall of Famers - the Clemenses, the Bondses, the Palmeros. Those cards became worthless both because of mass-production and because of steroids. I mean, the steroids, those guys that came up in the '80s, they're notorious - Jose Canseco, you could go on and on. Even Miguel Tejada. But it was a fun time. It was a great time. It still got a lot of people into collecting, and I think a lot of the collecting cards ended up leading into memorabilia, which is my strong point. I really started as a "baseball card guy" when I started my store in '92. And I became a serious collector when I was in…it wasn't cool to collect baseball cards after sixth grade, when I was growing

Just Out of Reach: The 1980s New York Yankees

up. So I kind of changed the curve, and I was collecting in the seventh and eighth grade - I was buying all of my friends' collections of cards that they had. They were going on to other things. But that's what it was - it was really a tremendous craze.

People always wanted Mattingly in the '80s - as far as "the modern." But as far as "the vintage," Reggie's rookie, Johnny Bench's rookie, Steve Carlton's rookie, Nolan Ryan's rookie, Tom Seaver's rookie - all of those guys. Henderson of course, Winfield was really, really big at that point, because everybody's always thinking somebody's going to go in the Hall of Fame. George Brett and Robin Yount were the keys to the '75 set [up until the early '80s, Topps was the main sports card company in the US]. And Winfield's rookie is the only real solid rookie in the '74. '73, Mike Schmidt was huge - everybody wanted to have a Schmidt rookie. '71 didn't really have too many really big rookies, and '72 would have been Carlton Fisk. Really, the Robin Yount rookie and the George Brett rookie, that actually started me in collecting when I picked that up. I would say I was in junior high school, and the cards were worth $1.00 or $1.50. That's when I really started to buy my friends' cards, for 50 cents. Kind of got the ball rolling for me.

I think it was 1981 that Fleer and Donruss came into fruition. First of all, the stock of their paper, it was definitely on the thinner side - just a thin stock paper. And they had a lot of errors back then. The "Craig Nettles" error. And to this day, I bet if you ask a lot of people that think they knew baseball, they would tell you Graig Nettles' name was *Craig* Nettles. I would say 20% of people would say that. So there were errors back then, and then people started collecting baseball cards for errors. There was even a big misconception when I was growing up in the '70s and the '80s, where if a card was off-centered and was mis-cut, that it was more valuable. Obviously, it's a myth, because in the baseball card world, if a card is off-centered, it can *devalue* a card.

So the early '80s, you had Topps, Donruss, and Fleer. And then you ended up with I think it was in 1981, they started the "traded sets." And then obviously, Fleer and Donruss came into that, and then you had the big rookies that really drove the trading market - the first big one would have been Cal Ripken, which showcased him alone, versus his 1982 regular issue card, which he shared with two other players. My recollection - because I'm just a maniac for cards - is he was card #21, Ripken's '82 rookie card [in the regular Topps set]. Which really, Ripken winning Rookie of the Year [in 1982] and MVP in '83 started a lot of that.

And then '83 came along, it was a great set - Topps was always the leader at that point, they were stronger than Donruss and Fleer in the collecting market, and it was Wade Boggs, Tony Gwynn, and Ryne Sandberg's rookie. And then the traded set that year would have featured Darryl Strawberry, which would drive that, and then in '84, Topps lost its hold on cards, and Donruss was by far leaps and bounds ahead, and Fleer followed behind them in collectibility. Topps actually lagged and lost its footholding in baseball cards. And Donruss, leaps and bounds, to this day, the 1984 Donruss, even though the market is so weaker in '80s cards, having the Don Mattingly rookie, which at the time was when Mattingly dominated baseball. Arguably, probably the most dominant player in that three or four year period of time. His rookie is still the best card in that set. Strawberry was there, paralleling him, but obviously, Strawberry's career got derailed…and Mattingly's got derailed to some degree, too.

Traded sets in those years, '84 Fleer was by far in the era of the '80s I think the #1 set. Very rare and showcasing Roger Clemens' rookie, Kirby Puckett's rookie, Dwight Gooden's rookie, and some other ones. But those were the keys. At one point, that set was going for in the $500-$600 range. Today, it probably sits in the $150 range. That still is one of the stronger sets. However, Puckett fell out of favor a little bit in collectibility, and steroids really crushed the market, so Clemens' stuff has become extremely soft. '85, I would say Fleer and Donruss paralleled each other, as far as the leaders, but Topps did have the Mark McGwire rookie. And that - later on in the late '90s - ended up catapulting that well ahead, just due to the "USA card" [that showed McGwire wearing a "USA" uniform

Just Out of Reach: The 1980s New York Yankees

and cap], which at one point, hit numbers in the $200-$300 range. *That McGwire card is now worth $5.* Again, having an impact of steroids. As you talk about the late '80s - '86 on - again, Donruss and Fleer sort of paralleled. Donruss had the best rookie card at the time - Jose Canseco. His Donruss rookie was by far the best - he was alone. I believe his '86 Fleer is shared with another player. He didn't have an '86 "natural" card in Topps, he had an '86 "traded" card. The same goes for Barry Bonds - he was "traded" in '86. Topps traded, Fleer update, and Donruss rookie sets, that's what they called themselves. Those cards were huge.

The first regular issued card of McGwire was '87 Topps, the first regular issued card of Bonds was Topps, but his '87 Fleer became like the poster child for cards also. That was one of the big ones. And Fleer made a regular issued set that year and they made a "tin set," which was a glossy set. I should have mentioned earlier that Topps did make glossy sets, which were called "Tiffany sets," which were exponentially more valuable than the regular issued, because they were much more limited. The average general Joe that decided to become a collector as we're getting into the '87s and '88s…everybody knew somebody who had like a candy store or tobacco wholesaler, and everybody decided to jump into the baseball card market, because it was kind of like the dot-coms - everything you touched turned to gold. People hoarded, there was money to be made everywhere, and everybody knew about baseball cards at that point to some degree - whether it was a larger degree or not - but they were going to shows and selling.

In 1988, Topps mass-produced cards. The '87 set too is mass-produced, but in '88, the Al Leiter rookie was something that drove the market - they had a wrong [photo], they had him as another player. So that card was driving the market at the time. Al Leiter, again, that touched on your '80s Yankees - Leiter came up as he was supposedly going to be a tremendous pitcher. He ended up having a very solid career. But the '80s, that's when everybody bought cases and cases of stuff. And today, when I get phone calls, it's always like, "Oh, I have all these cards. I put

Booming Baseball Card Biz 282

them away for my kids' college education fund. I've got cases and cases." And it's *always* '88, '89 Topps, which was mass-produced. All the stuff from the late '80s until the early '90s was just...I consider it almost like toilet paper. To give an example, a guy like Tom Glavine, who never did steroids and is a 300-win pitcher - but not very flashy - his regular base rookie cards are basically worthless. And it doesn't matter how great of a guy you were, it's just such a mass amount that there will never really be much of a value to it at all, unfortunately. I just see it today, because I get so many calls that say they have '80s cards, and I tell them, "I buy it by *weight,*" and people laugh. It's basically sold by weight! I was guilty and I think everybody was guilty of jumping into it at that point. I almost equate it to people who weren't even involved became involved. I think that anybody that grew up in the '80s, everybody jumped into baseball cards.

And then coming along and changing the game a lot was Upper Deck. They showcased in 1989 with Ken Griffey Jr. being the #1 card in the set, and that really catapulted people into baseball cards more. Tremendous impact after that. There were a lot of scandals with Upper Deck - there was a book written about this, about Upper Deck and how they kind of controlled cards ['Card Sharks: How Upper Deck Turned a Child's Hobby into a High-Stakes, Billion-Dollar Business' by Pete Williams]. I'm not talking about baseball now - they ended up making a '90 Upper Deck hockey, and they made a French hockey, and there was a lot of corruption behind that and a lot of control. Some of that became worth tremendous money, worth thousands. And today, worth pennies. It's mind-boggling. I'm sure there was millions and millions and millions of dollars made and lost - and on rookies that never made it. I'll go up to 1991 - the Phil Plantier rookie. He was a Red Sock and was supposed to be unbelievable. But there were so many guys, you can go '92 Yankees - Brien Taylor, who had the fight and never made it. He was supposed to be the next unbelievable pitcher. There are a tremendous amount of stories like that.

I forgot Score - Score came up in 1988. They had a very, very large set. Their '89 set, I think it was 900+ cards. They did

Just Out of Reach: The 1980s New York Yankees

do an '88 traded set at the time, which was strong - it had a Roberto Alomar and a Craig Biggio rookie. But like everything else, the '88 Score was mass-produced. In fact, to this day, it can be bought and sold for $1-$5. It's sad. But they mass-produced their product through the market. Again, the only real rookie in there I believe in a regular base set was Glavine, which isn't worth much.

A lot of baseball card shows [where sellers/traders set up displays] were popping up in the mid to late '80s, and baseball cards were strong in the '90s. It doesn't stop in the '80s - it became very paramount in the '80s, but it did carry on into the '90s. But those years were just mass-produced years. They did have some golden sets - that '89 Upper Deck still has a value of 50 or 60 bucks maybe. But at one point, it was $150 and the Ken Griffey Jr. was a $100 card. Randy Johnson's rookie is in there. But to be honest with you, Randy Johnson didn't do steroids or anything and had an incredible career, and his '89 Upper Deck is pretty much the rarest card, and it still only sells for a few dollars. It books for $20 but it really…price guides came in, the Beckett Magazine. People look at a price guide and go, "This card books for $20, I'll take $10," but unfortunately, it doesn't work like that. Back then it did, because there was no internet and there were only [baseball card] shows. That's how it went. Later on, the internet came into play with everything and baseball cards essentially got crushed in those years - it's more money to ship the stuff than it's worth.

California was always a leader [in baseball card shows]. A lot of the big annual shows were in California. I would say California and New York were the thriving forces in baseball cards. There were a lot of shows in churches, a lot of local shows. There was always the Gloria Rothstein show in White Plains. I went to school in Albany, and a guy named Ed Keetz ran a show for many, many years [at the Polish Community Center]. It was a pretty huge show, and I would go. He would have Ted Williams at the time, and I was like, "Ah, I don't want to spend $20 on Ted Williams' autograph. That's crazy." That was in the late '80s. It was a very big show - people traveled from all over to go to that show, and he always had great autograph guests. But yeah, *$20 for a Ted Williams autograph.* Wish you could go back in time to then, huh?

The White Plains/Gloria Rothstein show was always great, and became what's known as "The East Coast National," which now is not nowhere near as strong as it used to be. But it was tremendously strong in the late '80s and all through the '90s. The National, in its infancy, was most of the time in California, now it's all over. The last two out of three were actually in Baltimore, Maryland. But that's still a great place to go if you want to really see a tremendous amount of sports memorabilia and cards and the history of sports. That's the place to go and spend a few days.

The grading [of a card's condition] is scrutinized really heavily. I would say the leading grading card companies are as follows - PSA [Professional Sports Authenticator], SCG [Sportscard Guarantee], Beckett/BGS [Beckett Grading Services]. Cards are looked at under a high-powered magnifying glass - I think over a hundred times powered - by a team of about three people. And they're looked at for so many different reasons - the centering, the surface of the card, the glossiness, the color, the back. They also are looked at for the corners. If there is a print dot, it doesn't matter if it came out of the manufacturer like that, but those things all weigh in heavily into the grading of a card, and have a great factor. People are always quick to say to me, "Well, y'know Scott, how do you expect a card from the '50s to look like that?" Well, the grading card companies, they grade it whether it's a new card or an old card on a scale of one to ten. However, if a card is older - in the '50s or '60s - if it gets a strong grade, it will sell for exponential money. So the grades are true to what the condition is. But if you can find a card that's at a higher grade, you will see good money on that card.

Cards in the '80s and '90s, they should be nines and tens, but that comes as no surprise - unless, it's a difficult set, a la a 1971 Topps baseball set, which has black borders, and always shows all the wear. Certain cards are very hard to find centered - an example would be a 1979 Ozzie Smith rookie. Nearly

Just Out of Reach: The 1980s New York Yankees

impossible to find centered. And if you do find it centered, and you do grade it and it becomes something, you can get exponential money, meaning the card might be a $50/$60 card, but if you get that card graded in a high grade, you can sell it for upwards of $500-$1,000. Grading changed the game a lot in the late '90s/early 2000's, where it raised values of cards that were never going to get that kind of money. The person that really had beautiful cards stood to prosper. It even gave rise to trying to get a ten for a mediocre card, that if it got a ten, then maybe that card was worth a dollar, now it's worth $25. People get excited, lose their money, and don't realize what they're doing. Meanwhile, the grading companies are really making a tremendous amount of money. Corners [of a card] are very important. Like I said, corners, centering, printing, print dots, wax stains because they came in wax packs, so a lot of times in the '70s and '80s, there would be bubble gum stains [due to a stick of bubble gum being included inside the pack of cards]. Today, there's really no bubblegum in cards.

I'm still doing baseball cards today and baseball cards are an important thing, and are sort of "my roots." When I started the store, I had to have memorabilia. So I started doing it a little bit in the early '90s, and then it became stronger and stronger from there and I saw the demand for it. I became very savvy with autographs - I was actually considered an expert on authentication and consulted for some of the major authentication companies. I've been on a lot of TV shows - I did 'HBO Real Sports with Bryant Gumbel,' I was on the YES Network as a Mickey Mantle expert and a Ted Williams expert. I would say it started swaying [more towards memorabilia] in the days that Jeter came up. Jeter's autograph drove the market - everybody wanted a young Jeter, with the Yankees winning the World Series in '96, '98, '99, and 2000. That started changing the marketplace. People wanting the Marianos, the Jeters. Every great moment that people would witness, they would want a memory of.

Really, memorabilia grows out of experiencing something and seeing it with your father or family member, and remembering that moment. And wanting a piece of that history. Whether it be the 1986 World Series, seeing Jesse Orosco throw up his glove, Buckner/Wilson, the "Shot Heard 'Round the World," the Mantle/Maris race - these are things that people are privy to and remember watching, and going to the games. Baseball cards was remembering something, but memorabilia actually gave you a piece of the player and allowed you to feel closer to the game. It's amazing, even when times are bad...I remember having the store after 9-11, and being like, "What am I doing? I'm selling autographs and memorabilia. It's so not important in what is going on in the world today. Who's going to care? It's got to be the lowest thing on the food chain." But I remember going, "Wow. You know what? People are coming in and they're still buying this stuff." Sports is unifying in bringing people back to a place where they fell safe and remember their childhood. Maybe they lost their dad, maybe they go back and buy something because they remember watching or being at a game with their father.

It could have been you becoming a Dave Winfield fan, remembering how he hit line drives harder than anybody else, and hitting line drives that actually hit the outfield fence. There's nobody that turned on the ball and hit it harder than Dave Winfield at the time. The race between Mattingly and Winfield, there's always great pictures of those guys together, signed. The photos of Winfield, Mattingly, and Henderson together in Yankees uniforms - everybody remembers that. "The Bash Brothers" with McGwire and Canseco together, stuff like that. The Kirk Gibson home run, with the arm up, limping around the field. People want that. These moments people wanted to have, and started collecting and making their early "man caves." And everybody became heavily into memorabilia. A lot of people that were kids then go into college, and sometimes they sell their stuff back. Eventually, people come full circle and they come back to it. These memories, these moments, they drive memorabilia, and I think it's a natural fit if you're a collector or a fan, you want to be close to it. You want to put a baseball jersey on the wall of your favorite player, y'know?

chapter 32: old timers' day

One day each year, the '80s Yankees shared space with DiMaggio, Mantle, Rizzuto, and other all-time greats.

MIKE PAGLIARULO: I remember when I was at an Old Timers' Game - when I was an old timer - they asked me what my best day was as a Yankee. And guys were going around, "Oh, I had five hits here, a couple of home runs, and this guy had a one-hitter." It was Bill Madden who asked me, I think it was, and I said, "My best day? That was easy. It was in 1984, my first year with the Yankees, and they had Old Timers' Day." Now, I had never been to an Old Timers' Day before. I didn't even know what it was. All of a sudden, I go to the ballpark, and it's just a madhouse at 10:00 in the morning. I couldn't believe it. And that was when the old timers would be in the same locker room. Well, I walked in there, through this giant crowd in the locker room, and in my locker was Joe DiMaggio! I couldn't believe it, I'm like, "Oh my god, that's really him!" And he said, "Hey Mike, how are you doing?" I couldn't speak at first. I was like, "Um...*hi, Mr. DiMaggio.*" He was sitting in my chair in my locker, and my locker was in the back right corner, where Donnie's was. I didn't know what to do - I had to get my stuff, but I didn't want to disturb him. And he had all these writers around him. I said, "Mr. DiMaggio, do you mind if I get my socks out of there?" And he goes, "Oh yeah, anything you need. Hey, welcome to the club. If you need anything, just let me know." I couldn't believe what a nice guy he was, and he actually knew my name.

And all of a sudden, when Mickey Mantle shows up, people just kind of quiet down for a minute. At the front of the locker room, the two doors open, and in comes Billy Martin and Mickey Mantle. Everyone kind of quiets down for a second.

Now, you've got to picture all of these greatest legends of Yankees history, standing in this locker room, DiMaggio is standing next to me, talking to me, and in comes Mickey and Billy. Billy hits Mickey on the arm - and everyone is looking at them both - and Mickey raises his right arm, and goes, "Hey Billy, is that 'the kid' over there?" And he's pointing right at me. And he goes, "Yep." Now, all these legends, they turn, and they look. And I'm like, "What the hell did I do?" I look at Donnie, and say, "Did I break some bat? Did I go to Munson's locker? What did I do wrong?" I was scared to death. Here comes Mickey Mantle - and Billy Martin's just got this shit-eating grin on his face - and then Mickey grabs me in a headlock, and drags me into the training room, and starts punching me in the side and wrestling me! He goes, "Hey kid, how's it going? Man, I love the way you play. Welcome to the family. Anything I can do for you, just let me know, alright?" I couldn't believe it, I was wrestling with Mickey Mantle! I told Madden, I have no idea how I played that day, if I got any hits, if I made any errors. I don't know what happened that day. But by far, that was my best day.

MIKE EASLER: Mickey Mantle came in, Whitey Ford, Yogi Berra. Let me tell you, people don't understand - it's like royalty when you play for the Yankees. They treat all their former players well. I actually played in two of the Old Timers' Games myself. They are first class, and the way they treat their former players is amazing. A couple of years ago when I went, they brought in the families and the wives of some of the departed players. Just a great organization. They say "Once a Yankee, always a Yankee," and I feel that I was a part of that family.

STEVE BALBONI: Oh, it was great. I can't remember what year it was - it might have been '82 - I got called up, and we were on the road. I hardly had any sleep, and I had to take a 5:00 flight to leave where I was, to get to the stadium for the next day. So I got in there, and I went right to the ballpark. I was exhausted - I went in the players lounge, laid down, and fell asleep. I didn't

Just Out of Reach: The 1980s New York Yankees

know it was Old Timers' Day. So when I woke up, Yogi was in there, Mickey Mantle, all of the old timers were in there, in uniform. I just woke up, I didn't know where the hell I was, what had happened, or what was going on! And then I finally realized, it was Old Timers' Day. They were all in the clubhouse with us. That was my favorite day. I happened to be there again the next year, it was just great. Because one of them was in your locker with you. They were just great to talk to, great stories. It was just a lot of fun being around them.

GEORGE FRAZIER: I've got some autographed balls from the Old Timers' Games. Probably the best-known old timer that nobody talks about is Pete Sheehy, who was a clubhouse manager, that started out with the Yankees when Babe Ruth was still playing. And Pete's no longer with us [Sheehy passed away on August 13, 1985 at the age of 75]. But when Pete was there, and he was the head clubhouse man, when I played there it was always a thrill for me to sit down, and go, "Pete, 1948. Pete, 1952. 1958. 1964." And he would start telling stories about the Yankees. So when you had Old Timers' Day, you could match names with faces and stories that Pete had told me.

I've always been a big historian of the game - I love and respect the former players of the game. So to meet Joe DiMaggio, become friends with Mickey Mantle - those kind of guys that would come back and participate. Don Larsen, Yogi Berra was the coach with us. To be around people that had touched the game of baseball the way they had, to see who they are and see that they're still just great guys. I actually played in an Old Timers' Game a couple of years ago. To see Whitey Ford again, Yogi again - all those guys that came back for that was a great thrill for me. Because once you're a Yankee, you're always a Yankee - regardless of what your contribution was while you were there. You're always part of that fraternity.

DAVE LaROCHE: To me, I was still in awe - even at the end of my career. And I still am today if I meet old time players. I love hearing stories of the '40s and '50s and '60s - whatever I hear, I just love listening to those guys. And people are always asking me, "Don't you wish you were playing today, with the money?" And it would be great - don't get me wrong, if I made more money. But I would have loved to have played in the '50s and '60s - that's when I grew up and that's when I fell in love with the game. To pitch against Mickey Mantle and watch Sandy Koufax pitch, face Ernie Banks and Roberto Clemente, Stan Musial, Ted Williams...I could go on and on. It was great seeing those guys - on both teams. The Old Timers' Games, that was a great day in New York. I think all the players look forward to that day.

BRIAN FISHER: Whitey Ford was the nicest man I ever met. The first person I met in spring training - the guy sat down, and I'm like, "Oh my god. *I'm talking to Whitey Ford.*" It was just amazing the amount of superstars that walked through that place. That part was cool.

GARY ROENICKE: The 1986 season was a 25th anniversary of Murderers' Row, so I got to meet Mickey Mantle, he was there. I had him sign a ball - I wish now I had him sign *several* balls - but I got to listen to him talk a little bit. Yogi, I've known him for years before when he was coaching for the Yankees. Whitey Ford, he came in quite often, because he threw batting practice to us a lot of times in spring training - he could still throw well. Even Joe DiMaggio - he wasn't on that '61 team, but he showed up for that day. So that's something that I'll always remember - seeing those guys.

RON KITTLE: It was nice to see the old aura of Mickey Mantle, Billy Martin, Yogi Berra, Whitey Ford. Joe DiMaggio was there. Phil Rizzuto, they bring a cow out onto the field and the cow steps on his foot and trips him! I remember everything in detail. That's so sad - I can't remember a phone number, but I can tell you pretty much every pitch, every at-bat from other players, including myself.

Just Out of Reach: The 1980s New York Yankees

RON DAVIS: Heck, that was great when I played there. All the old guys would come in. But also, when I got to come back as an old timer and to get back in the locker room, it's a great feeling. Like, "Oh boy, I'm back in here again - back in the locker room." They'd set you up in your old locker where you originally were, so that was pretty neat. As a player having Old Timers' Games was outstanding, and coming back as an ex-player was outstanding, also.

BARRY FOOTE: I saw them all - Joe DiMaggio, we had Yogi on the ball club with us, Mantle, Maris. You name it, they came though. In the '80s, they were still alive and actively able to go out on the field. It just showed you the tradition - the other part of the game that was so great was that you had so many guys that were Hall of Famers. It was pretty incredible.

chapter 33: substances

With steroids a seemingly daily headline in the early 21st century, was it already on baseball players' radar back in the '80s?

BRIAN FISHER: Cocaine was a little bit more prevalent. Steroids was just toward the end of my career. I spanned '85 to '92/'93, steroids is a little bit later than me. I didn't see that much of it, but again, I wasn't really paying attention. It's one of those deals where if you're in that loop, you're in that loop - if you're out of that loop, you're out of that loop. And that wasn't a loop I was in - in either direction. It wasn't in the group of people that I was hanging out with, so I don't know. But I know steroids was at the tail end - Lenny Dykstra went from this little puny dude to a monster cat in one year. That was the biggest one I saw. I understand why they did it, I just wish they would have come clean after it was found out. I wish they just said, "You know what? I messed up. I made a mistake." People in New York are really forgiving if you just go, "Hey listen, here's why I was doing it." Some of the guys I can understand, there's some I can't. But I think people are forgiving.

It's an interesting life, it's a great life, and I get this question asked all the time - "Would you have if you could have three more years in your career?" Man, is that a tough question to answer. I don't know. Because I'm out of that era, but if you walked up and said, "Brian, you're going to get three more years in your career - at this lifestyle, at this level." What would you do? Tough question, isn't it? And baseball was turning a little bit of a blind eye to it. So I have a tough time with that question. I played three years with Barry Bonds. As big of a jerk he was, I defend him. I think he did it for a certain reason, because he was the greatest hitter in baseball at the time, and they were turning a

Just Out of Reach: The 1980s New York Yankees

blind eye to the other guys that were doing it, and he said, "Hey, I'm the greatest damn hitter." It's a tough place to be, when your ego's that big and you're in that kind of game and you're there...I don't know how to answer these questions for these people that think there's an easy answer why people were doing it. Monster egos, man - they are the best in the game.

REX HUDLER: No steroid use. There was pot. And I didn't see any cocaine. Of course, I was a young player. But we'd go into a young guy's room and we'd smoke some pot after games. But that was about it. And I can tell you that even in the '90s - I played all the way up to '98 - there was no talk really in the clubhouse of, "Oh, look at this guy. He's doing something." Of course, most guys were strong and buff anyway. If you're a baseball player for 162 games a year, you're in pretty good shape - outside of the pitchers' bodies. I never really heard a lot of that talk. So, to me, back in the '80s, the only thing that I was ever a witness to - or even participated in really - was just smoking some weed. And with the Expos in '88/'89/'90, Floyd Youmans, Tim Raines - there was some of that then [both Youmans and Raines were linked to cocaine use during the '80s]. However, I think it's just who you associate with maybe, as a teammate, because I never saw anybody doing it or saying, "Hey, you want to do any of it?" Never anything like that. So for me, some of that stuff was non-existent.

Y'know, greenies were always there. That was a thing that had been in the fabric of baseball for years. Amphetamines. But I never could do those. I did them one time. Because my metabolism is so high wire and wound tight...that that's what they give kids and people now that have ADD [attention deficit disorder]. So I took it one time, and I missed a couple of balls during a game - made a couple of errors. Johnny Oates was my skipper, and he said, "Hey kid, what was wrong with you tonight?" And I said, "Johnny, everything will be better tomorrow. *Don't worry about it."* But I remember guys were passing out pink hearts [amphetamine] in the clubhouse - that was in Triple A. I thought, "Ah, let me try one of those," but I swore off them. Then later, the FBI started coming to the teams and talking about the drug use and gambling and all that stuff. And then when he got to amphetamines, he said, "In some cases, if your metabolism is really worked up, it can bring you down." And I raised my hand in the meeting with the 25 players, they all laughed. I said, "That's what happened to me!" My teammates were going, "Well, give him a case of those then, because we can't shut him up!" But one time in 21 years did I ever do a greenie.

BOB WATSON: The '80s, back in those days, I was at the end of my career [Watson retired after the 1984 season], and I didn't really notice drug use. Guys used to drink, because that's what they could afford. I didn't see the drugs. And the weights and all that didn't come into play until the late '80s. In the '60s and '70s - probably even in the '50s - they didn't let you lift weights. The Oakland club, they went on an active weight program - they hired strength coaches. We didn't have a strength coach. So, I guess hanging out and doing all those weight things at the gyms, that's where the steroid stuff got started. But that wasn't an issue when I played. I think the thing that was an issue was the amphetamines - they did the greenies, and they did the drinking. It wasn't until after I retired that the Pirate thing came out with the cocaine [in 1985, several Pittsburgh Pirates - and several renowned players from other teams - were called before a grand jury to testify about cocaine use in MLB]. But again, I guess when I played the average salary was $50,000. Well, then the salaries jumped up into the hundreds of thousands of dollars, and guys could afford those recreational drugs.

ANDRE ROBERTSON: I didn't do drugs - if I took them, I'd probably jump over the centerfield fence or something! Just even going out to parties and whatever, that stuff was everywhere. I used an ammonia towel - ice water and ammonia, put it on my face, go about my business. I didn't stay out with a lot of the other guys. A lot of the other guys were married, I happened to be single for that most time. I didn't like to go out - I'd be

295 Just Out of Reach: The 1980s New York Yankees

emotionally drained after a game. So I stayed in a lot. But hey, everybody has their thing. I think the older guys, it was drinking - like Billy Martin and that era, we know what happened with Mickey Mantle, the cirrhosis [Mantle would pass away from cancer on August 13, 1995, at the age of 63 - although he also received a liver transplant shortly before his death, after he was diagnosed with cirrhosis and hepatitis C]. It's a progression. Each era had its little vices. But I just know going out, cocaine was prevalent back then. I saw a little pile - it was like the size of a dime, and about an inch high. I said, "How much is that?" Somebody told me, "$200." Well, that was enough to run me away from it, because I couldn't afford it. [Laughs]

RON KITTLE: I was so scared of my father, of doing something stupid, that my dad would have killed me. That was one of those things - that I had respect. I didn't interfere with anybody else's life if they were doing such things. But unless I saw them hurting themselves or hurting others, I would have said something. It's nice when you're 6'4"/250 pounds, you can put your foot down on some things. But I didn't see it. I went into other cities, the temptation is there. There's a lot of bad people on the outside trying to give you free stuff, and I know how the game works - you get it for free until you're hooked, then you've got to pay for it. But I don't think it was as strong as they thought. But MLB did a good job of trying to keep it out and keep it protected.

GARY ROENICKE: I didn't hear [about steroids] - even though Canseco was on that '86 [A's] team. Obviously, we know that he took it and he admitted it. But we didn't know it at that time. Never really heard who was on it or anything really about it until I was pretty much done - 1988 was my last year. But of course, what you mentioned [cocaine], some players getting in trouble for that, but we did hear the use about the amphetamines - a lot of the uppers. That was pretty...I don't know prevalent, it was prevalent that we heard of it. I don't know how many guys took it or what, but when you take something like that, it's just like taking a whole bunch of coffee.

STEVE JACOBSON: I knew the rumors about Canseco were around, the line was a "Canseco cocktail." I didn't see any of that. I was suspicious about stuff, but I never saw that around the Yankees. And Canseco, I had the brush with him briefly [Canseco played on the Yankees for part of 2000]. The Yankees were grasping at a lot of straws then. No, I don't have a strong image of that. Canseco was the poster boy for that.

STEVE BALBONI: Steroids was nothing that I knew about. I didn't see it or hear about it. It never even occurred to me. I mean, that was something that bodybuilders did and football players did. We didn't even have weights. The Yankees didn't want us to lift weights, because they wanted you to keep flexibility. So once Nautilus came out with those machines, they started promoting that a little bit, where you'd get a little stronger, but still keep flexibility. And they used to send people in and teach us how to do it. They didn't want guys bulking up - especially pitchers. They didn't want pitchers doing anything with their arms or shoulders. Mainly, they could lift with their legs. So that part of it wasn't really around then, that I know of. For me, it was mostly just a lot of drinking, the smoking of cigarettes, and coffee. Not the healthiest of diets. There wasn't a lot of drugs with the people that I was around.

GEORGE FRAZIER: I never did either one of them. I think it was just a phase of baseball. And steroids really didn't come in until the late '80s and early '90s - about the time I was retiring [Frazier retired after the 1987 season]. So I never saw much of that. As far as the cocaine side of things, all I ever heard was rumors of stuff. I never actually experienced it, saw it, or was in a room with it. I mean, you'd hear whispers about players, just like you hear whispers today of guys being on steroids - you'd hear whispers of guys using coke. But for me personally, I never saw it.

Just Out of Reach: The 1980s New York Yankees

MIKE EASLER: A lot of times, I was hearing about that. I never was involved in any of that. I heard rumors about it all around. And actually, you heard more rumors about some guys being bigger and stronger than they normally would early in their career. It kind of was at the beginning at the same time with the scandals with Pittsburgh and Philadelphia and St. Louis - some of the guys were caught to be doing some things like that with drugs. But it never really affected me, because I never really thought about it. I was married at the time and I was just trying to do my job. I was an extra player - I wasn't an everyday player. I couldn't slip - I had to keep a clean nose and walk a straight line. So a lot of times, I just wasn't involved in all that. I was kind of surprised when I heard some of the names come out, myself.

BOBBY MEACHAM: For whatever reason, I think I was just too worried about myself that I just didn't notice it. Now I think back and I talk to people about it, and I'm like, "I don't know how I missed it all." I didn't see all the drugs they were talking about. Now I can think back and, "Oh OK - *that's* why guys said 'Hey, did you go to dinner there? You need to stay out of there'." That type of thing. That's why guys seemed a little nervous about me being around this or that. It never dawned on me at the time. I was young when I was in the big leagues - I got there when I was 22 and I was done before I was 30. I was 28 my last year up there [1988]. So I just was trying to get my life together, my game together. And I just didn't see it. I heard whispers about stuff I remember at the very end of my career, when I was basically just an extra player in '88, and I remember hearing about steroids. All I knew about them was, "Nobody would do that. Nobody in baseball. First of all, you're not supposed to get big in baseball - that's going to hurt you. Second of all, that's for the football players." You heard about Lyle Alzado being sick from it and whatever, and you thought, "Oh gosh, that's for football guys that are a little bit overzealous and maybe for wrestlers who want to look [big]. But that would never work in baseball, to be big." It didn't make sense to me, so I didn't really concern myself with it.

RUDY MAY: Collectively, as an organization - and by that I mean not only the Yankees, but Major League Baseball - we were all warned about the drugs and the gambling. We were all warned to the extent that they said, "We understand that you guys aren't going to stop doing this. So what's going to happen is we're going to make an example of some of you. And when we do, we hope that gets your attention." And they did. And you know that, because those guys winded up doing time and being exposed by the public - that there is a gambling issue in baseball.

RON KITTLE: I don't believe in too many second chances. When you ruin it, you should be gone. That's the luxury of playing at the highest pinnacle you can.

chapter 34:
rivals

While the Red Sox will always be the Yankees' top rival, the '80s saw several other teams engage in fierce battles with the Bronx Bombers.

DAVE LaROCHE: Everybody in your division is [a rival]. Those are tough games. To me, a rivalry is something that for year to year, you have teams that you have tougher games with. But a rivalry is something that is over time. And the Yankee/Red Sox rivalry is in fathers and grandfathers, and passed on to kids, and in women and mothers and grandmothers. Our games with the Brewers, we knew they were going to be tough. Of course, with the Yankees, wherever you go, it's going to be a controversial attendance - the fans. Because it seems like wherever we go, it's half Yankee fans, and half people who hate the Yankees. The Yankees aren't like a lot of teams. If the Angels went in to Boston or wherever, there might be some Angels fans, and the Red Sox fans are rooting for their team. But when the Yankees went somewhere, it was like, people either loved them or hated them. There was very little in between. So that's what made them really unique. It's like Reggie - either you loved him or you hated him. Most fans came to see him either hit a home run or strikeout.

TOMMY JOHN: The Royals and the Brewers. Because the Brewers were in our division. Because it was east/west - Kansas City was in the west, Brewers were in the east. Boston was, but it wasn't that big as it is now. The best thing that happened to baseball was Boston winning the World Series [in 2004, after not winning a World Series since 1918]. Because it just makes the rivalry more intense. Which is great - I love it.

BARRY FOOTE: You had the Brewers, but it was nothing like the Red Sox thing. That was a big deal. Everybody knew about that traditional rivalry there - as far as for first place, you were usually battling the Brewers at that time in the '80s, because they were on the move as a ball club.

BRIAN FISHER: Orioles and Boston. All day long. Cal Ripken was in that group, Eddie Murray - stud teams in Baltimore at that time. Boston was just a blast to play in - the fans, everything, it was just great. That was fun. Milwaukee, yeah, they had good teams - they had Paul Molitor and Robin Yount. But it was nothing close to playing against Boston or even the Orioles on the east coast, that were relatively close to New York. Baltimore is just down the road and Boston is just up the road. You couldn't wait to go into those cities.

MIKE EASLER: It had to be the Red Sox. Everybody else was just a game. But the Red Sox, it was *a war.* [Laughs] And I enjoyed it. The players don't get into the hype as much as the fans and the media does, but when you play the Red Sox, it just upped your game a little bit higher, and you played a little bit harder. It's just like Pittsburgh and Philadelphia - we used to have kind of a quiet rival there, being from the same state. But the Yankees, let me tell you something, when you put on that Yankee hat and the pinstripes, it's like you died and went to heaven - baseball heaven. I'm just glad that I was able to end my career with New York [in 1987, before playing two more years in Japan], because it's a credit to my career and my father and my mother, and the way they brought me up to be a nice human being, as well as a good ballplayer. When you play for the Yankees, it seems like you've reached the pinnacle.

The Red Sox were great too, and I got a chance to meet my childhood hero, which was Ted Williams [Easler played on the Red Sox from 1984-1985, before coming to the Yankees]. And to me, that was the greatest thing. Plus, Fenway Park was made for Mike Easler - if I started my career at 21/22 like some of these kids now at Fenway Park, I definitely would have had

Just Out of Reach: The 1980s New York Yankees

3,000 hits. No doubt in my mind. Because that ballpark was made for my inside-out swing. They couldn't have gotten me out - it would have been impossible. [Laughs] But the ballpark was just made for left-handed hitters. Ted Williams, I heard he was a dead pull hitter and he was kind of stubborn a little bit. But Ted Williams, if he would have actually tried to go the other way, the way he wanted to, he would have hit .420/.430. That ballpark was just made for left-handed hitters. It helped my career tremendously. It was great for Mo Vaughn, Big Papi [David Ortiz], JD Drew played well when he was over there. It's just a left-handed hitters' ballpark. Right-handed hitters try to pull, and it gets them in a slump.

GEORGE FRAZIER: Boston was always - Fenway always will be. The Kansas City Royals were a big rivalry - home and road, regardless of where we played. Detroit was a good baseball team at the time. But more Boston/Kansas City than any other two teams I can think of.

ANDRE ROBERTSON: Boston. That's the number one rival. But also Baltimore. And then you had Toronto. That's in that East Division - it was a tough division. But Boston I'm sure, just like now, whenever those two teams play, I guess it goes back to Babe Ruth [the Red Sox sold Ruth's contract to the Yankees in 1919, resulting in the infamous superstition, "The Curse of the Bambino"]. It's always an awesome rivalry - that tension feels almost like a World Series attitude every time the two teams play.

GARY ROENICKE: When I was on the Yankees, it would be the Red Sox. It might not be as intense then as it is now - to us players it was, only because I don't know if it goes back to the rivalry of Babe Ruth coming over to New York. I don't know what turned that on. But you had two cities that loved their baseball teams. So that led to it. Nowadays, it may be more of a rivalry because of the media coverage. It's just so intensified and so much enhanced now than when I played, that it just makes it bigger. They talk about it - you have talk shows and pre-games and all this. And you didn't really have that then. Back then, it was basically just newspapers. ESPN was just starting out, so that has a lot to do with it.

RON KITTLE: Playing on the White Sox and other teams - the Boston/New York rivalry is big-time awesome. That's what you play the game for - to compete at the highest level, where the fans are involved. I think the Yankee fans are awesome - they know the game of baseball, and they dislike the Boston Red Sox fans even more. So it was tight tension, all the games were good...you knew there was going to be some tension out there. And it was even better when the stands were packed. I remember Jim Rice got his hat stolen one time, and he chased a guy through the stands in Yankee Stadium! It was competitive and it was loud - in both ballparks - when we played each other.

STEVE BALBONI: The Red Sox. Not so much the players - the players actually got along, the whole Yankees/Red Sox rivalry. We used to look forward [to it] - there would be three or four fights in the stands in either place! It was crazy. People throwing things...their fans would be throwing things at our players, our fans would be throwing things at their players. It was really a crazy situation. But it was fun. It was a fun thing to be part of.

RON DAVIS: I don't think that's ever changed [in response to being asked if the Yankees/Red Sox rivalry died down a bit in the '80s]. I think there's always been a little hatred there - no matter what goes on there. As far as rivals, as far as winning baseball games, it was definitely Milwaukee. Because they were up and coming and winning every year. Not that we hated them, but as players, Milwaukee. As the fans, it's always going to be Boston. The rivalry is between the fans, not the players.

DAVE LaROCHE: There's no doubt that the Red Sox were the top rival. They might not have been in the hunt [during the early

Just Out of Reach: The 1980s New York Yankees

'80s], but they had a really good line-up. They had a good team. They hadn't moved up in the standings to where they would normally be - or where they are now - but they had a great line-up. And just the rivalry. I grew up with the Dodger/Giant rivalry as a kid. I *still* do not like the Giants - I don't like orange and black. And then I played with the Cubs and saw the Cub/Cardinal rivalry, and then with the Yankees, the Red Sox/Yankee rivalry. Those I guess are three of the longest, strongest rivalries. And that was the big rivalry - there's no question. And it doesn't matter if they were in last and we were in first, or we were in last and they were in first - they were still always going to be bitter, tough, hard-fought games.

chapter 35:
crosstown nemesis

For the only decade in history, the Mets usurped the Yankees in the '80s...or did they?

STEVE JACOBSON: I thought [the '80s Yankees] were largely bland. That was the era that the Mets owned New York. I believe for seven or eight of those years, the Mets outdrew the Yankees. The '85/'86/'87/'88 Mets were quite good. They didn't get good until Keith Hernandez joined the team [midway through 1983], and then it burned out. They beat the Red Sox [in the 1986 World Series], and then it didn't happen again for them. They let some players go prematurely.

MIKE EASLER: The Yankees and the Mets always had the rivalry. The Yankees were a little more powerful - the way Steinbrenner went about getting players and buying free agents. There was always that rivalry in the city. And the Yankees probably did have a little better record during the '80s [during the '80s, the Yankees won 854 games, while the Mets won 816 games]. Steinbrenner was very flamboyant and was very vocal, so that's what made him and the Yankees probably the more popular team in the city. But the Mets back then had some good ball clubs, too. Davey Johnson put together a good set of ballplayers in '86, and that's when they won it.

But you've still got to say the Yankees were the dominant team of the century - between them, the Dodgers, and Cardinals, those are the three most winningest organizations in baseball. Steinbrenner would make sure that the manager - whoever managed that ball club - would have the ballplayers in line and lined up. He was going to have a star at every position if he could. That's why Steinbrenner won - he went out and spent the money, where a lot of clubs would get money and instead of spending on free agents, *who knows* what they were doing with the money. George was putting money back into his ball club.

MIKE PAGLIARULO: I thought it was great, because we actually played against a lot of the minor leaguers - Dykstra and some of the other guys coming up in the Mets system. I thought it would have been fabulous [if the Yankees played the Mets in a World Series during the '80s]. They had a great team. It would have been a lot of fun. It would have been crazy. I don't think either team was favored to win. You have a very strict line between Yankees fans and Mets fans. And that's never going to be disturbed. It's either black or white. It's all respect and it's all good.

We played them in an exhibition game at Shea Stadium. I'll tell you what, our owner, he did not like the Mets *at all*. As a matter of fact, it was pretty known that if you did bad during the Mets game, you were going to get traded. There was no doubt about it. They had the Triple A third baseman, Tucker Ashford, he was the MVP of the league [Ashford won the 1982 International League MVP Award], and he played terrible in a Mets game in spring training…that day, he was traded. That's what happens in New York. The owner is very demanding, and you know what he likes and you know what he doesn't like. So there were no surprises. That whole Mets thing was great, because when you're on the field and you're talking to those guys, it was pretty cool, because they had a good bunch of guys - really talented players and young players. They were going to be good for a while, it seemed, and so were we. So I thought, "This is going to be fun for years."

REX HUDLER: George, whenever we played the Mets in spring training, it was do-or-die. It was a "World Series game." It wasn't a regular season game - it was a World Series game. Especially when he was in attendance. And I remember being in that line-up and hearing the manager say, "Look, George is here. Make sure you hustle and don't have a bad game." I made two errors in one game against the Mets, and the next day in the newspaper, they had some quotes from George, and they brought up my name - the young prospect. "Oh yeah, Hudler? He's not ready. He'll go back and do some time - he'll be back in the minor leagues." That's what he did. Based on one game, one performance, if you didn't perform, you were gone. And I'll never forget that. It was "on." Like that clubhouse meeting I was sharing with you, it was about the Mets. "The Mets did this, and we're going to go along with them." He really competed against that crosstown team. So I got fired one spring because of that, too.

ANDRE ROBERTSON: I should have mentioned that, as far as rivalry. That was definitely there. I know people made the team by playing well against the Mets in spring training. But hey, they had a good team. You think of the Dwight Goodens, the Darryl Strawberrys - that's more so where you had the cocaine. Darryl and I had the same agent [Richie Bry], so I met him a few times, and that's how I met Dwight Gooden, also. But they had some good players. Hojo [Howard Johnson], José Oquendo - I just wanted to try and do better than him [Oquendo was the Mets' shortstop from 1983-1984]. That was a big rivalry back then too, even though we didn't play each other. It's a battle for fans, and I think some may have switched or some were loyal to both teams. But hey, that was as big a rivalry as Boston.

TOMMY JOHN: Could be [that the Mets usurped the Yankees in the '80s]. Because one, they had a hell of a manager managing when they won - Davey Johnson. Davey could manage, as you see now [Johnson managed the Washington Nationals from 2011-2013, winning "NL Manager of the Year" in 2012]. But players win and players lose - managers just stay out of the way and don't screw it up. And Davey was smart enough to know that. They had some pretty good pitching in those days - they had a good bullpen, Jesse Orosco. They had good pitching. Not so much power, but they had good hitters that could keep innings going. They'd get base hits, doubles, steal a base, they had good

Just Out of Reach: The 1980s New York Yankees

defense. The Mets - by and large - had a better team from probably about '84 to '89 than the Yankees did.

GARY ROENICKE: There probably wasn't a decade around where the Mets won more games than the Yankees. So if they did win the championship that year and the Yankees didn't, then you'd probably have to say that they had the edge. Because ultimately, we're in it to win.

MIKE EASLER: Even though I got traded from Boston, I was really rooting for the Red Sox [to beat the Mets in the 1986 World Series], because I played there two years, I had some awards there, I had one my best years there - my first year there in '84, I hit 27 home runs. I had a really successful time in Boston. I liked Boston, I liked the Red Sox. I was really rooting for Boston, but it just wasn't their time at that time [the Mets beat the Red Sox, four games to three, in one of the more thrilling World Series - best known for the infamous Bill Buckner/Mookie Wilson play in game six].

RON KITTLE: You always want to go for the American League team, just because if you can't beat them and be in it, hopefully the team that beats you gets to that point. It was a good Series. I'm not much of a fan of watching the game of baseball - I can pretty much read a box score and tell you what goes on with the game. I currently work for the Chicago White Sox, but I follow the good players. I follow the players who hustle, play hard - whether they make mistakes or not. I like that action of the game.

MIKE PAGLIARULO: What is interesting is I felt bad that we weren't in it [in '86]. So I couldn't root for anybody. But there was some players on the teams that I knew and liked to see play well. Guys that you played against or might have been part of your organization. We played against the Red Sox in the minor leagues coming up at a few different levels, so you got to know some of the guys on that team. There were guys you liked and didn't like. But there was not one particular team - no matter who won, it wasn't going to feel good.

DALE BERRA: As it turns out, the early '80s Mets stunk. When I played against them from '77 through '83 [with the Pirates]...Dwight Gooden just came up in '84, they hadn't really gotten Keith Hernandez yet. So they weren't any good. Lee Mazzilli was good - they had some good players. '84 would have been the start of their coming up. Did they out-perform the Yankees? I don't know, I bet you they didn't win more games than the Yankees over those years - if you took 1980 to 1989, I would doubt that the Mets won more games [again, during the '80s, the Yankees won 854 games, while the Mets won 816 games]. They did certainly win a World Series and they did what they did, and they had a good team. When I was on the Pirates, they didn't have much.

RON KITTLE: Living in Chicago, I know the competitiveness between the Cubs and White Sox. And I never paid attention to the Mets and the Yankees, who fought for the biggest back pages of newspapers. Both teams were good, but I think if you get a World Series ring out of it, compared to the Yankees not getting one in the '80s, I'd have to give the edge to the Mets at the time.

BRIAN FISHER: The only thing that can be said for that era of the Mets is that they won the World Series in '86. Other than that, I don't think anyone can put them in the same league as with the Yankees. Highest, pure dislike for the Mets - as a Yankee and as a Pirate, playing in that same division - great players at that time, but I don't think they would ever be considered in the ranks of the Yankees.

GEORGE FRAZIER: Two very good baseball teams that played great. They did win a World Series. I don't know - that's for other people to decide besides myself.

FRAN HEALY: See, '85 was a year I was more focused on the

Just Out of Reach: The 1980s New York Yankees

Mets, because I did a lot of their games, and they had Gooden, Strawberry, Carter came over that year, Hernandez. They had a terrific team, and they kind of went by the Yankees. But I will say this - the Mets are a terrific organization, but there's nothing like the Yankees. I'm not talking about just the Mets, I'm talking about any team - there's nothing like the Yankees. Every player that's ever gone into especially old Yankee Stadium was in awe, because of the "ghosts" of the old Yankee Stadium. Yankee Stadium was a cathedral, and Fenway Park and Wrigley Field weren't a ballpark, they were chapels. But the *cathedral* was Yankee Stadium.

chapter 36: why not?

One final question…despite being loaded with talented players, why did the Yankees teams of the '80s not win a World Series?

TOMMY JOHN: With the Yankees, they would make a trade in the early '80s, and then they would see that it wasn't a good trade, and then they would make *half a dozen* more trades to try to make up for that first trade, and they just kept going from bad to worse. But one of the [good] things that the Yankees did is when they brought Gene Michael in as general manager. He managed in '81 and then George fired him, and brought in Bob Lemon. Stick was like a scout or a confidant to George, and then George put him in as general manager in the early '90s. And all of a sudden, they started acquiring these draft choices, and all of a sudden, the Yankees' minor league started to flourish like they used to, and they could reach down and pull a guy up. I really thought that the resurgence of the Yankees [in the late '90s] was a direct result of Gene Michael being the general manager.

BOB WATSON: The thing is that they had not a stable management. From the top. Up until…I want to say Stick came in and had a say in '93 I guess [Michael served as Yankees GM twice, from 1980-1981 and 1991-1995], from that time going forward, that's when George wasn't there, so Buck and Stick and Joe Molloy, the son-in-law [of Steinbrenner], ran the team. And they ran it more stable than when George was there firing everybody. I don't know, how many managers did he have in the '80s? [The Yankees had a total of nine managers during the '80s, with a few making reappearances] That will tell you right off the top. The same with managers and pitching coaches and third base coaches - the people that are on the field every day, when you change all of those people, and then change people coming

Just Out of Reach: The 1980s New York Yankees

in and out with free agents and trades, you don't have any stability.

RUDY MAY: In some cases, this isn't going to be true, but I believe - and this is just me, now - in this case it will be true, I think that stability has a great deal to do with performance. And by that, I mean this - look at our country, look at our family structure, and you will see the offspring of these families that are together as a family with mom, dad, sister, brother, have a lot better chance of complete adult maturity that stay together. So here's a belief that I truly do believe - I believe that had our 1980 team stayed together along with the manager, we could have done a lot of great things, like Joe Torre and Joe Girardi in that sense. I look back, and I say, "Man, I played for *a lot* of managers."

      It was different in the '70s - the '70s Yankees teams that I played for - because I left there when they started playing in World Series under Billy. But after that, they started the musical chairs as far as the manager goes. Players have a tendency to look at that as negativity. And that's how I looked at it - "We don't have a 'father,' so I can get away with what I want to get away with. I'm playing for myself." And I think that had a lot to do with it. I'm not sure, but I do know that during that period of time that I was there and we didn't win, we pretty much didn't feel like a family. I know I did when I was with Dick Howser. I remember Howser used to tell me, "Hey man, you need a ride home? Where are you going?" And Mike Ferraro, those guys were just tremendous people - Stan Williams, Whitey Ford. But we weren't together long, we didn't have any history together. I think that's the reason.

BRIAN FISHER: I think when they stabilized the managerial thing with Joe Torre, you saw the big difference. They kept bringing guys in and out. I mean, pitching coaches like crazy. We were winning one year - I think it was '86, six weeks in - and they fired the pitching coach! We had a winning record and a pretty decent ERA. If you ask me, "Who was your pitching coach?" I'd say, "I *think* Mark Connor." I remember Mark Connor, because he was there the longest. That's it. I'd have to go back and look at the damn pitchers to remember who the pitching coaches were. We were winning, we didn't have losing records - we were always above .500 by quite a stretch - and we were firing people. So I think when they stabilized the managerial position, you saw what kind of Yankee teams could be put together. Plus, they got the greatest reliever that ever lived on the planet. [Laughs] The one regret is that I wish I learned how to throw a damned cutter. [Laughs] But fun to watch - they've always been fun to watch. And playing for them was absolutely wonderful and a life-changing experience.

BOBBY MEACHAM: The one thing that always stuck in my mind, I remember a quote - and I'll get it wrong somewhere - but I remember [Dan] Plesac, I actually remember the guy who said it because I was in spring training, and like I said, the Eastern Division was so close. Everybody was so good - the Brewers were good, Boston was good, Detroit was phenomenal, Toronto was on the way up. Everybody was good in the East. And I remember a quote in spring training asking him who was going to win the East, and he said, "There's very little room to separate all of these teams. The very little things are going to determine again."

I remember him saying reasons why we're going to be better than this team and better than that team, and one of his reasons was all of the distractions in New York. I remember him saying, "They're the best team, but the distractions they put up with in New York, I think that puts us right with them - neck-and-neck with them. It takes wins away from what they do on the field." What he meant from that is all the media frenzy over us not winning in a while, George kind of getting crazy about that, the firing of...I mean, I played for *six managers in six years,* and more hitting coaches and more pitching coaches than that. Just the distractions there I think added up to we didn't quite win enough. Not because we weren't better, it just took away.

313 Just Out of Reach: The 1980s New York Yankees

I used to tell my wife sometimes - she would ask me the same question you're asking - and I'd say, "Sometimes I feel like we're worried about other stuff, and the Brewers are worried about beating our brains out. And we're worried about what the press said or what George is doing or who got fired. We're kind of not pointed in the right direction all the time. We're distracted a lot." The young guys, I don't think it bothered - myself, Pagliarulo, and Mattingly. That's all we knew, as far as we knew. And I never played for anybody else. So as far as I knew, that was just the big leagues. But I think the older guys, you could see it - not the Guidrys and the Randolphs because they were always there, too. But the Winfields and the Griffeys. And Rick Rhoden, the new pitchers. Toby Harrah…guys that came in who were good players - Smalley and Wynegar - all of a sudden, they weren't on point as much. Or maybe they were, it just seemed like they would be distracted by it. So I think that cost us a couple of games here and there, and that's all it took to keep us out of the playoffs.

DAVE RIGHETTI: I think it's pretty simple - you look at our road record during those times. Until Rickey got there, we didn't have any speed, hardly. I mean, we didn't use it. Jerry Mumphrey could run a little bit, and he was really a solid hitter. But again, we didn't steal a lot of bases. There was a lot of "waiting for the three-run homer." We didn't manufacture runs. There were a couple of years there where we were really good, and they all got hurt - it seemed like Rickey went down, Claudell [Washington] went down. Just guys getting hurt left and right. And we didn't have enough depth. But it really came down to I think our team speed a little bit. And our road record has got to be…the predominantly left-handed pitching, I think. I know it helped us at home, but I don't think it helped us on the road. But again, those guys were great. Nobody else was winning a hundred games every year. Baltimore did it once maybe, and Detroit did it. But for the most part, we thought we had to win 95 every year. We just came up short.

GOOSE GOSSAGE: Well, I think there was a fine line between winning and losing. I think there was a time - through expansion - that you could really buy what the great teams of the Yankees...that wasn't a tough division, there were a lot of doormats. A lot of weak teams in the league. I just don't think it was as hard then as it was when we played. That Eastern Division remained tough - clear through the late '70s and the mid '80s. It was always the toughest division in baseball. I don't think you'd get an argument out of anybody. Maybe the Eastern Division of the National League was also very tough. But man, that Eastern Division was just the beast of the east. It was unbelievable.

PHIL NIEKRO: I just guess there was another club better than we were. I mean, '84/'85, we had a good ball club. If you look at that line-up, gee, we were *stacked*. I don't know. Sometimes, the best team doesn't get the pennant or in the Series.

GARY ROENICKE: You mentioned the wild card - that could be a big reason. Because baseball - even with the wild card now, and having two wild card teams - is still the toughest sport to win a championship, because fewer teams get in the playoffs than any of the other major sports. So back then, you only had four. I was guilty of that in 1980 with the wild card - I won a hundred games as an Oriole. We had the second best record in baseball, and didn't even get into the playoffs, because the Yankees had the better record [the Yankees finished 103-59, while the Orioles finished 100-62]. So that had a lot to do with it. And another thing, the American League East is by far and away during that time - the late '70s and then most of the '80s - the best division in all of baseball. Just go down and every year, somebody different would win or be in it. It was just very difficult to repeat.

RON KITTLE: We had a really good hitting team. We had some good defense. We just didn't have that sure pitcher that went out there, that you knew you were going to have a chance

Just Out of Reach: The 1980s New York Yankees

to win a ballgame if he took the mound. I mean, we had Charlie Hudson who had a great arm, Drabek was there. You had some people that had great success in the past - they were getting just a little bit old. And nobody really took charge on the mound. I mean, don't get me wrong, their gut and their heart were on the mound, but they just didn't have that capability of shutting something down and stopping a losing streak. It was a battle.

TOMMY JOHN: '80 was the best team in that era that I saw with the Yankees. We just didn't pitch well at the time that we were supposed to. But we could pitch, we could field, we could hit, we could run, Gossage could close. We had everything. We had all the guns. In fact, we even had Gaylord Perry in 1980! But I think that right there tells you the quality of the pitching that the Yankees were going after. Like I said, a 43-year-old man made the staff in 1986, and Gaylord was well into his forties in the '80s. He was at the tail end, and they were looking for anybody. We brought Rick Reuschel in - they were bringing guys in to try to fill a hole. It's just those were not the right people. But for the time, for a short period of time, it was. Because young pitchers were never allowed to be "a young pitcher." You were never allowed to go up and make mistakes, because with the Yankees, winning was a must. A must. *You must win.* And with George, he just made it tough on bringing a young kid up. Because young pitchers are going to make mistakes - that's part of the deal. But you learn from them, and you teach them from that. But you were never allowed to make mistakes.

GEORGE FRAZIER: I think the biggest thing with George and the organization at the time, they wanted veteran guys that had proven what they'd been doing. They didn't want to bring a young kid up and have him hit a buck eighty, and then send him back down, and never hear from him again. They want guys that come up, and when they come up, they're superstars, they stay there or they trade for them or they sign them through free agency, because it's a proven commodity. It's kind of like, "Do I go buy this car that just came out on the market, or do I go buy the Mercedes-Benz, that's been here for 200 years?" And that's kind of the philosophy they had there.

REX HUDLER: 100% and I wasn't the only one [who felt the Yankees fell into a habit of trading away young talent for veteran players]. Willie McGee? I mean, could you see Willie patrolling centerfield in Yankee Stadium? He had a great career with the Cardinals - he was a world champion, a batting title guy, an MVP. Steve Balboni. I mean, they weren't patient with Bonesy, either. But Bonesy, Italian - perfect fit there. Even though he was a right-handed hitter, he had plenty of pop for that stadium. But that was when they still had the big left centerfield though. There were a bunch of guys - Doug Drabek, Jimmy Deshaies, Greg Gagne. There was a ton of world-class talent, but I remember one of the reasons I was six years in A Ball is no one moved. He would buy free agents - that was his deal. He had more money than anybody, then he would buy his top free agents - whenever there was a spot open - and it would logjam the system. That's what made it frustrating. Al Leiter, there's probably some more that are sleepers that I can't think of [another prospect the Yankees traded in the '80s was first baseman Fred McGriff, who went on to have a long and successful career for several teams]. But I've named a couple of world champions for you that left there. Gagne was a heck of a shortstop. But I remember that there was a logjam of players and talent. That minor league system that he had was full of blue chip guys, and had he been a little more patient with the development, I believe that they would have had some World Series winners, mid to late '80s - to go along with the '90s.

STEVE BALBONI: [Leiter] was up when I was there, he came up and pitched a couple of games. He pitched really good - he ended up getting blisters. He had a real blister problem, and he had to come out of the games. But his talent, it was unquestionable how great he was.

Just Out of Reach: The 1980s New York Yankees

RON KITTLE: Drabek, [Bob] Tewksbury - a lot of good pitchers at that time. But all he wanted to do was win, and you can't blame ownership for that. He wanted to win, he wanted to win quickly. I just think sometimes those "puzzle moves" kind of bit him in the butt a few times.

BRIAN FISHER: Even though the era of the '80s wasn't the Yankees' best, they weren't that bad. The Yankees, even though those were down years, I think the only "down" that I saw is our starting rotations weren't that strong - at least for '85 and '86. We didn't have super-strong starting pitching. But offensively, we were very strong. In fact, I remember I couldn't wait to go out and watch BP, because these guys would just *mangle* baseballs all over the place. Those would be the kind of thoughts that I would remember about '85 and '86.

Guidry would give you seven or eight strong innings, but then after that, I don't remember those many guys going that deep into the innings. So the bullpen was working pretty hard - Shirley, myself, and Righetti. It seemed like we had a lot of innings. Even in those days, a lot of our saves were three inning saves and two inning saves. Even Dave Righetti was getting two inning saves - not one inning situations. That's what I would see. And then you could think about trading myself and Doug Drabek [to the Pittsburgh Pirates, for Rick Rhoden, Cecilio Guante, and Pat Clements, after the 1986 season].

You traded away a Cy Young Award winner [Drabek won the NL Cy Young Award in 1990] that had twelve to fifteen years in the big leagues of huge success after his rookie season for the Yankees. That part I never understood. He was a starter, and that would have definitely boosted the Yankee rotation through those years, because Doug ended up being a pretty solid pitcher from '86 through '98. It was tough, it was a lot of pressure, everybody wanted to win. They wanted the veteran player. You didn't have a ton of rookies stick around - that's also what it felt like. A lot of it was older guys with some time in, that could play. Definitely an older clubhouse - one of the oldest ones I played in. That's truly what I remember. Again, I had a great time, an absolute blast. You're talking about a 23-year-old kid in New York City, going, "Yeah, this is pretty good - wearing the pinstripes!"

DALE BERRA: It came down to pitching, always. We just weren't quite as strong as whoever they had - we didn't have a "number one starter" who was a guaranteed 20 game winner, like Clemens and Stieb for Boston and Toronto. Righetti out of the bullpen was good. But probably didn't quite have the pitching.

STEVE BALBONI: I know their starting pitching, they always seemed to have problems with starting pitching. Either guys didn't do well that had done well before, guys got hurt. I know they had a lot of injuries with starters, where they would go in with five guys, and they never seemed to have five guys very long. They always had to end up making changes. But if there was a wild card, it could have been completely different. Because it seems like going through those mid-'80s, when I was with the Royals, the Yankees seemed to be second every year. They were a great team, and Toronto beat them in '85, in '86 the Red Sox beat them out. It seemed like they were "second" - they'd win ninety-something games every year, and there was always one team better.

ANDRE ROBERTSON: We had the chance in '85, but we had to sweep Toronto, and that's a funny story too, because we won the first game, then Doyle Alexander beat us. Well, he was still on our payroll I think. He was traded in the middle of the year [1983] and beat us in that game. We won two or three, but lost by two games. That's when we got Rickey Henderson. I think we should have won that year. Some of the problems we had, some of the players couldn't play there. You've got to have a certain attitude to play there. It's like, you're right in the media blitz, and I think Ed Whitson was one of the pitchers - he was great in San Diego, he struggled when he got to New York. Rick Reuschel. They had people there that could play, but I think they were getting toward the end of their careers. Steve Kemp, Omar

Just Out of Reach: The 1980s New York Yankees

Moreno. A lot of guys came in, and they were more towards the end of their careers, and I think that's what hurt us back then.

STEVE KEMP: The teams in the '80s, it seemed like they always had good talent. They just couldn't quite push it over and get into the World Series. Baseball is a funny game. There's 160 games, and anything can happen. I mean, the one year, we had a good ball club and the Tigers - who were all my friends over there - I don't know what they started off...28-4 or something? [The 1984 Tigers opened the season 9-0, and then posted a 35-5 record after 40 games] They were just *on fire* at the beginning of the season, and all they had to do was play .500 ball the rest of the year from after that first month, five weeks into the season. That's what I think is great about today's game, is you've got the wild card, because you keep battling away and try to make up ground, but basically, one team was going to the playoffs - that's it - from our division. If you look at that team, I'm disappointed in what happened with me - if it was injuries - but my performance, I would say I was a part of why that team didn't achieve what it could have achieved, because I was brought there to do some things that I had done in the past, but I can't control what happens as far as things that are on the field and injuries that come from that.

DAVE LaROCHE: Getting the right talent and getting the right chemistry. You can go back and say, "If we'd have kept Reggie longer, would that have made a difference?" You just don't know. It was a cold spell. It's really tough to answer those questions.

RON DAVIS: The reason why they didn't win was because of the chemistry. They got rid of Jackson after the '81 Series, they got rid of me after the '81 Series. They brought in other great ballplayers, don't get me wrong - they brought in Ken Griffey, Dave Collins in '82. Then they got rid of Bucky, a clubhouse leader. You were just a game short of the World Series in '81 [actually two] and then you start dismantling it for other people.

It changes the chemistry. I think what Mr. Steinbrenner did in the '80s, he thought he had just to go get players out there on the market, instead of "What's best for my team as far as guys that are teammates?" Think about it - at one time, we had Lou Piniella, Bobby Murcer, Reggie Jackson, Dave Winfield, all those guys. I think '84, they traded Nettles and Gossage. You're getting rid of chemistry. And then by the '84/'85 season, the only guy that was left from the '70s would have been Willie Randolph. So from '79 say, when Thurman was there, to the last guy who played with Thurman would have been Randolph. And I think [Guidry] was there until '88. But Guidry being a starting pitcher once every fifth day, that's why pitchers don't make MVP's a lot.

MIKE PAGLIARULO: Looking back, some organizations say, "We're going to have to redo the organization. We're going to have to develop everything, we're going to have to restructure." I think there was a restructuring going on. I know for a fact there was. And there was a lot of learning. And what it did was it helped get the right players. It helped get the Jeters and the players that they need to contend every year. I feel that it was a transition that it had to go through. And restructured the right way. Today, teams restructure, but they just flip bodies around, and there's no remnants of them anywhere. There's nothing that is long-lasting. When you restructure, you should do it the right way, build it the right way, and when you do it the right way, it will last for a long time. Otherwise, you're not really restructuring - you're just full of crap. [Laughs]

You don't just try things - you're talking about the elite, highest level of the industry. You have to try and do it the right way. When you have all that money out there, there is no reason why you can't. It just takes time. And I think that the Yankees showed that they not only develop players, but develop front office personnel, develop scouts, develop player development people, develop the media. And the owner, that personality, his goals and mission - as well as the people that he hired. Development is all about challenge. If you're not challenged, you

Just Out of Reach: The 1980s New York Yankees

can't develop anything. That's what George wanted, and that's what George got - he got people to challenge each other. It wasn't like everybody agreed. If everybody agreed, you don't need any other people, right? But they were diverse minds that challenge you on the field, challenge your coaching theories, and also your managing theories.

And there were some great people, great scouts - Bill Livesey, to name one, who was George's right hand man at the time. I think it was Jack Butterfield before that. They came in together and worked with George closely, and they had some GM's in New York - Bob Watson at the time, and Gene Michael. So there are a lot of parts to that, and a lot of different areas of the organization, which was pretty vast back then - bigger than most organizations back then. And the way that they collaborated was unique. I don't know how they did it, but I believe it was right what they did, and George created it. I think it developed a structure - they've got some great, great players, some great representatives for New York and for the Yankees, of the last 20 years.

BARRY FOOTE: I just think they were in one of those spirals. I think probably it was a learning curve for Steinbrenner - the way he ran the ball club. It was a combination of things. The perfect manager for George Steinbrenner was probably Joe Torre. You've got the perfect shortstop who was a good-looking kid that could do a lot of things and play for the Yankees in Jeter. A lot of the pieces started coming together. George was probably a better owner then than he was earlier - like most people get better at what they do. It was just a combination, and I think the Yankees were a little short of talent through that '80s period. I learned something many, many years ago, when I was managing in the minor leagues and I thought I was a pretty good manager, and where clubs are always winning. There was a guy named Walt Dixon, who had been a manager in the minor leagues for like 40 years, he said, "Let me just remind you of one thing. In baseball, when you've got the horses, you win. And when you've got the mules, you lose."

And I think that when the Yankees finally put it together...and let me give you one point that I think was very important - I think they finally learned that there were certain role guys that needed to be role guys. You couldn't have 15 star players on one team. You needed your star players, you needed your starting guys, and you needed role guys. And if you look at those teams that the Yankees had when they won, they had great role guys. You had the star guys, but you also had guys that were role guys, that when they weren't playing, they weren't causing any issues within the ball club. They knew what their role was, they performed it well. I just think they put it all together, and during that period of time, Joe Torre was the perfect guy to deal with Steinbrenner. He was a low-key guy. But he was probably firm when he wanted things done. It was just a perfect combination of things, whereas during that period of the '80s, you had Piniella, you had Martin, you had all these different guys managing the ball club. I think you saw the beginning of the turnaround with [Buck] Showalter, and then basically handed over the reins to Torre, and that's why they became "the team" of the late '90s and early 2000's.

STEVE KEMP: It's like that Tigers team in '84, all those guys came up through the minor leagues together, or they were in the minor leagues at the same time. They might not have been playing at the same level like A Ball, Double A, Triple A. But Ralph Houk, he's the one that really enabled - and me, I was one of the first ones, and Jason Thompson and Mark Fidrych - us just to play. We never felt like, "Oh god, if we don't do good, maybe they're going to send us back to the minors." I remember when Trammell and Whitaker first came up, and he wanted to protect Whitaker, because he would only play those two together and they would not play against left-handed pitchers. You'd say, "Well, that's not fair to Trammell" - Trammell could hit right-handers and Lou could hit left-handers. But Ralph wanted them to get more comfortable, and not just throw them to the wolves and say, "OK Lou, you and Trammell are going to be out there every day." He felt like, "I want to get their feet wet and bring

Just Out of Reach: The 1980s New York Yankees

them along slow." Obviously, those two are probably the longest playing double play combination in my day. I don't know how many years they played together - 15? [Whitaker and Trammell played together for 18 years] They both went on to have great careers. And it was hard to get into the playoffs in those days. Only one team was going from each division. We only had an East and a West. You had to win the whole thing. That made it more difficult for teams. Look at, you bring in Torre, and he did such a phenomenal job and he had the whole nucleus that you just keep together. And Torre is running the show. You know what you got, you know what you're capable of doing, you don't doubt somebody, you've got confidence in the other players on your team. It makes a difference, also.

FRAN HEALY: Once you get in the playoffs - as far as I'm concerned - you've got to hope the team stays hot, or three people stay hot, or four people stay hot. But if everybody goes cold for three games or four games, *you're dead.* And I've seen it numerous times. The Dodgers, when Gibson hit the home run [in the 1988 World Series], wasn't that team much weaker than the Oakland A's? The Oakland A's weren't playing like they played during the season. And it happens. It has nothing to do with, "Oh, it's the World Series." Because during the season, you can have a week of bad play or two weeks of bad play. That's why I get a kick out of, people go, "This player doesn't belong in the Hall of Fame because of the World Series." Are you kidding me? Or, "This guy didn't win." To me, it's what he did as an individual.

MIKE PAGLIARULO: I always felt that the Yankees tried to do everything they could to win. We were maybe one player away or one pitcher away, it seemed - just something like that. But what a lot of people don't know is in baseball today, a lot of the front offices now - the entire San Francisco front office for instance - are Yankee executives. And what was going on at the time, which I realized in probably the last five to ten years, is that during that time they were building a structure and a

Why Not? 324

process that is still revealed from what is on the field today. Which was Derek Jeter, Bernie Williams, Jorge Posada, Mariano Rivera - those players, they built an organization to draft those types of guys. It was specifically designed to do that, and to build those types of guys. If you look at the history of who they had at centerfield, with Deion Sanders, Roberto Kelly, and Bernie Williams, what the Yankees had was they really designed a championship model. And they drafted on that and they scouted around that.

They had a system - I know this, because in my private business, I hired some of the Yankees that did exactly that. For two years, I wrote down how they built it. It made sense to me later, because I used to ask a ton of questions. I asked, "Why is it we always went to one place and developed in that one place during the year, no one touched us, no one bothered us, and then if we did good, then we went to the next level?" And the response was, "Well, that's how it's supposed to be. That's how you develop baseball players. There is no such thing as a 'fast track.' You don't get a tree and plant it here and plant it there. You leave it in one place and you let it grow. And that's development." They had all these analogies and things that they used to build it, and they used the championship teams as an example. It was very clear that, "Hey Pags, if you mess up, we're going to send you down, and we have five guys right behind you, that look just like you and play just like you." And it was true - Mike Blowers, Hensley Meulens, and Mike Lowell. They were behind and they drafted all those guys, and those guys were all over baseball.

I think at the end of the '80s, there were more Yankee players in the major league than any other team, and that was because they worked very hard - that was the owner, George. He demanded that. And part of that was the Rickey deal. They traded *a lot* of guys to get Rickey. Rickey is a great player and a great guy - it's just that when you trade five good players, you need to replace that. So, the organization itself was challenged with restocking and building, and they couldn't miss. Drafting in the amateurs is so damn hard. Really hard. And they just had a

325   Just Out of Reach: The 1980s New York Yankees

way of doing that. Fred Ferreira, the guy who drafted me, has got like 70 guys in the major leagues. He's been with championship clubs everywhere. I was just at the winter meetings last year, and he was honored for his services. They had all these great scouts and great player development guys. We had guys that played major league baseball coaching us - we didn't have just "other guys." They weren't just guys that played in the minors and didn't play major league baseball. And the thought was, if you had a question about what it was like to play in the major leagues, that question had to be answered. And that was demanded by the owner. That's how he built it. And it was great to be in that, because it challenged you every day - it challenged you to be better. You always had someone pushing you, and nothing was handed to you. You had to earn it. That's a great way to be and a great way to play. It gets you ready.

So they expected when you got up there that there was no grace period - there might be a couple of hiccups here and there, but you were ready to play. And every place that I played in the minor leagues, we won a championship. So they also taught that at the minor league level. That was part of the development and part of the culture, also. I've been asked about the '80s before and playing in the '80s, and I'm very proud about the fact that there was a lot going on with the Yankees - in the organization itself. And they have a ton of executives all over baseball, they have a ton of players all over baseball. Because they did things right - player development. There's so much to player development that I'm learning today, that I'm just glad to be part of that.

GEORGE FRAZIER: Everybody kept saying, "Well, George bought his ball club," when realistically, the mainstays of those teams - Jorge Posada, original Yankee. Derek Jeter, original Yankee. Robinson Cano, original Yankee. Bernie Williams, original Yankee. And then the one guy that held the anchor more than anything was Mariano Rivera - an original Yankee. And there's others, but those guys were original Yankees. Andy Pettitte. I mean, there's guys that came to the big leagues with the

New York Yankees that were the hub of that wheel. And they turned that wheel.

STEVE JACOBSON: Simply, they weren't good enough. They were good enough to contend, not good enough to win. There were better teams in the division, and the Yankees won consistently - for second place.

MIKE PAGLIARULO: Maybe there were more homegrown guys, and we were very, very proud of that. In fact, I was born a Yankee - not many people can say that. That's a different kind of tide for the organization. It was a different kind of relationship you had with the guys that were Yankees before. When they talk about family, "Welcome to the family," you have in-laws and then you have real blood. So I guess you could say that we were blood. And that, to me, is what real Yankees are. And granted, you can't win without having free agents. And I don't mean to ever slight any free agent acquisition - that's how you win championships. You have to do that. But as far as my relationship and how I feel about it, that's how I feel about it - that's my personal opinion. And I know there are other guys that are very proud of that fact, also. I know Donnie is and other players that were brought up through the Yankees.

DAVE RIGHETTI: But I wouldn't trade it, playing with Donnie, Willie, Winfield, Baylor, Rickey Henderson, and the pitchers, the players, the Hall of Famers. We were just in the wrong place at the wrong time - we weren't in the Western Division, where you could win maybe 85/87 games, and you were going to go. We were playing against Boston, Detroit, Toronto, Baltimore. And if you look at the last five or ten years of Hall of Famers going in, there is somebody from that division, from that era, going in every year. And there probably should be a couple more. So that's the way I look at it. It was just that time, and nobody could get on a run because of how good all the teams were, beating each other up. And if you look back at our record during that time, we weren't a great road team. I think a

Just Out of Reach: The 1980s New York Yankees

lot of it was we didn't have a lot of team speed, and we were very left-handed. We didn't have a lot of good, strong, right-handed pitching. Especially young. Anyway, it was a great time, and *a lot* of stuff went on. [Laughs] But some great memories.

TOBY HARRAH: The Yankee organization, you couldn't be treated better by anyone. They were just first-class all the way. Everyone should play for the Yankees one time in their career. I can only have positive things to say about that ball club.

RON KITTLE: If I had to look back, I'd say I am definitely glad I had a chance to play for the New York Yankees.

chapter 37: today

A look at what everyone is up to today.

STEVE BALBONI: I'm doing advanced scouting for the San Francisco Giants.

DALE BERRA: I've been clean and sober for 20 years. I work with kids about them making good decisions. I, along with my brother Timmy, run the Berra family business, which is called LTD Enterprises [yogi-berra.com], which we take care of all the Berra business. We have no more agents, no more brokers - you want anything to do with the Berra business, my dad's endorsements, his signings, the use of his name and image and likeness, all that stuff comes through me and my brother. Everything is kept within the family.

RON DAVIS: I'm just up to normal. [Laughs] I'm getting ready to see my son play, Isaac. So that's what I do. It's fun to go see your son get to play a little bit. Being a father that played in the big leagues and then having a son that's playing in the big leagues, it's probably the greatest thing ever. Basically, I don't work anymore, so I get a lot of fishing and hunting in and a little bit of golf, and I get to watch my son play.

MIKE EASLER: I was working with the Mets organization as a Triple A hitting coach, in Buffalo. I got hit with a ball about two years ago, so I got a herniated disc in my neck and my lower back. So a year ago, I had back surgery. They took out two discs, I think, and they had to fuse the level of the discs in my lower back. I still have the herniated disc in my neck, so I'm kind of limited to what I can do now. I'm here in Vegas, semi-retired. My grandson plays, so I watch him. And sometimes I'll go in the

329   Just Out of Reach: The 1980s New York Yankees

batting cages and give instructions and help out with kids and some of the coaches. I'm just trying to stay young and stay busy [Easler works with On Deck Baseball Academy - ondeckba.com].

BRIAN FISHER: I'm a sales guy in Colorado. I've got two kids and the same wife - I went to high school with my wife. I enjoy playing tennis and golf, and I play a little baseball. Nothing really hurts that bad - I have a few aches and pains, and my knees are shot, but I'm happy. I sit on the Board of Major League Baseball Alumni, so I'm in touch with trying to help retired baseball players. I've been on the Board - their headquarters are in Colorado Springs, which is right down the road, but I've been trying to stay in touch with that part of the game on the retired side. I try to stay relatively busy and I'm relatively happy. And playing for the Yankees has always been a bonus - it opened more doors. You just say the word "Yankees" and you're instantly a celebrity. Even though I was a minor player for two years, it still opens doors that wouldn't open if I hadn't have played for the Yankees.

BARRY FOOTE: I've been in various businesses. I got into the oil and gas business in Alaska, and we did well in Alaska in the natural gas business, especially. We did two large gas deals up there. And then I'm in the wireless communications business. We are right now getting ready to roll out a system that we developed - and these are companies that I founded - a manner to wirelessly from an airborne platform, such as a drone or an unmanned aerial vehicle, read gas, water, and electric meters. And we're also going to take that out to the rural community, to allow them to get broadband services to the home. F2 Technologies, LLC [f2technologies.com] - that's my main company now.

GEORGE FRAZIER: I'm a broadcaster and have been for 17 years with the Colorado Rockies. Very proud of the fact of representing the Rockie organization for FoxSports for 16 years, and then the last couple of years for Root Sports. So, broadcasting, and still very involved in the game of baseball.

GOOSE GOSSAGE: I'm currently retired. I do a lot of speaking engagements, a lot of corporate events around the country. I meet a lot of great fans that used to love what we did. It keeps me out there, it keeps me busy and I still have my life here. I have had three or four opportunities to coach at the big league level - pitching coach - and I just don't want to get back into the grind. Anybody can count pitches and take them out after 100 pitches, and righty-righty, lefty-lefty. It's all out of a book today, coaching. Whatever the computer spits out is the way the game is. They don't pay coaches, and I'm not going to get into that grind and do the things that I did for 25 years. I'm enjoying being out of it.

TOBY HARRAH: I just turned 65 and I just retired. I'd been with the Tigers for eleven years, I've been their minor league hitting coordinator, and for the last year-and-a-half, I've been their assistant hitting coach with the big league team. Last year, we went to the World Series, and this year, we made the final four. It was disappointing not making it to the World Series. But the Tigers, Dave Dombrowski is the GM there, the president and CEO. He's kind of the leader there, and he knows what it takes to win. It's a super franchise and a super major league team that I think is going to win for a number of years to come.

FRAN HEALY: We're with Madison Square Garden, and we're doing three different things - a show on Hall of Famers called 'Halls of Fame,' it's 25 years old this year. Doing a show called 'The Game 365,' which is in its eighth year, and we started about four or five years ago a thing called 'The Lineup.' The first thing we did that led into 'The Lineup' was there was a movie called 'The Bronx is Burning' - ESPN put it out. We aired that movie on MSG, and then they asked me to build programming around it with my teammates, so I did that. In fact, it won the Emmy here in New York.

Just Out of Reach: The 1980s New York Yankees

REX HUDLER: Second year, just finished doing 142 games as the color commentator for the Kansas City Royals. It's interesting how the Kansas City Royals hate the New York Yankees - all the fanbase there, because of all those years they got beat [by the Yankees]. The Royals won in '85 - they beat the Cardinals - but earlier, it was the Yankees that were knocking the Royals out. I retired in '98 from the Phillies, and then broadcasted for eleven years with the Angels, and I'm now in my second year with the Royals. Just having a gas, just talking and sharing baseball with young people [Rex's site is rexhudler.com].

STEVE JACOBSON: I wrote a book that was supposed to be about [former Yankees pitchers] Fritz Peterson and Mike Kekich - about the wife swap that they had, and it was supposed to run when...Ben Affleck had bought the rights to Peterson's [story]. And my book was supposed to be the rest of the story. Affleck was going to make it a charming laugh movie, and Peterson's [story] has been anything but. But now that I have written that part of it, Affleck has not gone forward with the movie, and the agent can't find a publisher. So I've spent some time on that, and now, I'm trying to work on another book about compulsive gambling. And I wrote another book in the meantime that I am proud of, called 'Carrying Jackie's Torch,' about the black players in the period after Jackie Robinson, when America thinks baseball and sports opened its doors and arms to black players, when the truth is that they tried to push the door shut for a long time [Steve's site is stevejacobson.net].

TOMMY JOHN: Retired, checking in, making sure there are assisted living homes on golf courses, so I can move in and play golf. I just want to play golf and ride out my sunset years and try to get as good as I can, and go on vacations. Just retired. It's a pitching academy [Tommy John Pitching Academy - tommyjohnpitchingacademy.com], and we do a lot of fundraisers and stuff with that. It's to raise money for charities and for the organizations that we're doing. Our thing for the pitching academy is we can't teach you how to throw a hundred miles per hour, but we'll teach you how to get batters out. And I think that's overlooked in baseball nowadays - everybody wants a hundred-mile-an-hour-thrower, and nobody wants a pitcher that can pitch six/seven/eight innings, and get batters out with less than great stuff.

STEVE KEMP: I'm retired. I stlll have a little interest with the Tigers. I do a fantasy camp for them and a couple of other things that they ask me. But I'm trying to just stay above water and enjoy the opportunities that are there for me.

RON KITTLE: I am an ambassador for the Chicago White Sox. I travel around the world and do motivational speaking for many groups. Then I do custom baseball art design. There's nothing I can't make - I always tell everybody I played baseball for a hobby, but I'm a woodworker/steelworker at heart. I make humidors, beds, benches - you name it, I can make it [Ron's site is ronkittle.com].

DAVE LaROCHE: I'm retired and my wife just retired, and relaxing and enjoying watching my kids play. Andy currently is in Buffalo with the Blue Jays and Adam in Washington really enjoys the atmosphere there. They had a great year last year and hoping to get it going again, get back in the playoffs, and finish what they started last year.

BILLY MARTIN JR. is a certified baseball agent with Pro Agents, Inc - proagentsinc.com.

RUDY MAY: In May, I just retired from my second profession - I worked as a marketing consultant, a franchise business consultant for British Petroleum, BP, out here on the west coast. And out here, we know it as ARCO/ampm. So I worked for them from the late '80s/early '90s, up until this year, when I was 68. So now I'm completely retired. I've had some medical problems that I've since got fixed - as a matter of fact, I just got out of the hospital on Thursday. So I'm retired and not doing anything - I'm trying to play a little golf every day...maybe. [Laughs]

BOBBY MEACHAM: I'm still in baseball. I'm a lifer - I've managed in the minor leagues seven or eight years. Last year, I managed A Ball with the Blue Jays in Dunedin. I've been coaching in the big leagues before that - three years with Houston [first base coach], one year with the Yankees coaching third in '08, '07 I was coaching with the Padres at first base, and then the Marlins in '06. I was with Girardi two different times, which was great. Last year was my 17th year coaching or managing in the minor leagues. I'll be back in the big leagues soon - my goal is to manage and follow in the footsteps of my boy, Billy, and manage a big league team.

PHIL NIEKRO: I live on a lake, down here in Lake Lanier, a little northeast of Atlanta. I fish a lot, play golf, have a couple of charities going. I'm involved with an organization called Operation One Voice [operationonevoice.org]. What we do is we raise money to take care of the families of the special operation forces all over the country. The guys that have been lost, we bring their families in, we bring the guys in that have been shot, and amputees, double amputees - and we wine them and dine them for three or four days. And another one up in Gainesville, Georgia, I've been having golf tournaments for the Edmondson-Telford Center for Children [etcenterforchildren.org], which is for neglected and abused children. I've been doing that for about 18 years now.

MIKE PAGLIARULO: What I'm doing now is I started to get back on the field and do some coaching. For me, it brings me full circle in the baseball industry, because as a player, I got to experience that, and then I wanted to see my kids grow up. I started an international scouting business, which helped get Hideki Matsui to the Yankees and a bunch of other Japan and American relationships. And then I was an advanced scout for the Angels, and then in this off-season...after taking care of my mother the last couple of years - she had ALS. One of the prouder things I have to say about my mother, when they diagnosed her with ALS, she said, "My son played for the Yankees, and so did Lou Gehrig." She was almost proud to have ALS. We lost her about a year-and-a-half ago. So now, I was approached by a couple of teams last fall and interviewed, and I said, "I think I'm ready. My daughter has graduated college, my son graduated college - my son lives in Manhattan and my daughter just graduated from Rollins College in Florida. So I can commit to it, and hopefully it will help bring me full circle - and help me be a better person in the industry." [Pagliarulo works as a hitting coach for the Pittsburgh Pirates' Triple A team, the Indianapolis Indians]

DAVE RIGHETTI: The same thing I've been doing the last 15 years - coaching with the Giants. I've been a pitching coach for the last 15 years with them. Right now, I've just been working out, rehabbing - trying to get my arm fixed. After all these years, I tore it years ago when I was pitching with the Yankees, never fixed it, and just let it scar down. Until finally, it got to the point where I couldn't throw BP anymore. I finally had elbow surgery, so I'm rehabbing it. I'm playing against Donnie now - I've got to beat his ass with the Dodgers. [Laughs]

ANDRE ROBERTSON: Today I work for Dupont. I'm the head of a chemical plant, and hopefully no more than seven more years. I'm about to make 56 in October. I have a seventeen-year-old, he's diabetic, so I'm working now for insurance. Hopefully he can get a job and get himself taken care of. But I'm always asked questions about the game. Me, I think I'm more of a humble type person. I don't bring up what I did, but everybody else does. "He used to play for the Yankees" and "Oh I saw your picture over there in the restaurant." Restaurants here have got pictures of me with my big afro, which I don't have enough hair now to even say it's up there. It was a great time, and now I'm on to my second career and I'm trying to do well in that, as I tried to do well in baseball. What was instilled to me by my father -

Just Out of Reach: The 1980s New York Yankees

"Don't start nothing you can't finish." I think I said that the whole time I was playing, and I'll say it here. Sometimes it's harder here than dealing with George! But it's the industry - try to keep yourself afloat in it. And that's what I'm doing now.

GARY ROENICKE: I've been a baseball scout for a lot of years. I scouted with the Padres for eight years, scouted with the Orioles for eight years, Milwaukee last year. This year, I couldn't find a job, so I'm not presently working. My son [Josh] pitches for the Minnesota Twins, so we've seen him a few times - went to Minnesota for the first time since 1986. And then I'm presently doing a lot of fishing. And I'm also trying to get a job for next year - I'm trying to get in touch with teams again. When you've been doing it for 18 years and you're still only 58...baseball's been my life. You realize that when you get out and you try to find other types of work. People nowadays want experienced people, which I understand - that's why I'm trying my best to get back in it.

BOB WATSON: I'm retired. I do special assignment stuff for Major League Baseball, such as with youth. The youth academies, I go and teach coaches how to coach. But I have formed a partnership with the Roberto Clemente Foundation and with Roberto Clemente Jr., and we are working on the concussion side of sports - both professional and in youth. And please believe me, we are working real hard. We've done a number of things to get concussions out of the dark ages - from when you got a concussion and they would ask you, "How many fingers do I have up? What's your name? What city are you in?" To now, really taking a serious look. There are some technical breakthroughs and equipment that you can do a scan, and in three minutes it can tell you if you have a concussion or a bleed. We're pushing forward to get that involved in little league, all high schools, all colleges, and I think that will come to fruition here pretty soon.

Made in the USA
San Bernardino, CA
31 March 2014